CW00743348

BIOCHEMICAL SOCIETY SYMPOSIA

No. 76

DNA DAMAGE: FROM CAUSES TO CURES

BIOCHEMICAL SOCIETY SYMPOSIUM No. 76
held at Robinson College, Cambridge, December 2008

DNA Damage: from Causes to Cures

ORGANISED AND EDITED BY
RICHARD P. BOWATER,
RHONA H. BORTS
AND MALCOLM F. WHITE

PORTLAND PRESS

Published by Portland Press Ltd on behalf of the Biochemical Society
Portland Press Limited
Third Floor, Eagle House
16 Procter Street
London WC1V 6NX
U.K.
Tel.: +44 (0)20 7280 4110
Fax: +44 (0)20 7280 4169
Email: editorial@portlandpress.com
www.portlandpress.com

ISBN 978 1 85578 173 3
ISSN (print) 0067 8694

British Library Cataloguing-in-Publication Data
A catalogue record for this book is available from the British Library

Typeset by Aptara Inc., New Delhi, India
Printed in Great Britain by Latimer Trend Ltd, Plymouth

Contents

Preface

All cells contain a diverse range of repair pathways that have evolved to optimize their survival following damage to their DNA. These pathways involve the co-ordinated actions of a large number of proteins that remove and repair the damage and maintain genome stability. Clearly, when these processes do not function correctly, a likely result will be instability of the genome. The 2008 Biochemical Society Annual Symposium provided a showcase for studies of DNA repair and genome instability. Entitled 'DNA Damage: from Causes to Cures', it was held at Robinson College, University of Cambridge, on 15–17 December 2008.

As was evident from the wide range of talks and poster presentations, this research field is providing significant advances to our understanding of important biological issues. These extend from improved knowledge of processes that drive evolution to mechanisms that are involved in a range of human diseases, including many cancers. Notably, basic and applied biochemical studies have provided significant developments across this range of topics.

The Symposium highlighted recent advances in areas that are of significance to human diseases. A particular focus was to report on progress in understanding biochemical details of how DNA repair intersects with cellular pathways that lead to cancer or aging. The meeting was particularly timely since it is now apparent that certain DNA-repair processes offer significant potential for novel therapies to treat diseases such as cancer. The U.K. has a large body of active researchers at the forefront of biochemical analysis of these processes. This is demonstrated perfectly by the fact that this research community supplied four of the recipients of Biochemical Society Awards for 2008.

The meeting brought together almost 200 researchers, and an important aim was to identify topics that will provide the next areas to focus on for the field, particularly as basic research translates into more clinical applications. Thus the scope of presentations was wide, covering studies in model organisms through to functional analysis of purified proteins, as well as applied and translational research.

In addition to the main invited speakers, whose contributions are collected in this volume[1], the meeting also featured lectures by the aforementioned Biochemical Society Award winners[2], talks by ten younger scientists and

---

[1]These chapters are available online at http://symposia.biochemistry.org.
[2]Articles by the Award Lecturers who presented at the Annual Symposium have been published in *Biochemical Society Transactions* volume 37, part 3 (http://www.biochemsoctrans.org), as have the articles published in this book.

80 presented posters[3]. The high quality and superb science delivered by all presentations demonstrated the strength in depth within this research field.

Links to cancer

A large body of experimental data has demonstrated that genetic instability causes a variety of human diseases. However, the evidence is particularly strong with cancer, where recent studies suggest that many cancers are linked to DNA damage or malfunction of DNA-repair pathways. The use of contemporary genomic technologies in identifying links between cancer, DNA repair and the cell cycle is highlighted in this volume by Janet Hall (Chapter 1). Insights into the involvement of DNA repair in specific forms of cancer are provided by Ian Hickson in relation to Bloom's syndrome (Chapter 5) and by Fred Alt in relation to the role of DNA double-strand breaks in the formation of some lymphomas (Chapter 6). DNA-repair proteins and pathways provide plausible targets for therapeutic treatment of cancer, and the significant progress that is being made in this area formed is covered by Thomas Helleday (Chapter 12).

New insights into human physiology

For several years, it has been clear that appropriate regulation of DNA-repair pathways is important for maintaining a balance between increased prevalence of cancer or early onset of aging. The link to natural aging is becoming greater and an important component of this connection is maintenance of the length of telomeres at the end of chromosomes; Nicola Royle (Chapter 10) reports on the significance of recombination in these processes.

As we understand more about the biochemistry and physiology of DNA-repair pathways, additional links to human diseases are being identified. Interestingly, recent unrelated studies have identified different mechanisms by which formation and repair of single-strand breaks in DNA lead to specific inherited disorders. Tomas Lindahl (Chapter 2) describes how mutations in TREX1 (3′ repair exonuclease 1) lead to a specific type of inflammatory disease, Aicardi–Goutières syndrome. The links between repair of single-stranded DNA breaks and neurodegenerative disease are outlined by Keith Caldecott (Chapter 8).

Studies using model systems

One reason that there has been such rapid recent progress in the field of DNA repair is that excellent model systems are available for experimental studies. These range from *in vivo* studies in prokaryotic and eukaryotic cells to high-resolution structural analysis of macromolecular complexes that are influenced by protein–protein and protein–DNA interactions. Penny Jeggo (Chapter 7) outlines recent advances in understanding how DNA double-strand break repair

---

[3] Abstracts submitted for all oral presentations and posters are hosted on the web pages for the Annual Symposium (http://www.biochemistry.org/meetings/programme.cfm?Meeting_No=SA084).

is influenced by the chromatin state of the genome. Several chapters address the significance of guanine repeats in relation to the formation of unusual DNA structures and DNA repair. With a focus on therapeutic strategies, this topic is covered by Stephen Neidle (Chapter 9) in relation to telomeres and Kevin Hiom (Chapter 11) in relation to increased understanding of the roles of BRCA1 (breast cancer 1 early-onset) in the DNA-damage response.

High-resolution structural studies of DNA repair pathways form the basis of Chapter 3 in which Aidan Doherty discusses non-homologous end-joining in prokaryotes. Malcolm White (Chapter 4) describes how studies of archaea that grow under extreme conditions are providing an improved understanding of the roles of specific proteins in nucleotide excision repair.

Summary

We thank everyone who ensured that the Symposium was a success. Generous sponsorship was received from Portland Press and a number of pharmaceutical and molecular biology-focused companies, and excellent organization, co-ordinated by Silvia Rabar, was provided by the Biochemical Society's Meetings Office. Most importantly, we thank all of the authors for their scholarly contributions, and Ed Elloway and his colleagues at Portland Press for their assistance in the publication process. The articles in this volume provide a snapshot of recent important findings within the field of DNA repair, and we look forward to further exciting developments.

Richard Bowater, Rhona Borts
and Malcolm White

Abbreviations

AEP	archaeo-eukaryotic primase
AGS	Aicardi–Goutières syndrome
AID	activation-induced cytidine deaminase
ALT	alternative lengthening of telomeres
AOA1	ataxia oculomotor apraxia-1
APB	ALT-associated promyelocytic leukaemia body
APLF	aprataxin- and polynucleotide kinase-like factor
A-T	ataxia telangiectasia
ATM	ataxia telangiectasia mutated
ATMi	ATM inhibitor
ATR	ATM- and Rad3-related
BARD1	BRCA1-associated RING domain 1
BER	base excision repair
BIR	break-induced replication
BLM	Bloom's syndrome protein
BRCA	breast cancer, early-onset
BRCA1	breast cancer 1 early-onset
BRCT	BRCA1 C-terminal
BS	Bloom's syndrome
BTR	BLM–topoisomerase III–RMI1/2
CAF1	chromatin assembly factor 1
CDK	cyclin-dependent kinase
CDKN	cyclin-dependent kinase inhibitor
CHEK2	checkpoint kinase 2 checkpoint homologue
CI	confidence interval
CS	Cockayne's syndrome
csPCNA	cancer-specific PCNA
CSR	class switch recombination
CtIP	CtBP (C-terminal binding protein)-interacting protein
DAPI	4′,6-diamidino-2-phenylindole
DHJ	double Holliday junction
DinG	damage-inducible G
D-loop	displacement loop
DNA-PK	DNA-dependent protein kinase
DNMT1	DNA methyltransferase 1
DSB	double-strand break
DSBR	double-strand break repair

dsDNA	double-stranded DNA
EC-DSB	DSB located within euchromatic DNA
ECTR	extrachromosomal telomeric repeat
ER	endoplasmic reticulum
ESCO	establishment of cohesion
EXO1	exonuclease 1
exoX	exonuclease X
FA	Fanconi's anaemia
Fanc (or FANC)	Fanconi's anaemia complementation group
FancJ	Fanconi's anaemia complementation group J
FEN1	flap endonuclease-1
FHA	forkhead-associated
FPRP	false-positive report probability
FSp53	fully spliced p53
Gadd45	growth-arrest and DNA-damage-inducible protein 45
GFP	green fluorescent protein
γH2AX	phosphorylated histone H2AX
H3K9ac	histone H3 acetylated at Lys^9
H3K9me	histone H3 methylated at Lys^9
H3K9me3	histone H3 trimethylated at Lys^9
HC-DSB	DSB located within or close to heterochromatic DNA
HDAC	histone deacetylase
Hdm2	human double minute 2
HIT	histidine triad
HP1	heterochromatin protein 1
HR	homologous recombination
HRDC	helicase and RNaseD C-terminal
HRR	homologous recombination repair
IgH	Ig heavy chain
IgL	Ig light chain
IL-4	interleukin 4
IR	ionizing radiation
IRIF	ionization-radiation-induced foci
KAP-1	KRAB (Krüppel-associated box) domain-associated protein 1
Lig3α	DNA ligase IIIα
LigD	ligase D
LigDom	ligase domain of LigD
LOH	loss of heterozygosity
LPS	lipopolysaccharide
mAID	mouse AID
MD	Molecular Dynamics
MDC1	mediator of DNA-damage checkpoint 1
MEF	mouse embryonic fibroblast
MGMT	O^6-methylguanine DNA-methyltransferase
miRNA	microRNA
MLH1	MutL homologue 1

MM-PBSA	Molecular Mechanics and the Poisson–Boltzmann surface area approximation
MMR	mismatch repair
MRE11	meiotic recombination 11
MRN	MRE11–Rad50–NBS1
MRX	MRE11–Rad50–Xrs2
MSH	MutS homologue
Mt	*Mycobacterium tuberculosis*
NBS1	Nijmegen breakage syndrome 1
NER	nucleotide excision repair
NHEJ	non-homologous end-joining
NucDom	nuclease domain of LigD
OR	odds ratio
PCNA	proliferating-cell nuclear antigen
PD	population doubling
PFGE	pulsed-field gel electrophoresis
PICH	Plk1 (Polo-like kinase 1)-interacting checkpoint helicase
PIP-box	PCNA-interaction protein box
PKA	protein kinase A
PML	promyelocytic leukaemia
PNK	polynucleotide kinase
Pol	polymerase
Polβ	polymerase β
PolDom	polymerase domain of LigD
PolyPhen	Polymorphism Phenotyping
POT1	protection of telomeres 1
pRb	retinoblastoma protein
Rap1	repressor activator protein 1
RAP80	receptor-associated protein 80
Rb	retinoblastoma protein
RFC	replication factor C
RING	really interesting new gene
RMSD	root mean square deviation
RNF8	RING finger protein 8
ROS	reactive oxygen species
RPA	replication protein A
RQC	RecQ C-terminal
RR	relative risk
RTEL	regular of telomere length
RVCL	retinal vasculopathy with cerebral leukodystrophy
S	switch
SCE	sister-chromatid exchange
SHM	somatic hypermutation
SIFT	Sorting Intolerant From Tolerant
siRNA	small interfering RNA
SNP	single nucleotide polymorphism

SSB	single-strand break
SSBR	single-strand break repair
ssDNA	single-stranded DNA
SUMO	small ubiquitin-related modifier
Suv39H1/2	suppressor of variegation 3–9 homologue 1/2.
TdT	terminal deoxynucleotidyltransferase
TFIIH	transcription factor II H
TIN2	TRF1-interacting nuclear factor 2
TLS	translesion synthesis
TMD	transmembrane domain
TMM	telomere maintenance mechanism
TP53	tumour protein 53
TREX1	3′ repair exonuclease 1.
TRF	telomeric-repeat-binding factor
T-SCE	telomere sister-chromatid exchange
TTD	trichothiodystrophy
UBM	ubiquitin-binding motif
UFB	ultrafine bridge
UIM	ubiquitin-binding motif
UTR	untranslated region
WRN	Werner's syndrome protein
WT	wild-type
XLF	XRCC4-like factor
XP	xeroderma pigmentosum
XPB	xeroderma pigmentosum complementation group B
XPD	xeroderma pigmentosum complementation group D
XPG	xeroderma pigmentosum complementation group G
XRCC	X-ray repair complementing defective repair in Chinese-hamster cells.
$XS\mu$	*Xenopus* $S\mu$
zAID	zebrafish AID.

Biochem. Soc. Symp. 76
Citation reference: Biochem. Soc. Trans. (2009) **37**, 527–533.

1

The associations of sequence variants in DNA-repair and cell-cycle genes with cancer risk: genotype–phenotype correlations

Janet Hall*†[1], Virginie Marcel‡, Celeste Bolin*†, Marie Fernet*†, Laurence Tartier*†, Laurence Vaslin*† and Pierre Hainaut‡

*Institut Curie-Recherche, Bats 110–112, Centre Universitaire, 91405, Orsay, France, †INSERM U612, Centre Universitaire, Bats 110–112, 91405, Orsay, France, and ‡International Agency for Research on Cancer, 150, cours Albert Thomas, 69372, Lyon, France

Abstract

DNA-repair systems maintain the integrity of the human genome, and cell-cycle checkpoints are a critical component of the cellular response to DNA damage. Thus the presence of sequence variants in genes involved in these pathways that modulate their activity might have an impact on cancer risk. Many molecular epidemiological studies have investigated the association between sequence variants, particularly SNPs (single nucleotide polymorphisms), and cancer risk. For instance, *ATM* (ataxia telangiectasia mutated) SNPs have been associated with increased risk of breast, prostate, leukaemia, colon and

[1] To whom correspondence should be addressed
(email janet.hall@curie.u-psud.fr).

early-onset lung cancer, and the intron 3 16-bp repeat in *TP53* (tumour protein 53) is associated with an increased risk of lung cancer. In contrast, the variant allele of the rare *CHEK2* (checkpoint kinase 2 checkpoint homologue) missense variant (accession number rs17879961) was significantly associated with a lower incidence of lung and upper aerodigestive cancers. For some sequence variants, a strong gene–environment interaction has also been noted. For instance, a greater absolute risk reduction of lung and upper aerodigestive cancers in smokers than in non-smokers carrying the I157T *CHEK2* variant has been observed, as has an interaction between *TP53* intron 3 16-bp repeats and multiple X-ray exposures on lung cancer risk. The challenge now is to understand the molecular mechanisms underlying these associations.

Introduction: genes and sequence variants

DNA-repair systems provide a critical defence mechanism against exogenous DNA-damaging agents, such as the human carcinogen ionizing radiation and those found in tobacco smoke, and endogenous sources such as ROS (reactive oxygen species) generated from normal cellular metabolism. Many types of DNA lesion result from such exposures including SSBs (single-strand breaks), DSBs (double-strand breaks), mismatches, chemical modifications of the bases and sugars as well as inter- and intra-strand cross-links. To avoid the deleterious consequences of damage accumulation and thus maintain the integrity of the human genome, cells have developed a co-ordinated damage response involving the recognition of the damage, signalling of its presence to effector molecules and activation of cell-cycle checkpoints. Cell-cycle progression is halted in order to allow time for DNA-repair processes to remove the damage before cellular replication. If the damage is too extensive, the cell dies by apoptosis or necrosis, so that the resulting mutations or chromosomal aberrations do not result in genomic instability and cancer formation [1].

The particular repair mechanism used depends on the type of DNA lesion. Base damage and SSBs, caused by oxidative damage, ionizing radiation and many alkylating agents, are repaired by the BER (base excision repair) pathway. In mammalian cells, the highly mutagenic methylated-DNA lesion O^6-methylguanine is dealt with by the so-called suicide enzyme MGMT (O^6-methylguanine DNA-methyltransferase). Bulky DNA adducts and intrastrand cross-links, formed by carcinogenic metabolites, UV light and platinum-based chemotherapy agents, are repaired by the NER (nucleotide excision repair) pathway. Replication errors result in mismatches and insertion or deletion loops, which are repaired by the mismatch repair pathway. DSBs, the lethal lesions caused by ionizing radiation and topoisomerase II inhibitors, are repaired by homologous recombination, non-homologous end-joining and single strand annealing. The majority of these pathways involve several proteins that function in a co-ordinated fashion to remove and replace the damaged nucleoside residues and interact with the signalling pathways that regulate proliferation. The inability of a cell to properly regulate its proliferation in the presence of DNA damage would also increase the risk of the accumulation of gene mutations. The transitions between different phases of the cell cycle are driven by changes in cyclin–CDK (cyclin-dependent kinase) pairs. To ensure the completion of each phase before entry into the next, surveillance mechanisms or cell-cycle checkpoints monitor the progress. If errors or defects are detected, progression is reversibly halted by CDK inhibitors.

The deleterious clinical consequences of inherited defects in DNA-repair systems are apparent from several human syndromes. Increased cancer predisposition is found in patients with XP (xeroderma pigmentosum) (NER-compromised), A-T (ataxia telangiectasia) and Nijmegen breakage syndrome (DSB detection and repair compromised) as well as Li–Fraumeni syndrome (p53 suppressive function impaired) [2–4]. Defects in some repair processes manifest themselves as premature aging syndromes such as Werner's syndrome [5]. Others, particularly those associated with ROS-induced DNA damage, manifest themselves primarily in neuronal tissues and are associated with neurodegenerative diseases such as ataxia with oculomotor apraxia 1 and spinocerebellar ataxia with axonal neuropathy 1 [6]. In addition to rare deleterious mutations, there is evidence that genetic predisposition to cancer acts via a combination of sequence variants in a set of low- and medium-penetrance genes. Recent genetic association studies on cancer risk have focused on identifying the effects of SNPs (single nucleotide polymorphisms) in candidate genes, among which DNA-repair and cell-cycle-control genes are increasingly studied because of their critical role in maintaining genome integrity. A growing body of literature demonstrating that certain SNPs can alter the expression and functional properties of the corresponding enzymes supports the implication of SNPs as genetic risk factors.

SNPs are the most frequently found form of genetic variation. It is estimated that there are approx. 10 million SNPs in the human genome and they account for most of the known genetic variation between individuals. They may fall within coding sequences of genes, non-coding regions of genes such as the promoter region, introns or the 3′-UTR (untranslated region), or the non-coding regions between genes. Those within a coding sequence may or may not change the amino acid sequence of the protein produced (non-synonymous and synonymous SNPs respectively), owing to degeneracy of the genetic code. SNPs outside the protein-coding regions can modify transcriptional or translational control, e.g. polymorphisms within miRNA (microRNA)-binding sites in the UTRs of mRNAs (discussed below). Over the last 15 years, the association between the presence of SNPs and the risk of cancer development at a number of different sites has been investigated in case-control studies using a candidate gene approach [7]. Genes studied have been selected based on several criteria including the likely environmental exposures of the population, knowledge of the chemistry of the suspected carcinogens and their interaction with DNA, and an understanding of the cellular processes activated in response to the DNA damage produced. For instance, several studies investigating the association of sequence variants with bladder cancer have focused on SNPs in the NER genes because of the implication of aromatic amines in bladder cancer aetiology. SNPs in BER genes have also been investigated, because exposure to cigarette smoke, which produces alkylating and oxidative DNA damage, is a known risk factor [8–11]. However, results for certain SNPs have been inconsistent, possibly because of (i) low statistical power for detecting a moderate effect, (ii) false-positive results, (iii) heterogeneity across study populations, (iv) failure to consider effect modifiers such as environmental exposures, and (v) publication bias.

The last few years have seen an explosion in the development of genome-analysis technology and analytical tools with larger cohorts being more comprehensively genotyped. Several recent meta-analyses and pooled analyses have attempted to evaluate the contribution of candidate genes to the genetic susceptibility of cancer. For instance, Dong et al. [7] reviewed the results obtained in 161 analyses, each including at least 500 cases, covering 18 cancer sites and 99 genes. Taking into account the FPRP (false-positive report probability), 13 gene-variant cancer associations remained noteworthy (FPRP <0.2) including *XPD* (xeroderma pigmentosum complementation group D) K751Q and lung cancer [OR (odds ratio) 1.3, $P = 2 \times 10^{-4}$], *XRCC1* (X-ray repair complementing defective repair in Chinese-hamster cells 1) R399Q and lung cancer (OR 1.3, $P = 5.2 \times 10^{-5}$) and *CHEK2* (checkpoint kinase 2 checkpoint homologue) *1100delC and breast cancer (OR 2.4, $P = 2.5 \times 10^{-9}$). Assuming a very low probability of 10^{-6}, similar to a probability assumed for a randomly selected SNP in a genome-wide association study, and statistical power to detect an OR of 1.5, four highly significant associations were found involving not a SNP, but a deletion variant of the GSTMI (glutathione transferase Mu 1) metabolizing enzyme. A number of genome-wide association studies have been reported in prostate, breast, colon and bladder cancers, where hundreds of thousands of variants have been genotyped across the whole genome, allowing capture of 65–75% of common genetic variation (for a recent review of genome-wide association studies, see [12]). These studies have identified statistically significant variants that had not been identified previously as they mostly did not reside in 'interesting' candidate regions.

Genetic variants in DNA-damage-detection and DNA-repair genes associated with altered cancer risk: functional considerations

Although many DNA-damage-detection, DNA-repair or cell-cycle-control genes have been characterized at the functional level, and the consequences of their absence has been assessed using mutant cell lines and RNAi (RNA interference) approaches, the impact of many sequence variants remains to be established. Many amino acid substitution variants identified in DNA-repair genes during human population screenings are predicted to have an impact on protein function using algorithms such as SIFT (Sorting Intolerant From Tolerant) and PolyPhen (Polymorphism Phenotyping). Xi et al. [13] reviewed 520 different amino acid substitution variants in 91 human DNA-repair genes using both algorithms and predicted that 21–31% of the variant proteins would exhibit reduced activity. Refinements of such *in silico* approaches have been reported. For instance, Tavtigian et al. [14] have developed an extension of the original Grantham difference by including multiple sequence alignments. Their algorithm, Align-GVGD (http://agvgd.iarc.fr/) allows the prediction of where missense substitutions in genes of interest fall in a spectrum from enriched deleterious to enriched neutral for genes including the clinically relevant *ATM* (ataxia telangiectasia mutated), *BRCA1* (breast cancer early-onset 1) and *BRCA2*, *CHEK2* and *TP53* (tumour protein 53) genes.

Much of the difficulty in establishing predictive functional assays is knowing which of the biochemical functions of an often multifunctional protein is important for carcinogenesis and should be assayed (see examples in [15]). For instance, even for a relatively 'simple enzyme' such as the MGMT protein that repairs the O^6-methylguanine via the irreversible transfer of a methyl adduct to the sulfur of the active-site cysteine residue, there are several distinct aspects of regulation and function that should be considered as potential points of polymorphic regulation. For the *MGMT* gene, there are reports that the C458A SNP in the promoter may modulate expression, but also that the variant allele at amino acid 143 changes the reactivity towards other O^6-alkyl species and sequence context repair. In addition, polymorphisms must be considered in the context of the haplotype structure. Over the approx. 300 kb genomic structure of *MGMT*, 509 SNPs were genotyped in Caucasians and, among these, 321 had a minor allele frequency of >0.05 (reviewed recently in [16]).

Impact on splicing: cyclin D1 and TP53 sequence variants

Some SNPs do not influence the amino acid context of the corresponding protein, but result in alternative splicing (Figure 1). Molecular epidemiological studies have shown that the 870A allele of the cyclin D1 gene (*CCND1*) (accession number rs603965) is associated with an increased risk of several cancers (reviewed in [17]). Cyclin D1 is a regulator of cell-cycle progression which interacts with and activates the G_1 CDKs, CDK4 and CDK6. Inactivation of cyclin D1 arrests cells in the G_1-phase of the cell cycle. The cyclin D1–CDK4 or CDK6 complex phosphorylates Rb (retinoblastoma protein) and releases the cell cycle into S-phase, p16 binds to the cyclin D1–CDK4 complex and inhibits phosphorylation of Rb thus blocking the cell cycle at the G_1/S border. Hung et al. [18] found no association between this SNP and lung cancer risk. However, the dose–response relationship between lung cancer risk and X-ray exposures was modified by the *CCND1* genotype. No lung cancer risk from X-ray exposures was observed among subjects with the G/G genotype, intermediate risk was

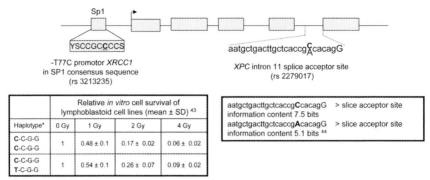

Haplotype*	Relative in vitro cell survival of lymphoblastoid cell lines (mean ± SD) [43]			
	0 Gy	1 Gy	2 Gy	4 Gy
C-C-G-G C-C-G-G	1	0.48 ± 0.1	0.17 ± 0.02	0.06 ± 0.02
C-C-G-G T-C-G-G	1	0.54 ± 0.1	0.26 ± 0.07	0.09 ± 0.02

* -77, codons 194, 280, 399

Figure 1. Examples of SNPs in promoter sequences and intron/exon boundaries and their consequences

The −T77C SNP in the Sp1 (specificity protein)-binding site of the *XRCC1* promoter modulates the risk of developing an adverse effect to radiotherapy: the *XRCC1* haplotype with the T allele at position −77 and the wild-type alleles at codons 194, 280 and 399 is radioprotective (OR 0.39, 95% CI 0.2–0.9) compared with the haplotype with the C allele at this position. In agreement with this observation, lymphoblastoid cell lines heterozygous for the −77 SNP show a higher *in vitro* radiosensitivity [43]. The *XPC* (xeroderma pigmentosum complementation group C) intron 11 splice acceptor polymorphism located at the −5 position of the intron 11 splice acceptor changes the splice acceptor information content from 7.5 bits to 5.1 bits. Cells with AA at this position have 2.6-fold more mRNA without exon 12 than CC cells, and the AA cells had a lower DNA repair capacity, providing a possible explanation for the increased head and neck cancer risk in carriers of the A allele [44].

observed among subjects with the G/A genotype, and the highest risk was observed among subjects with A/A genotypes [trend OR for X-rays 1.16, 95% CI (confidence interval) 1.12–1.49]. Two major cyclin D1 transcripts are found in mammalian cells: cyclin D1a and D1b. The cyclin D1a transcript is encoded by exons 1–5, whereas the cyclin D1b transcript is encoded by exons 1–4 and sequences from intron 4. Molecular studies have shown that the abundance of the cyclin D1b is regulated by the G870A allele which is located at the exon 4/intron 4 boundary. The presence of the A allele favours the alternative splicing, giving rise to cyclin D1b. It has been shown that, unlike cyclin D1a, the alternative transcript D1b by itself has the capacity to transform fibroblasts *in vitro*, and Rojas et al. [19] have shown using a transgenic mouse model that mice expressing cyclin D1b have enhanced skin carcinogenesis. Because cyclin D1b does not contain the Thr^{286} phosphorylation site that is required for nuclear export and regulated degradation, one of the major differences between cyclin D1a and cyclin D1b is their localization. Unlike cyclin D1a, which is exported into the cytoplasm during S-phase, cyclin D1b remains in the nucleus during the cell cycle, where its constitutive expression is probably associated with its oncogenic potential and modifications of the cellular responses to ionizing radiation, although the exact mechanisms remain to be elucidated.

Another variant that appears to influence splicing and which was found to modify the effect of X-rays on lung cancer risk is a 16 bp duplication in intron 3 (p53*PIN3*) (rs17878362) of the *TP53* tumour-suppressor gene [18]. The A2 allele, carrying the G-rich duplication, is present in approx. 20% of the Caucasian population [20] and has been associated with an increased risk of cancers at several sites (http://www-p53.iarc.fr/index.html) [21]. The biology of the *TP53* gene is complex. In addition to being probably the most frequently mutated gene in human cancers, it is highly polymorphic and is expressed as several isoforms with a conserved DNA-binding domain, but different N- and C-termini [22].

The main proximal promoter generates transcripts with two different 5′ regions, FSp53 (fully spliced p53) and p53I2. FSp53 mRNA encodes the canonical p53 protein, which exerts tumour-suppressor activities. The p53I2 mRNA is an alternatively spliced variant retaining intron 2, which contains stop codons [23,24]. The use of the ATG at codon 40 as an alternative translation start site either from the FSp53 or p53I2 mRNAs produces the ΔNp53 isoform which lacks 39 amino acids [23,25]. As a consequence, ΔNp53 is deficient in its capacity to transactivate p53-target genes and is a stable protein, since it escapes Hdm2 (human double minute 2)-dependent degradation owing to the lack of the Hdm2-binding site (residues 17–22) [23,25]. When expressed in excess, as compared with p53, ΔNp53 inhibits p53 transcriptional activity and interferes in cell-cycle control and apoptosis by exerting a negative effect possibly through hetero-oligomerization [23,25,26]. Thus the levels of ΔNp53 expression in cells may have a profound impact on p53 activation in response to stress and on its functional consequences for growth suppression.

Several years ago, we showed that lymphoblastoid cell lines carrying the A2/A2 alleles had reduced p53 mRNA levels compared with A1/A1 cells, suggesting that the p53*PIN3* polymorphism may regulate the expression of p53 mRNA [27]. In recent studies, we have investigated whether the levels of ΔNp53 and p53 are different, depending on the p53*PIN3* statute. Making use of the fact that the DO-7 monoclonal antibody recognizes an epitope contained only in p53 and the CM1 polyclonal antibody recognizes both p53 and ΔNp53, we quantified the expression of p53 protein isoforms in A1 (no duplication) and A2 (duplication) cells by Western blotting (Figure 2). DO-7 detected a major band corresponding to p53 in cell lines carrying either the A1 or A2 homozygous genotypes. Compared with A1 cells, the p53 migration was slightly delayed in A2 cells, in agreement with the presence of, in addition to the intron 3 duplication, a proline residue instead of arginine at codon 72. However in the four A2 cell lines tested, p53 levels were decreased by approx. 15% compared with the four A1 cells. The CM1 antibody detected a 53 kDa protein, corresponding to p53, and a 40 kDa protein, which was not recognized by DO-7, indicating that it lacks the N-terminus and therefore corresponds to ΔNp53. This isoform is more abundant in A2 than in A1 cells (approx. 10% increase). Overall, these results show that presence of the p53*PIN3* duplication is concordant with a reduction in p53 expression and a relative increase in ΔNp53. The molecular basis of this alternative splicing is not fully understood, but it is

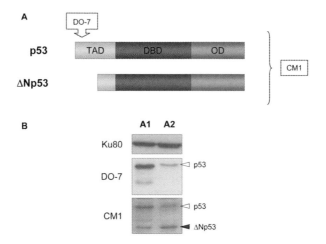

Figure 2. *TP53* isoforms and expression levels in relation to the p53*PIN3* polymorphism
(**A**) Schematic representation of p53 and ΔNp53 isoform. The p53 protein contains a transactivation domain (TAD), a central DNA-binding domain (DBD) and an oligomerization domain (OD). In contrast with p53, the ΔNp53 isoform lacks part of the TAD. The regions of p53 recognized by the two anti-p53 antibodies are indicated. (**B**) Expression level of p53 and ΔNp53 in relation to the p53*PIN3* polymorphism. Proteins were extracted from non-treated lymphoblastoid cell lines carrying either the A1 or A2 allele. In A2 cells, the p53 expression level is reduced, whereas the expression level of ΔNp53 is weakly increased compared with A1 cells.

interesting to note that the 112-bp-long intron 3, which is only separated from intron 2 by the very short exon 3 (20 bp), is guanine-rich (33%). Our present working hypothesis is that the p53*PIN3* sequence is involved in the formation of G-quadruplexes, a common type of structure known to regulate alternative splicing [28,29] and may provide a new mechanistic basis to explain the genetic susceptibility associated with the p53*PIN3* polymorphism. That an interaction between this variant and X-ray exposure was observed in lung cancer patients [18] might be related to the negative biological functions of the ΔNp53 protein (Figure 3) [30].

Impact on gene expression and mRNA stability: variants in the 5′- and 3′-UTRs

In addition to a direct impact on function through amino acid substitutions or via alternative splicing, polymorphisms may affect gene expression directly (Figure 1). In a survey of data available for 108 DNA-repair genes that have been systematically screened for sequence variation, an average of 3.3 SNPs per gene were found to exist at a variant allele frequency of at least 0.02 in the region 2 kb upstream of the 5′-UTR region [31]. These were located both in CpG islands and within predicted promoter elements and could thus exacerbate the impact of amino acid substitution variants on the activity of proteins

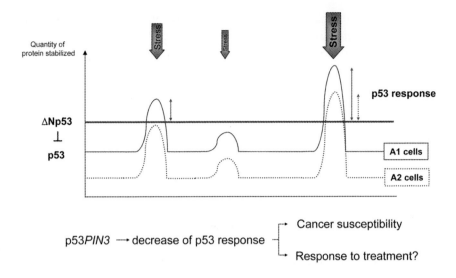

Figure 3. Role of p53*PIN3* polymorphism in cancer susceptibility
The ΔNp53 isoform is a stable protein that acts as an inhibitor of p53 suppressive function. Under genotoxic stress, p53 is stabilized, and a p53 response may be observed only if the quantity of stabilized p53 is higher than ΔNp53. In A2 cells, p53 expression level is reduced, and a decrease of p53 response may be expected.

by modulating expression levels. Among the post-transcriptional regulation mechanisms that can modulate gene expression, miRNAs play a key role. These non-coding, small (approx. 22 nucleotides) RNAs regulate expression by pairing to the 3'-UTRs of mRNAs of target genes, resulting in the cleavage of target mRNAs or repression of their productive translation. A growing body of evidence has implicated miRNAs in a regulatory role in a variety of biological processes, including embryonic development, cell proliferation, cell differentiation, apoptosis and cancer development [32]. Polymorphisms in both the miRNAs themselves and in the miRNA target sites (miRNA-binding SNP) have been documented [33]. These latter SNPs can either abolish existing binding sites by disrupting the thermodynamics of the RNA–RNA interaction between the miRNA and its target mRNA or create illegitimate binding sites, resulting in the deregulation of the target gene expression. Approx. 20000 SNPs located in miRNA-binding sites have been catalogued in databases such as PolymiRTS (http://compbio.utmem.edu/miRSNP) and Patrocles (http://www.patrocles.org) (reviewed in [34]). Possible associations between miRNA-binding SNPs and cancer risk have been investigated, and cancer-associated aberrant allele frequencies have been identified. For example, Landi et al. [35] identified 57 putative SNPs in miRNA-binding sites in 104 colorectal cancer candidate genes and evaluated them for their ability to affect the binding of the miRNA with its target by assessing the variation of Gibbs free energy between the two alleles of each SNP. Eight were subsequently evaluated in a case/control association study of colorectal cancer, and it was found that variant alleles of the *CD86* and *INSR* (insulin receptor) genes were associated with increased cancer risk [35]. Similar screens have identified miRNA-binding SNPs in DNA-repair genes that will either modify miRNA binding at existing sites or create new sites, and might, as predicted by Chen et al. [36], provide a gold mine for molecular epidemiology in the future.

Gene–environment interactions: carrying variant alleles can be beneficial

Gene–environment interactions can also be beneficial for the carrier of variant alleles. The heterozygous T/C genotype of the *CHEK2* gene variant (rs17879961, I157T) was found to be associated with a lower incidence of lung cancer than the common T/T genotype [RR (relative risk) T/C compared with T/T 0.44, 95% CI 0.31–0.63, for lung cancer of any histological type] and with a significantly lower risk of upper aerodigestive cancer (RR 0.44, 95% CI 0.26–0.73, all were squamous cell carcinomas) [37]. This unexpected halving of tobacco-related cancers, replicated independently [38], implies much greater absolute risk reduction in smokers than in non-smokers. If this association is causal, i.e. a functional defect in one copy of *CHEK2* actually causes smokers to have a lower cancer risk, then the mechanistic basis must be novel and it can only be speculated as to what this might be. The *CHEK2* gene encodes a multifunctional protein kinase that can have opposite effects on damaged cells. It can hold back cell division until any DNA damage has been repaired, or it can activate cell death by apoptosis if there is unrepairable damage. Brennan et al. [37] have suggested a possible mechanism. In response to DNA damage, stem cells undergo apoptosis, forcing nearby stem cells to divide before they have repaired their own DNA damage from tobacco smoke. If so, reducing the rate of apoptosis by reducing CHEK2 activity could be protective. Although, as the authors point out, not smoking would be far more protective. Interestingly, a modest protective effect was also seen among smokers and for tobacco-related histologies for the *XRCC3* T241M SNP [39]. Whether this variant modulates similar cellular processes remains to be established. Some alleles in the *ATM* gene have also been found to be associated with an anti-neoplastic effect under certain circumstances. Mutations in this gene are associated with the autosomal recessive cancer-prone syndrome A-T, and carriers of A-T, although clinically asymptomatic, have an increased risk of developing breast cancer (reviewed in [40]). Carriers of common *ATM* variants have been reported to have an increased risk of breast, prostate, leukaemia, colon and early-onset lung cancer, but the relationship between individual SNPs and cancer risk appears to be complex. For instance, the ATM P1054R variant (rs1800057), which is predicted to have a deleterious effect on protein structure on the basis of either SIFT or PolyPhen, was not associated with an increased risk of primary breast cancer, but was associated with a significantly decreased risk of second primary breast cancers in the WECARE study [41]. Functional studies of ATM activity in cells from carriers of these variant alleles should help to resolve their effects.

Conclusions

Molecular epidemiological studies have identified several sequence variants in DNA-repair and cell-cycle genes that show statistically significant associations with cancer risk. The findings of Landi et al. [35] that SNPs within miRNA-binding sites are associated with colorectal cancer will surely lead to a close examination of variants in the 3′-UTRs of many genes. A handful of recent studies have linked miRNAs to the genotoxic stress response. For instance, p53 is a transactivator of *miR-34* which itself can promote apoptosis or cell-growth arrest (reviewed recently in [42]). Preliminary *in silico* studies have identified several SNPs that will modify miRNA binding in DNA-repair genes, and it is reasonable to predict that they will play a role in modulating responses to DNA damage. The challenge will remain: to understand the underlying molecular mechanisms.

Funding

V.M. was supported by a Fellowship from La Ligue Nationale Contre le Cancer, M.F. received financial support from Electricité de France [grant number 2006-01], L.T. was supported by the French Ministry of Health [grant number PHRC 2006-AOM06158] and C.B. was supported by a postdoctoral fellowship from Institut Curie.

References

1. Hoeijmakers, J.H. (2001) Genome maintenance mechanisms for preventing cancer. *Nature* **411**, 366–374

2. Kraemer, K.H., Patronas, N.J., Schiffmann, R., Brooks, B.P., Tamura, D. & DiGiovanna, J.J. (2007) Xeroderma pigmentosum, trichothiodystrophy and Cockayne syndrome: a complex genotype–phenotype relationship. *Neuroscience* **145**, 1388–1396

3. Lavin, M.F. & Kozlov, S. (2007) DNA damage-induced signalling in ataxia-telangiectasia and related syndromes. *Radiother. Oncol.* **83**, 231–237

4. Petitjean, A., Achatz, M.I., Borresen-Dale, A.L., Hainaut, P. & Olivier, M. (2007) TP53 mutations in human cancers: functional selection and impact on cancer prognosis and outcomes. *Oncogene* **26**, 2157–2165

5. Muftuoglu, M., Oshima, J., von Kobbe, C., Cheng, W.H., Leistritz, D.F. & Bohr, V.A. (2008) The clinical characteristics of Werner syndrome: molecular and biochemical diagnosis. *Hum. Genet.* **124**, 369–377

6. Caldecott, K.W. (2008) Single-strand break repair and genetic disease. *Nat. Rev. Genet.* **9**, 619–631

7. Dong, L.M., Potter, J.D., White, E., Ulrich, C.M., Cardon, L.R. & Peters, U. (2008) Genetic susceptibility to cancer: the role of polymorphisms in candidate genes. *JAMA, J. Am. Med. Assoc.* **299**, 2423–2436

8. Figueroa, J.D., Malats, N., Real, F.X., Silverman, D., Kogevinas, M., Chanock, S., Welch, R., Dosemeci, M., Tardon, A., Serra, C. et al. (2007) Genetic variation in the base excision repair pathway and bladder cancer risk. *Hum. Genet.* **121**, 233–242

9. Garcia-Closas, M., Malats, N., Real, F.X., Welch, R., Kogevinas, M., Chatterjee, N., Pfeiffer, R., Silverman, D., Dosemeci, M., Tardon, A. et al. (2006) Genetic variation in the nucleotide excision repair pathway and bladder cancer risk. *Cancer Epidemiol. Biomarkers Prev.* **15**, 536–542

10. Sak, S.C., Barrett, J.H., Paul, A.B., Bishop, D.T. & Kiltie, A.E. (2006) Comprehensive analysis of 22 XPC polymorphisms and bladder cancer risk. *Cancer Epidemiol. Biomarkers Prev.* **15**, 2537–2541

11. Wu, X., Gu, J., Grossman, H.B., Amos, C.I., Etzel, C., Huang, M., Zhang, Q., Millikan, R.E., Lerner, S., Dinney, C.P. et al. (2006) Bladder cancer predisposition: a multigenic approach to DNA-repair and cell-cycle-control genes. *Am. J. Hum. Genet.* **78**, 464–479

12. Lango, H. & Weedon, M.N. (2008) What will whole genome searches for susceptibility genes for common complex disease offer to clinical practice? *J. Intern. Med.* **263**, 16–27

13. Xi, T., Jones, I.M. & Mohrenweiser, H.W. (2004) Many amino acid substitution variants identified in DNA repair genes during human population screenings are predicted to impact protein function. *Genomics* **83**, 970–979

14. Tavtigian, S.V., Greenblatt, M.S., Lesueur, F. & Byrnes, G.B. (2008) *In silico* analysis of missense substitutions using sequence-alignment based methods. *Hum. Mutat.* **29**, 1327–1336

15. Couch, F.J., Rasmussen, L.J., Hofstra, R., Monteiro, A.N., Greenblatt, M.S. & de Wind, N. (2008) Assessment of functional effects of unclassified genetic variants. *Hum. Mutat.* **29**, 1314–1326

16. Bugni, J.M., Han, J., Tsai, M.S., Hunter, D.J. & Samson, L.D. (2007) Genetic association and functional studies of major polymorphic variants of MGMT. *DNA Repair* **6**, 1116–1126

17. Knudsen, K.E., Diehl, J.A., Haiman, C.A. & Knudsen, E.S. (2006) Cyclin D1: polymorphism, aberrant splicing and cancer risk. *Oncogene* **25**, 1620–1628

18. Hung, R.J., Boffetta, P., Canzian, F., Moullan, N., Szeszenia-Dabrowska, N., Zaridze, D., Lissowska, J., Rudnai, P., Fabianova, E., Mates, D. et al. (2006) Sequence variants in cell cycle control pathway, X-ray exposure, and lung cancer risk: a multicenter case-control study in Central Europe. *Cancer Res.* **66**, 8280–8286

19. Rojas, P., Benavides, F., Blando, J., Perez, C., Cardenas, K., Richie, E., Knudsen, E.S., Johnson, D.G., Senderowicz, A.M., Rodriguez-Puebla, M.L. et al. (2008) *Enhanced skin carcinogenesis and lack of thymus hyperplasia in transgenic mice expressing human cyclin D1b (CCND1b).* Mol. Carcinog., doi:10.1002/mc.20489

20. Lazar, V., Hazard, F., Bertin, F., Janin, N., Bellet, D. & Bressac, B. (1993) Simple sequence repeat polymorphism within the p53 gene. *Oncogene* **8**, 1703–1705

21. Petitjean, A., Mathe, E., Kato, S., Ishioka, C., Tavtigian, S.V., Hainaut, P. & Olivier, M. (2007) Impact of mutant p53 functional properties on TP53 mutation patterns and tumor phenotype: lessons from recent developments in the IARC TP53 database. *Hum. Mutat.* **28**, 622–629

22. Bourdon, J.C., Fernandes, K., Murray-Zmijewski, F., Liu, G., Diot, A., Xirodimas, D.P., Saville, M.K. & Lane, D.P. (2005) p53 isoforms can regulate p53 transcriptional activity. *Genes Dev.* **19**, 2122–2137

23. Ghosh, A., Stewart, D. & Matlashewski, G. (2004) Regulation of human p53 activity and cell localization by alternative splicing. *Mol. Cell. Biol.* **24**, 7987–7997

24. Matlashewski, G., Pim, D., Banks, L. & Crawford, L. (1987) Alternative splicing of human p53 transcripts. *Oncogene Res.* **1**, 77–85

25. Courtois, S., Verhaegh, G., North, S., Luciani, M.G., Lassus, P., Hibner, U., Oren, M. & Hainaut, P. (2002) ΔN-p53, a natural isoform of p53 lacking the first transactivation domain, counteracts growth suppression by wild-type p53. *Oncogene* **21**, 6722–6728

26. Yin, Y., Stephen, C.W., Luciani, M.G. & Fahraeus, R. (2002) p53 stability and activity is regulated by Mdm2-mediated induction of alternative p53 translation products. *Nat. Cell Biol.* **4**, 462–467

27. Gemignani, F., Moreno, V., Landi, S., Moullan, N., Chabrier, A., Gutierrez Enriquez, S., Hall, J., Guino, E., Peinado, M.A., Capella, G. et al. (2004) A TP53 polymorphism is associated with increased risk of colorectal cancer and with reduced levels of TP53 mRNA. *Oncogene* **23**, 1954–1956

28. Cogan, J.D., Prince, M.A., Lekhakula, S., Bundey, S., Futrakul, A., McCarthy, E.M. & Phillips, 3rd, J.A. (1997) A novel mechanism of aberrant pre-mRNA splicing in humans. *Hum. Mol. Genet.* **6**, 909–912

29. Gomez, D., Lemarteleur, T., Lacroix, L., Mailliet, P., Mergny, J.L. & Riou, J.F. (2004) Telomerase downregulation induced by the G-quadruplex ligand 12459 in A549 cells is mediated by hTERT RNA alternative splicing. *Nucleic Acids Res.* **32**, 371–379

30. Marcel, V. & Hainaut, P. (2009) p53 isoforms: a conspiracy to kidnap p53 tumor suppressor activity? *Cell. Mol. Life Sci.* **66**, 391–406

31. Mohrenweiser, H. (2007) Survey of polymorphic sequence variation in the immediate 5′ region of human DNA repair genes. *Mutat. Res.* **616**, 221–226

32. Bartel, D.P. (2004) MicroRNAs: genomics, biogenesis, mechanism, and function. *Cell* **116**, 281–297

33. Yu, Z., Li, Z., Jolicoeur, N., Zhang, L., Fortin, Y., Wang, E., Wu, M. & Shen, S.H. (2007) Aberrant allele frequencies of the SNPs located in microRNA target sites are potentially associated with human cancers. *Nucleic Acids Res.* **35**, 4535–4541

34. Sethupathy, P. & Collins, F.S. (2008) MicroRNA target site polymorphisms and human disease. *Trends Genet.* **24**, 489–497

35. Landi, D., Gemignani, F., Naccarati, A., Pardini, B., Vodicka, P., Vodickova, L., Novotny, J., Forsti, A., Hemminki, K., Canzian, F. et al. (2008) Polymorphisms within micro-RNA-binding sites and risk of sporadic colorectal cancer. *Carcinogenesis* **29**, 579–584

36. Chen, K., Song, F., Calin, G.A., Wei, Q., Hao, X. & Zhang, W. (2008) Polymorphisms in microRNA targets: a gold mine for molecular epidemiology. *Carcinogenesis* **29**, 1306–1311

37. Brennan, P., McKay, J., Moore, L., Zaridze, D., Mukeria, A., Szeszenia-Dabrowska, N., Lissowska, J., Rudnai, P., Fabianova, E., Mates, D. et al. (2007) Uncommon CHEK2 mis-sense variant and reduced risk of tobacco-related cancers: case control study. *Hum. Mol. Genet.* **16**, 1794–1801

38. Cybulski, C., Masojc, B., Oszutowska, D., Jaworowska, E., Grodzki, T., Waloszczyk, P., Serwatowski, P., Pankowski, J., Huzarski, T., Byrski, T. et al. (2008) Constitutional CHEK2 mutations are associated with a decreased risk of lung and laryngeal cancers. *Carcinogenesis* **29**, 762–765

39. Hung, R.J., Christiani, D.C., Risch, A., Popanda, O., Haugen, A., Zienolddiny, S., Benhamou, S., Bouchardy, C., Lan, Q., Spitz, M.R. et al. (2008) International lung cancer consortium: pooled analysis of sequence variants in DNA repair and cell cycle pathways. *Cancer Epidemiol. Biomarkers Prev.* **17**, 3081–3089

40. Hall, J. (2005) The ataxia-telangiectasia mutated gene and breast cancer: gene expression profiles and sequence variants. *Cancer Lett.* **227**, 105–114

41. Concannon, P., Haile, R.W., Borresen-Dale, A.L., Rosenstein, B.S., Gatti, R.A., Teraoka, S.N., Diep, T.A., Jansen, L., Atencio, D.P., Langholz, B. et al. (2008) Variants in the ATM gene associated with a reduced risk of contralateral breast cancer. *Cancer Res.* **68**, 6486–6491

42. Babar, I.A., Slack, F.J. & Weidhaas, J.B. (2008) miRNA modulation of the cellular stress response. *Future Oncol.* **4**, 289–298

43. Brem, R., Cox, D.G., Chapot, B., Moullan, N., Romestaing, P., Gérard, J.-P., Pisani, P. & Hall, J. (2006) The XRCC1 − 77T>C variant: haplotypes, breast cancer risk and response to radiotherapy and the cellular response to DNA damage. *Carcinogenesis* **27**, 2469–2474

44. Khan, S.G., Muniz-Medina, V., Shahlavi, T., Baker, C.C., Inui, H., Ueda, T., Emmert, S., Schneider, T.D. & Kraemer, K.H. (2002) The human XPC DNA repair gene: arrangement, splice site information content and influence of a single nucleotide polymorphism in a splice acceptor site on alternative splicing and function. *Nucleic Acids Res.* **30**, 3624–3631

Biochem. Soc. Symp. 76
Citation reference: Biochem. Soc. Trans. (2009) **37**, 535–538.
© The Authors. Journal compilation © 2009 The Biochemical Society

2

Biochemical properties of mammalian TREX1 and its association with DNA replication and inherited inflammatory disease

Tomas Lindahl*[1], Deborah E. Barnes*, Yun-Gui Yang† and Peter Robins*

*Clare Hall Laboratories, Cancer Research UK London Research Institute, South Mimms, Herts. EN6 3LD, U.K., and †Beijing Institute of Genomics, Chinese Academy of Sciences, 7 Beitucheng West Road, Chaoyang District, Beijing 100029, China

Abstract

The major DNA-specific 3′–5′ exonuclease of mammalian cells is TREX1 (3′ repair exonuclease 1; previously called DNase III). The human enzyme is encoded by a single exon and, like many 3′ exonucleases, exists as a homodimer. TREX1 degrades ssDNA (single-stranded DNA) more efficiently than dsDNA (double-stranded DNA), and its catalytic properties are similar to those of *Escherichia coli* exonuclease X. However, TREX1 is only found in mammals and has an extended C-terminal domain containing a leucine-rich sequence required for its association with the endoplasmic reticulum. In normal S-phase and also in response to genotoxic stress, TREX1 at least partly

[1] To whom correspondence should be addressed
(email tomas.lindahl@cancer.org.uk).

redistributes to the cell nucleus. In a collaborative project, we have demonstrated TREX1 enzyme deficiency in Aicardi–Goutières syndrome. Subsequently, we have shown that AGS1 cells exhibit chronic ATM (ataxia telangiectasia mutated)-dependent checkpoint activation, and these TREX1-deficient cells accumulate ssDNA fragments of a distinct size generated during DNA replication. Other groups have shown that the syndromes of familial chilblain lupus as well as systemic lupus erythematosus, and the distinct neurovascular disorder retinal vasculopathy with cerebral leukodystrophy, can be caused by dominant mutations at different sites within the *TREX1* gene.

Introduction

In an early biochemical survey of mammalian enzymes that act on strand breaks in DNA, we discovered and characterized two major exonucleases, TREX1 (3′ repair exonuclease 1) and FEN1 (flap endonuclease-1) (initially called DNase III and DNase IV respectively). Until recently, TREX1 was by far the least studied of these enzymes. However, this situation changed as a consequence of the cloning and expression of the human *TREX1* gene, which is located to chromosome 3p21 [1,2], the establishment of an unexpected autoimmune phenotype in *Trex1*-knockout mice [3], and the finding of inactivating mutations of *TREX1* in a recessively inherited human disease related to systemic lupus erythematosus known as AGS (Aicardi–Goutières syndrome) [4].

Enzymology of TREX1

TREX1 functions as a 3′→5′ exonuclease specific for DNA; it acts 3–4-fold more efficiently on ssDNA (single-stranded DNA) than on dsDNA (double-stranded DNA), but is totally devoid of endonuclease activity [5]. TREX1 has sequence similarities to several other 3′ exonucleases in prokaryotes and eukaryotes and is related to the *Escherichia coli* DnaQ/MutD protein, which contains the editing function of the multisubunit replicative DNA polymerase III. However, TREX1 does not remove mismatched nucleotides during DNA replication, but plays a different role [3]. In biochemical assays, TREX1 is more similar to the little-studied *E. coli* exoX (exonuclease X) [6] than DnaQ, exoI and other *E. coli* exonucleases; both TREX1 and exoX display catalytic preference for ssDNA and bind unusually tightly to ssDNA. *E. coli* exoX has an accessory and apparently redundant role in DNA repair and homologous recombination and may serve to confer genetic stability to tandem repeat sequences [6,7]. Surprisingly, a similar 3′ exonuclease has not been detected in budding yeast (*Saccharomyces cerevisiae*) or fission yeast (*Schizosaccharomyces pombe*); TREX1 is only found in mammalian cells. These cells also contain a closely related enzyme, TREX2, which is smaller than TREX1 [2]. Other higher eukaryotes such as *Xenopus laevis* have only one enzyme of this type, which appears to be more similar to TREX2 than TREX1, at least with regard to the C-terminal region [8,9].

The three-dimensional structure of the catalytic domain of TREX1 was solved recently by two independent groups [10,11]. The active enzyme occurs as a homodimer. Similarly to several other 3' exonucleases, TREX1 contains three distinct conserved sequence motifs for binding of the obligatory Mg^{2+} (or Mn^{2+}) cofactor through aspartate residues. Furthermore, a polyproline II helix occurs, which, among related exonucleases, is unique to TREX1. This flexible region might be employed for interactions with other proteins. However, no distinct protein partners of TREX1 have been identified with certainty to date. In this regard, it was reported that one function of TREX1 may be as a component of the large SET (suppressor of variation 3–9, enhancer of zeste, trithorax protein) complex active in caspase-independent apoptosis [12]. The structure of the deoxynucleotide-binding pocket in TREX1 explains the previously observed inability of the enzyme to excise an altered 3'-terminal DNA residue at a single-strand interruption, such as a phosphoglycolate caused by ionizing radiation. Recently, a detailed assessment of the hydrolytic mechanism of the 3' exonuclease activity of TREX1 and the *E. coli* DnaQ protein was made by quantum mechanics/molecular mechanics calculations, considering conserved important amino acid residues, with the reasonable assumption that a water molecule bound to the catalytic bivalent metal acts as the nucleophile for hydrolysis of the phosphodiester bond [13].

The unique C-terminal hydrophobic region of TREX1

TREX1 differs from TREX2, exoX and other members of the DnaQ/MutD family of 3' exonucleases in having an extended C-terminal region of approx. 70 amino acid residues [1,2]. The origin of this C-terminal region of the mammalian TREX1 enzyme is unclear, because no similar sequence has been detected in available protein databases. Surprisingly for an enzyme acting on DNA, TREX1 is predominantly cytosolic and localizes to the ER (endoplasmic reticulum). Only a very small proportion of the protein is present in the cell nucleus, although this proportion increases in S-phase and after apoptotic or genotoxic stress. Other groups have also shown the ER localization and its dependence on the C-terminal region of TREX1 [12,14]. In the present article, we provide a further detailed analysis of studies that systematically mutated the TREX1 C-terminal region [1,15].

A series of N-terminally-tagged GFP (green fluorescent protein) constructs encoding C-terminal deletions of TREX1 were generated to identify the residues that are required for its ER association (Figure 1). The subcellular localization of these GFP–TREX1 mutant proteins was investigated following transfection of the deletion constructs into MEFs (mouse embryonic fibroblasts) (Figure 1, upper panel). The expression of similar levels of protein of expected molecular mass was verified by Western blotting (results not shown). As observed for the

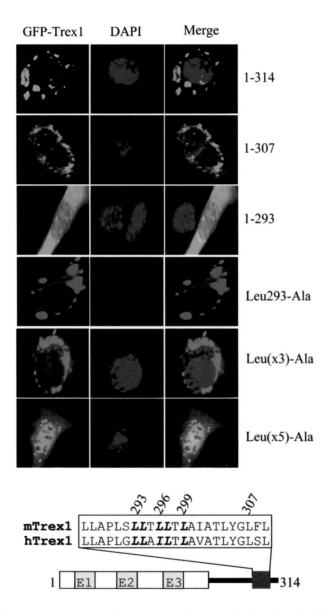

Figure 1. Site-specific mutagenesis analysis of the contribution of the TREX1 C-terminal domain to the subcellular distribution of the protein

Five key hydrophobic leucine residues occur within residues 293–307 of TREX1. Upper panel: subcellular localization of GFP–TREX1 truncations and point mutants. Lower panel: schematic diagram of TREX1 protein. Conserved exonuclease motifs are indicated (E1–E3). The putative TMD is shown as a boxed sequence, and the core hydrophobic leucine residues are highlighted in bold italics; this sequence is highly conserved in humans (h) and mice (m). The five leucine residues (Leu[293], Leu[294], Leu[296], Leu[297] and Leu[299]) were sequentially mutated to alanine in GFP–TREX1 [15]. All mutants were transfected into MEFs; 24 h later, TREX1 localization was observed by immunofluorescence microscopy. Note the loss of ER localization in the TREX1 TMD Leu(×5)-Ala mutant in which all five leucine residues were converted into alanine.

full-length GFP–TREX1 (amino acids 1–314), GFP–TREX1-(1–307) lacking the C-terminal seven amino acids still localizes in a perinuclear pattern. However, deletion of a further 14 amino acids abolished this characteristic TREX1 localization and the GFP–TREX1-(1–293) protein was diffusely distributed; cellular fractionation experiments indicated that GFP–TREX1-(1–293) was still entirely in the cytoplasm. The truncated TREX1-(1–293) enzyme remained in the cytoplasm even in cells exposed to ionizing radiation, whereas the full-length enzyme translocated from the ER to the nucleus after radiation (results not shown). Thus the region between amino acids 293 and 307 plays a critical function in the ER localization of TREX1. There is very limited homology of the C-terminal region in all the available mammalian TREX1 cDNA sequences, except for the most C-terminal 30 amino acids, which are almost entirely conserved. This region is extremely hydrophobic and probably hampers expression of soluble full-length recombinant TREX1 protein. Examination of the murine TREX1 open reading frame using either the PSORTII (http://www. psort.org) or SMART (http://smart.embl-heidelberg.de/) programs identified a leucine-rich motif within this C-terminal sequence as a putative TMD (transmembrane domain). This TMD-like element spans amino acids 287–309 of murine TREX1 (Figure 1, lower panel) and leucine residues 293, 294, 296, 297 and 299 were identified as the key hydrophobic elements for the functional TMD. Four of these five leucine residues are conserved in all of the available mammalian cDNA sequences, including human TREX1 (Figure 1, lower panel); only the murine sequence encodes leucine at position 296, but the equivalent amino acids are invariably a hydrophobic residue. To experimentally determine the contribution of this leucine-rich motif to the subcellular localization of TREX1, we generated GFP–TREX1 constructs in which the conserved hydrophobic leucine residues were mutated within the TMD (Figure 1, upper panel). Converting these five leucine residues into alanine, either singly or in combination, did not significantly affect the ER localization of TREX1 unless all five were mutated. In this case, the GFP–TREX1 mutant protein became diffusely distributed throughout the cytoplasm as had the GFP–TREX1-(1–293) truncation. All of the GFP–TREX1 TMD point mutants were expressed efficiently and were of the expected size (results not shown). Our data indicate that the C-terminal hydrophobic motif determines the association of TREX1 with the ER. As this motif is so highly conserved between species, the specific subcellular localization of TREX1 would be anticipated to be essential for its biological function. The nuclear form of TREX1 appears to show higher catalytic activity than the ER-associated form, presumably due to post-translational modification of the enzyme, or to dimerization of monomers released from the ER.

TREX1 deficiency and human disease

Insights into the functional role of TREX1 were initially obtained by the construction and investigation of *Trex1*-knockout mice [3]. These mice showed a greatly reduced lifespan and inflammatory myocarditis. By re-derivation of pathogen-free animals, it was demonstrated that the cause of the disease was not a virus or some other infectious agent, but rather an autoimmune condition.

Human genetics and biochemical studies on relevant families identified TREX1 deficiency as a major cause of AGS [4,16]. The *Trex1*-knockout mice provide an excellent animal model system for human AGS. Inherited systemic lupus erythematosus, variant forms of AGS and related clinical diseases with TREX1 dominant mutations have also been described [17,18]. These studies have been reviewed in [19–21]. In a subsequent development, cloning of the gene deficient in patients with the neurovascular disorder RVCL (retinal vasculopathy with cerebral leukodystrophy) showed that this was also due to dominant mutations in the *TREX1* gene [14,21]. Interestingly, mutations in AGS1 are usually located to the catalytic domain of TREX1 and lead to loss of enzymatic activity, whereas TREX1 mutations in RVCL are found in the C-terminal domain and lead to loss of the perinuclear localization of catalytically active TREX1, as shown in the model system in Figure 1. The relative activity of mutated forms of TREX1 on ssDNA compared with dsDNA might also affect the disease pattern [22].

Checkpoint activation in *TREX1*-knockout cells

Murine and human *TREX1*-knockout cell lines and primary fibroblasts exhibit chronic checkpoint activation dependent on the ATM (ataxia telangiectasia mutated) protein kinase, similar to that seen transiently in normal cells exposed to ionizing radiation. The properties and features of this response have been reported and reviewed recently [15,19,20]. Our data indicate that the checkpoint activation in *TREX1*-knockout cells is due to intracellular accumulation of ssDNA fragments. These would be efficiently degraded in normal TREX1-positive cells, which may explain why they have not been detected previously. The accumulated ssDNA was found to be of a discrete length of 60–65 nt. Our data [15] indicate that these ssDNA fragments seen in AGS1 cells are generated during lagging-strand DNA synthesis. An additional source of ssDNA was proposed recently by Stetson et al. [23], who reported that the ssDNA in TREX1-negative mouse heart tissue may largely represent activated retroelements. It is noteworthy, however, that the cytoplasmic accumulation of ssDNA of 60–65 nt that we detect in TREX1-negative cells could be sufficient to trigger the innate immune system in mice and humans; this observation provides a possible link between the pathological inflammatory response in AGS and TREX1 deficiency.

References

1. Höss, M., Robins, P., Naven, P., Pappin, D., Sgouros, J. & Lindahl, T. (1999) A human DNA editing enzyme homologous to the *Escherichia coli* DnaQ/MutD protein. *EMBO J.* **18**, 3868–3875

2. Mazur, D.J. & Perrino, F.W. (1999) Identification and expression of the TREX1 and TREX2 cDNA sequences encoding mammalian 3'→5' exonucleases. *J. Biol. Chem.* **274**, 19655–19660

3. Morita, M., Stamp, G., Robins, P., Dulic, A., Rosewell, I., Hrivnak, G., Daly, G., Lindahl, T. & Barnes, D.E. (2004) Gene-targeted mice lacking the Trex1 (DNase III) 3'→5' DNA exonuclease develop inflammatory myocarditis. *Mol. Cell. Biol.* **24**, 6719–6727

4. Crow, Y.J., Hayward, B.E., Parmar, R., Robins, P., Leitch, A., Ali, M., Black, D.N., van Bokhoven, H., Brunner, H.G., Hamel, B.C. et al. (2006) Mutations in the gene encoding the 3' to 5' DNA exonuclease TREX1 cause Aicardi–Goutières syndrome at the AGS1 locus. *Nat. Genet.* **38**, 917–920

5. Lindahl, T., Gally, J.A. & Edelman, G.M. (1969) Properties of deoxyribonuclease III from mammalian tissues, J. *Biol. Chem.* **224**, 5014–5019

6. Viswanathan, M. & Lovett, S.T. (1999) Exonuclease X of *Escherichia coli*: a novel 3'–5' DNase and DnaQ superfamily member involved in DNA repair. *J. Biol. Chem.* **274**, 30094–30100

7. Feschenko, V.V., Rajman, L.A. & Lovett, S.T. (2003) Stabilization of perfect and imperfect tandem repeats by single-strand DNA exonucleases. *Proc. Natl. Acad. Sci. U.S.A.* **100**, 1134–1139

8. Mazur, D.J. & Perrino, F.W. (2001) Structure and expression of the TREX1 and TREX2 3'→5' exonuclease genes. *J. Biol. Chem.* **276**, 14718–14727

9. Mazur, D.J. & Perrino, F.W. (2001) Excision of 3' termini by the Trex1 and TREX2 3'→5' exonucleases: characterization of the recombinant proteins. *J. Biol. Chem.* **276**, 17022–17029

10. de Silva, U., Choudury, S., Baily, S.L., Harvey, S., Perrino, F.W. & Hollis, T. (2007) The crystal structure of TREX1 explains the 3' nucleotide specificity and reveals a polyproline II helix for protein partnering. *J. Biol. Chem.* **282**, 10537–10543

11. Brucet, M., Querol-Audi, J., Serra, M., Ramirez-Espain, X., Bertlik, K., Ruiz, L., Lloberas, J., Macias, M.J., Fita, I. & Celada, A. (2007) Structure of the dimeric exonuclease TREX1 in complex with DNA displays a proline-rich binding site for WW domains. *J. Biol. Chem.* **282**, 14547–14557

12. Chowdhury, D., Beresford, P.J., Zhu, P., Zhang, D., Sung, J.-S., Demple, B., Perrino, F.W. & Lieberman, J. (2006) The exonuclease TREX1 is in the SET complex and acts in concert with NM23-H1 to degrade DNA during granzyme A-mediated cell death. *Mol. Cell* **23**, 133–142

13. Cisneros, G.A., Perera, L., Schaaper, R.M., Pedersen, L.C., London, R.E., Pedersen, L.G. & Darden, T.A. (2009) Reaction mechanism of the ε subunit of *E. coli* DNA polymerase III: insights into active site metal coordination and catalytically significant residues. *J. Am. Chem. Soc.* **131**, 1550–1556

14. Richard, A., van den Maagdenberg, A.M., Jen, J.C., Kavanagh, D., Bertram, P., Spitzer, D., Liszewski, M.K., Barilla-Labarca, M.L., Terwindt, G.M., Kasai, Y. et al. (2007) Truncations in the carboxyl-terminus of human 3'–5' DNA exonuclease TREX1 cause retinal vasculopathy with cerebral leukodystrophy. *Nat. Genet.* **39**, 1068–1070

15. Yang, Y.-G., Lindahl, T. & Barnes, D.E. (2007) Trex1 exonuclease degrades ssDNA to prevent chronic checkpoint activation and autoimmune disease. *Cell* **131**, 873–886

16. Rice, G., Patrick, T., Parmar, R., Taylor, C.F., Aeby, A., Aicardi, J., Artuch, R., Montalto, S.A., Bacino, C.A. et al. (2007) Clinical and molecular phenotype of Aicardi–Goutières syndrome. *Am. J. Hum. Genet.* **81**, 713–725

17. Lee-Kirsch, M.A., Gong, M., Chowdhury, D., Senenko, L., Engel, K., Lee, Y.A., de Silva, U., Bailey, S.L., Witte, T., Vyse, T.J. et al. (2007) Mutations in the gene encoding the 3'–5' DNA exonuclease TREX1 are associated with systemic lupus erythematosus. *Nat. Genet.* **39**, 1065–1067

18. Rice, G., Newman, W.G., Dean, J., Patrick, T., Parmar, R., Flintoff, K., Robins, P., Harvey, S., Hollis, T., O'Hara, A. et al. (2007) Heterozygous mutations in *TREX1* cause familial chilblain lupus and dominant Aicardi–Goutières syndrome. *Am. J. Hum. Genet.* **80**, 811–815

19. O'Driscoll, M. (2008) TREX1 DNA exonuclease deficiency, accumulation of single stranded DNA and complex human genetic disorders. *DNA Repair* **7**, 997–1003

20. Rigby, R.E., Leitch, A. & Jackson, A.P. (2008) Nucleic acid-mediated inflammatory diseases. *BioEssays* **30**, 833–842

21. Kavanagh, D., Spitzer, D., Kothari, P.H., Shaikh, A., Liszewski, M.K., Richards, A. & Atkinson, J.P. (2008) New roles for the major human 3′–5′ exonuclease TREX1 in human disease. *Cell Cycle* **7**, 1–8

22. Lehtinen, D.A., Harvey, S., Mulcahy, M.J., Hollis, T. & Perrino, F.W. (2008) The TREX1 double-stranded DNA degradation activity is defective in dominant mutations associated with autoimmune disease. *J. Biol. Chem.* **46**, 31649–31656

23. Stetson, D.B., Ko, J.S., Heidmann, T. & Medzhitov, R. (2008) Trex1 prevents cell-intrinsic initiation of autoimmunity. *Cell* **134**, 587–598

Biochem. Soc. Symp. 76
Citation reference: Biochem. Soc. Trans. (2009) **37**, 539–545.

3

Repairing DNA double-strand breaks by the prokaryotic non-homologous end-joining pathway

Nigel C. Brissett and Aidan J. Doherty[1]

Genome Damage and Stability Centre, University of Sussex, Brighton BN1 9RQ, U.K.

Abstract

The NHEJ (non-homologous end-joining) pathway is one of the major mechanisms for repairing DSBs (double-strand breaks) that occur in genomic DNA. In common with eukaryotic organisms, many prokaryotes possess a conserved NHEJ apparatus that is essential for the repair of DSBs arising in the stationary phase of the cell cycle. Although the bacterial NHEJ complex is much more minimal than its eukaryotic counterpart, both pathways share a number of common mechanistic features. The relative simplicity of the prokaryotic NHEJ complex makes it a tractable model system for investigating the cellular and molecular mechanisms of DSB repair. The present review describes recent advances in our understanding of prokaryotic end-joining, focusing primarily on biochemical, structural and cellular aspects of the mycobacterial NHEJ repair pathway.

Introduction

DSBs (double-strand breaks) in DNA represent a lethal form of cellular damage, but evolution has arrived at various solutions to repair such deleterious

[1] *To whom correspondence should be addressed (email ajd21@sussex.ac.uk).*

lesions, thus maintaining the integrity of genomic DNA. Breaks can arise from many sources, including endogenous metabolic processes and exogenous environmental stresses. Two major DSB-repair processes are deployed by cells: HR (homologous recombination) and NHEJ (non-homologous end-joining) [1,2]. HR relies on the pairing of one of the broken strands with a complementary region on the sister chromatid by the HR repair machinery and this 'templating' process faithfully guides subsequent HR-mediated break repair [1]. In contrast, NHEJ break repair is a non-template-directed process that occurs between the non-homologous termini of a DSB and is therefore considered to be more error-prone [1,2]. HR is favoured as the major DSB repair pathway in dividing cells, where the sister chromatid is available to direct accurate repair and prevent the propagation of genetic errors. In contrast, NHEJ is the dominant break repair pathway in G_1/quiescent cells, where a homologous DNA template is not available and the requirement for end-joining to prevent chromosomal instability overrides the need for accurate break repair.

Conceptually, the basic mechanism of NHEJ is relatively uncomplicated. First, the broken ends are identified, the termini are then brought together (synapsis), processed by polymerase and nucleolytic activities (if required to restore complementarity) and, finally, the remaining nicks are ligated together to restore the integrity of the DNA duplex [1,2] (Figure 1). Eukaryotic NHEJ is mediated by numerous factors with more than eight core factors involved in this DSB repair process [2]. The heterodimeric Ku70–Ku80 complex, which is responsible for recognizing and stabilizing the DNA ends, forms a toroidal-shaped ring structure with a large central hole through which the DNA passes and binds to the break termini in a sequence-independent manner [3]. Ku recruits a large DNA-PK (DNA-dependent protein kinase), which in turn promotes end-bridging and intermolecular ligation by the DNA ligase IV–XRCC4 (X-ray repair complementing defective repair in Chinese-hamster cells 4)–XLF (XRCC4-like factor) complex [2] (Figure 1A). Other accessory factors are also recruited to the break to aid in end-processing, including PNK (polynucleotide kinase; a 5′ DNA kinase and 3′ phosphatase) and Artemis (a 5′→3′ exonuclease) (Figure 1A). After alignment and processing of the break has occurred, short gaps may need to be remodelled by DNA synthesis to produce ligatable ends. This polymerase-based processing is performed by members of the Pol (polymerase) X family [Pol μ, Pol λ and TdT (terminal deoxynucleotidyltransferase)], which are recruited to the break by DNA-bound Ku [1,2].

Discovery of prokaryotic NHEJ

For many years, the process of NHEJ was considered not to exist in prokaryotes. However, recent bioinformatic studies have identified the existence of bacterial orthologues of Ku [4,5], now considered to be encoded by the majority of

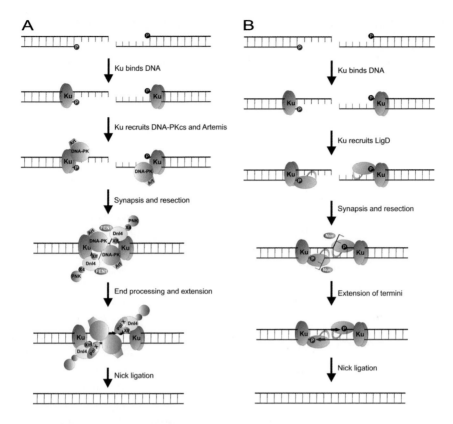

Figure 1. DSB repair by the NHEJ pathway

(**A**) Mechanism of NHEJ in higher eukaryotes. The Ku70–Ku80 heterodimer binds to the ends of a DSB. The catalytic subunit of DNA-PK (DNA-PK$_{cs}$) and Artemis (Art) are recruited, and the phosphorylation activity of DNA-PK$_{cs}$ is initiated. The DNA-PK complex brings about end-bridging and DNA ligase IV (Dnl4) and its associated factors [XRCC4 (X4) and XLF] are recruited to the assembly. PNK is also recruited to the break site via direct interactions with XRCC4. Artemis and Pol X process the break termini, if required, to restore complementary ends. Finally, ligation of the remaining nicks by Dnl4 completes the break repair process. FEN1, flap endonuclease 1. (**B**) Mechanism of NHEJ in prokaryotes. A Ku homodimer binds to the ends of the DNA break and recruits LigD. The polymerase domain of LigD specifically binds to a 5′-phosphate (P) and, together with Ku, promotes end-synapsis. The nuclease and polymerase activities of LigD, and possibly other factors, process the break termini, if required, to restore complementary ends. Finally, ligation of the nicks by LigD repairs the break.

prokaryotic genomes. Unlike the multifactor complex deployed by eukaryotes, bacteria appear to possess only a few NHEJ-specific genes, including a gene encoding a homodimeric Ku (Figure 1B). Notably, the prokaryotic Ku genes typically reside in operons containing a conserved ATP-dependent DNA ligase, LigD (ligase D) [5,6]. This operonic association suggested that prokaryotic NHEJ involves Ku homologues recruiting a repair ligase to DSBs, which has now been proven experimentally [7,8] (Figure 1B). In addition to a ligase domain, most LigDs also contain nuclease and polymerase domains [5,6]. It has been demonstrated that *Mt* (*Mycobacterium tuberculosis*) LigD possesses all of the end-processing, gap-filling and ligation activities required to repair DSBs [7–10]. In essence, bacterial NHEJ is mediated by a two-component Ku–ligase break repair complex [7,8], although it is likely that other factors participate in this DSB repair pathway.

Significantly, not all prokaryotes possess a NHEJ pathway, as the Ku and LigD genes are absent from many bacterial species, including *Escherichia coli* [5,11]. Currently, no clear link explaining the distribution pattern of NHEJ in prokaryotes has been discovered. This raises the question as to how bacteria acquired the NHEJ machinery and in what form did they inherit it? One possibility is that NHEJ genes were acquired by bacteria via horizontal gene transfer. The evidence for such gene transfer is exemplified by the distribution of NHEJ genes in phylogenetically distant organisms, such as proteobacteria, actinomycetes, *Parachlamydia* and low-GC Gram-positive bacteria [5,11]. It is notable that, with one exception, NHEJ genes are not present in the third kingdom of life, archaea. Another possible explanation is that NHEJ genes arose first in prokaryotes and bacteriophages, and were subsequently lost by some bacteria over evolutionary time.

Domain structure of bacterial NHEJ DNA-repair ligases

As discussed, the prokaryotic NHEJ repair apparatus is a two-component system, comprising Ku and LigD, which together possess the majority of the activities required for break recognition, end-processing and ligation [7,8]. In many bacterial species, including *Mycobacterium*, LigD is a multidomain protein encoded on a single polypeptide consisting of an N-terminal polymerase domain (PolDom), a central nuclease domain (NucDom) and a C-terminal ATP-dependent ligase domain (LigDom) [5,6,12], although the order of these domains varies from species to species [5,6]. Indeed, in many bacteria (especially in thermophilic species), these domains are encoded as individual polypeptides rather than as multidomain proteins. The most studied and versatile activity on LigD resides in PolDom (discussed below), the DNA primase/polymerase domain. Significantly, PolDom exhibits the combined polymerase activities of eukaryotic Pol X family members, which have been implicated in NHEJ end-processing in eukaryotes [8,13,14]. NucDom possesses a novel 3′–5′ nucleolytic activity capable of resecting 3′-ends and appears to be required for end-processing before ligation [8,15,16]. Finally, LigD contains a 'minimal'-sized ligase (LigDom) that is capable of sealing nicked breaks that are formed following synapsis and processing of the DSB [7,8].

Bacterial NHEJ polymerases belong to the eukaryotic DNA primase superfamily

In both sequence and structural terms, the bacterial NHEJ polymerases are members of the AEPs (archaeo-eukaryotic primases) [5,6,17], a large conserved family of polymerases that are essential components of DNA replication in all eukaryotic organisms. Primases initiate replication of new DNA strands by first synthesizing a dinucleotide product, which is subsequently elongated by up to 14 ribonucleotides [18]. The resultant 3′-hydroxy group of this RNA primes extension by the replicative DNA polymerases, as these enzymes are unable to initiate DNA strand synthesis *de novo* [17,18]. Although classified as a DNA primase, PolDom possesses a remarkable and unique assortment of nucleotidyltransferase activities, including DNA-dependent RNA primase, terminal transferase and DNA-dependent RNA/DNA gap-filling polymerase activities (Figure 2) [8,13,14]. All of these polymerase activities have

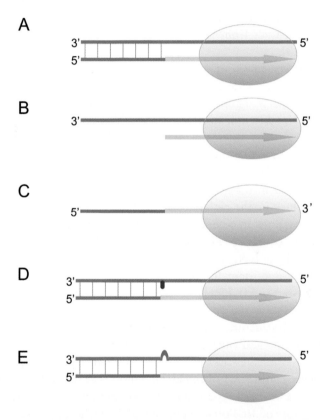

Figure 2. acterial NHEJ polymerase possesses a variety of nucleotidyltransferase activities
(**A**) PolDom (green) can fill in short single-stranded gaps and extend 3′-resected DNA termini (blue arrow) in a template-dependent fashion. (**B**) This polymerase can synthesize RNA primers *de novo* using a ssDNA template. (**C**) PolDom has terminal transferase activity, adding several nucleotides to the end of ssDNA or blunt-ended dsDNA in a template-independent manner. (**D**) PolDom can insert nucleotides opposite base lesions (red oval) and readily extend from these or mismatched base-paired ends. (**E**) PolDom has the ability to dislocate and realign the template strand (loop structure) to bypass lesions or abasic sites. In all cases, PolDom preferentially inserts ribonucleotides.

a requirement for bivalent metal ions and, with the exception of the priming activity, are directly relevant to NHEJ-mediated DSB-repair processing [9–11].

DNA primases are generally split into two major superfamilies that have no evolutionary relationship, despite being related functionally [17,18]. The DnaG family comprises primases from bacteria and bacteriophages, whereas the other family is made up of AEPs. The AEP family is typically characterized by the small subunit of the heterodimeric eukaryotic primases, which associates with the DNA Pol α and B subunits to form the Pol α primase complex. More robust sequence alignment methods have expanded the superfamily to include homologous primases from archaea, viruses and bacteria [5–7,17]. PolDom is a member of a subfamily of AEPs implicated in NHEJ. Functional studies have established that this divergent clade of NHEJ 'primases' have evolved specific structural and biochemical features required for their specific role in DSB break repair that are distinct from the basic activities required for priming DNA synthesis [8,13,19].

The crystal structures of a number of PolDoms have been elucidated, both as apo and nucleotide-bound forms (Figure 3A), which confirmed that these primases share significant structural homology with the replicative AEPs [13,19]. Notably, not only are the catalytic cores of the NHEJ AEPs conserved, but also so are many of the peripheral helices, which strongly suggests a common evolutionary ancestry with the more divergent members of the AEP family [13,17,19]. The catalytic triad of metal-binding aspartate residues, conserved in the NHEJ AEPs, maintain the same geometry as the equivalent residues in the active sites of other AEPs [3,19]. The co-crystal structures of PolDoms in complex with various nucleotides has identified the mode of binding of NTPs (Figure 3A) and dNTPs in the active sites of the prokaryotic NHEJ polymerase/primases and identified many of the conserved residues that are important for both nucleotide recognition and subsequent nucleotidyltransferase activities [13,19]. In addition, these structures established the molecular basis for the preferential binding of NTPs over dNTPs. In the Mt-PolDom–GTP structure, a specific interaction of the 2'-hydroxy group with conserved threonine and histidine residues in the active site stabilizes NTP binding and also orientates the sugar moiety to enhance the stacking interaction of the base with a conserved phenylalanine residue [13]. Lack of a 2'-hydroxy group results in a less well occupied nucleotide-binding site, as observed in the co-crystal structure of Mt-PolDom bound to dGTP where the binding of dNTP is only stabilized by the triphosphate tail and base-stacking interactions. The biological significance of this preferential binding of NTPs by these polymerases is discussed below.

On the basis of various primary sequence and structural alignments, AEPs have been shown to have a catalytic core convergent with the Pol X family of DNA polymerases [17,20,21]. There appears to be no topological convergence between these two families, with the catalytic residues sitting on a parallel β-sheet in the Pol Xs, whereas the equivalent residues are arranged on

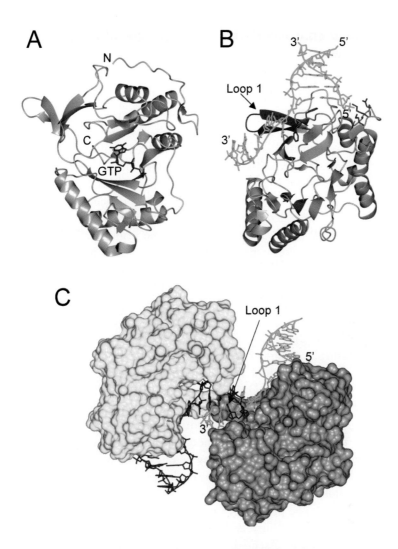

Figure 3. Co-crystal structures of the mycobacterial NHEJ polymerase
(**A**) The crystal structure of *Mt*-PolDom is depicted in ribbon form (blue) with GTP bound in the active site (PDB code 2IRX). (**B**) Crystal structure of a *Mt*-PolDom monomer complexed with DNA containing a 3′-protruding overhang. The enzyme makes limited contact with the DNA. The recessed 5′-phosphate is bound by a cluster of lysine residues and two phenylalanine residues stack against bases of the template strand. The position of loop 1, which plays a direct role in end-synapsis, is shown in red. (**C**) Structure of a polymerase-mediated DNA synaptic complex. A solvent-accessible surface representation of the synaptic complex of *Mt*-PolDom (blue and yellow) with DNA (green and red) (PDB code 2R9L). A homodimeric arrangement of PolDoms (via loop 1) promotes the association of the 3′-ends of two DNA molecules, forming a microhomology-mediated connection that stabilizes the synaptic complex.

antiparallel structural elements in the AEPs. Despite these differences, the spatial relationship of the three catalytic carboxylates is highly convergent between members of the two polymerase families, indicating that, not only do the AEPs bind the NTPs in a similar way as Pol Xs, but also they probably share a similar catalytic pathway for nucleotidyl transfer [21].

Biochemical characteristics of the bacterial NHEJ polymerases

As discussed, NHEJ polymerases possess a unique variety of DNA-extension activities, presumably reflecting the requirements for an assortment of extension activities during NHEJ-mediated end processing (Figure 2). PolDom can extend dsDNA (double-stranded DNA) (with 5′-overhangs) and fill in gapped dsDNA substrates in a template-dependent manner [8,12–14]. PolDom also displays template-independent terminal transferase activity on ssDNA (single-stranded DNA) and blunt-ended dsDNA substrates, although this activity is restricted to the addition of a few nucleotides [8,13]. DNA-dependent RNA primase activity has also been demonstrated for PolDom [8,13,14], confirming that these atypical AEP family members retain some primordial primase activity. Mutation of the conserved aspartate residues, involved in metal co-ordination, abolishes all of these polymerase activities, suggesting that one active site catalyses all of the distinct extension activities [8,12,14]. PolDom also possesses additional activities that are relevant for processing of DSBs, including nucleotide insertion opposite 8-oxoguanine and lesion bypass via template dislocation and realignment (Figure 2) [13].

PolDoms display a marked preference for the insertion of NTPs over dNTPs *in vitro*, with a ~20–70-fold difference in its preference for incorporation of NTPs over dNTPs into DNA, depending on the templating base [8,13]. In stationary cells, intracellular pools of NTPs are much higher than dNTPs (>10:1), suggesting that preferential incorporation of ribonucleotides is likely to occur *in vivo*, although this has not been demonstrated. This preference for incorporating NTPs into DNA may be one reason a primase fold has been adopted as the NHEJ polymerase by the prokarya. If this process occurs *in vivo*, what is the cellular fate of the short stretches of RNA introduced into the sites of repaired DSBs? The presence of patches of RNA in DNA would severely compromise genome stability and therefore a pathway that 'repairs' DNA–RNA hybrids would be essential. A candidate enzyme capable of recognizing and excising short RNA patches from DNA is type II RNase H, which can process short tracts of RNA introduced into newly synthesized DNA [22].

DNA-break recognition by the prokaryotic NHEJ polymerases

In addition to a wide diversity of extension activities, PolDoms possess other attributes that enable it to participate in atypical polymerase activities associated with DNA end-joining. The major determinant for specific binding of PolDom to DNA is the presence of a 5′-phosphate [13], located on the recessed end of the break site, and NHEJ AEPs have little affinity for DNA ends in the absence of a 5′-phosphate moiety. Phosphate interaction significantly enhances nucleotide selection and polymerization, as well as promoting end remodelling

[13]. Although structurally unrelated, the eukaryotic NHEJ polymerases (Pol μ and Pol λ) possess a related ability to bind 5′-phosphated ends via a helix–hairpin–helix domain [23,24]. PolDom lacks this phosphate-binding domain, but utilizes a novel structural feature to interact with a 5′-phosphate (Figure 3B) [25].

The elucidation of the crystal structure of the Mt-PolDom in complex with dsDNA (containing a recessed 5′-phosphate and a 3′-overhang) has provided significant insights into DNA recognition by this family of NHEJ DNA-repair polymerases (Figures 3B and 3C) [25]. The structure revealed that the 5′-phosphate of the duplex strand is bound by a conserved positively charged pocket on the surface of the protein (Figure 3B). PolDom induces a bending of the template strand (by over ~90°) via specific contacts with the surface of the enzyme. As discussed above, PolDom possesses many of the combined NHEJ activities present in the eukaryotic NHEJ polymerases (Pol λ, Pol μ and TdT), some of which contain a surface-exposed structural loop (loop 1) that promotes connectivity between the two discontinuous ends [24,26,27]. The PolDom–DNA co-crystal structure revealed that the bacterial NHEJ polymerases also possess a functionally analogous structural element, and this surface loop plays an important role in facilitating end-synapsis [25] (Figures 3B and 3C). In this structure, a homodimeric arrangement of the polymerases promotes the direct interaction of the 3′-overhanging termini of two DNA 'ends' (Figure 3C). Loop 1 acts as a molecular 'match-maker' promoting base-pairing, base-flipping, base-stacking and other interactions to occur between the 3′-termini, which results in stable synaptic complex formation between the opposing ends of a DNA break. This complex has also been shown to exist in solution and to be functionally relevant and important for templated extension of the termini of DSBs. It has been proposed that this arrangement may be required to mediate the processing of 'difficult' breaks, such as 3′-overhangs [25]. Mutation of loop 1 ablated the formation of the synaptic intermediates on termini with 3′-overhanging ends [25], implicating PolDom directly in the end-synapsis process. Further structural and functional studies are required to understand how LigD and Ku co-operate to promote break-synapsis and choreograph end-processing and ligation.

Processing and repair of non-homologous DNA breaks

Higher eukaryotes require a large number of factors to repair DSBs by NHEJ (Figure 1A) [2]. In contrast, the prokaryotic two-component NHEJ apparatus appears to possess most of the processing activities required for remodelling and repair of DSBs [9], and therefore the simplicity of this break repair apparatus makes it an ideal model system for studying the molecular mechanisms of the end-joining process. As discussed, the bacterial NHEJ complex is capable of bringing two discontinuous DNA ends together, processing the termini and ligating the resulting complementary ends to restore genome integrity (Figure 1B) [7–10]. Examination of the sequence of repaired break junctions provides insights into the molecular processes that drive NHEJ. During eukaryotic NHEJ, short stretches of DNA sequence homology (microhomologies) are often exploited to align the termini of non-homologous breaks [1,2]. Similarly, bacterial NHEJ preferentially exploits DNA sequence microhomologies, internal to the overhangs of incompatible ends, to promote end-synapsis, resection, resynthesis and ligation of DSBs [8,25,28]. Co-ordination of the nucleotidyltransferase and ligase activities of LigD is highlighted by its preference for filling-in of DNA duplexes containing gaps adjacent to regions of microhomology, before ligation of these intermediates [8,28]. As discussed, the polymerase domain of LigD plays a direct role in promoting the connection between break termini [25], especially 3'-ends, and it is likely that it plays a general role in promoting microhomology-mediated end-joining.

Terminal transferase activity has also been implicated in NHEJ repair, especially when at least one of the DSB termini is blunt-ended. When blunt-ended DNA is joined to a termini containing a 3'-overhang [8,25,28], the polymerase activity of LigD often performs a non-templated base addition to the 3'-terminus of the blunt-end as it cannot extend 5'-recessed ends, as DNA polymerases operate in a 5'–3' direction. This *de novo* synthesis activity is even more crucial when both ends are blunt-ended. During *in vivo* repair assays, where both ends of a DSB are blunt-ended, ~50% of the DSB repair events resulted in a mutagenic outcome where a single frameshift mutation was observed [28]. This frameshift is the result of one blunt end undergoing non-templated base addition at the 3'-terminus and templated addition occurring at the other blunt end before ligation.

LigD also possesses 3'-ribonuclease and 3'-phosphatase activities, exemplified by the removal of 3'-phosphates and nucleotide flaps, the latter intermediates are often a product of microhomology-mediated synapsis events [8,15,16]. The nucleolytic activities of LigD reside in the NucDom, which has a preference for cleaving recessed 3'-ends and is relatively poor at cleaving 3'-overhangs [16]. The probable role for the 3'-phosphatase activity in DSB repair is to process 3'-phosphated termini that have been generated during DNA breakage. Removal of the 3'-phosphate is essential to restore the 3'-hydroxy group that acts as the essential nucleophile for nucleotide addition and ligation reactions. In contrast, 3'-resection activity in DSB repair appears to be less obvious, although it has been observed in various *in vitro* and *in vivo* LigD-dependent NHEJ repair assays [8,28]. As discussed, PolDom can promote the bridging of 3'-protruding ends leading to the formation of DNA synaptic intermediates [25], which contain unpaired 3'-ends. These termini would require 3'-resectioning to enable gap-filling and ligation to complete the break-repair process. Stringent regulation of this nuclease activity would be required to prevent excessive resectioning that could lead to the loss of genetic information, therefore it is likely that this activity is not deployed unless absolutely required.

In summary, if the ends of DNA breaks are precise then only Ku and the ligase activity are required to repair them. However, if the DSBs are imprecise breaks, Ku and the polymerase activity are needed to promote the synapsis of the non-homologous ends, before end-processing and ligation. When available, bacterial NHEJ utilizes microhomologies on the opposing termini to direct this synapsis process. Realignment of the ends via microhomology-mediated end-bridging is certainly the preferred option, thus reducing the loss of excessive genetic information. In the absence of microhomology (e.g. blunt-ended DSBs) LigD employs other back-up activities, such as terminal transferase activity, to create *de novo* connections between the termini. After formation of the synaptic complex, the termini are ready to be processed in a sequential manner by the polymerase and nuclease activities before ligation.

Physiological importance of bacterial NHEJ

NHEJ break repair is not conserved in all bacterial species, suggesting that this repair pathway may not be essential for cell survival [11]. If this is the case, then why has NHEJ been retained by the vast majority of prokaryotic organisms? Recent reports suggest that NHEJ plays an essential role in the survival of both sporulating and non-sporulating bacteria. Although NHEJ mutant strains (*ligD* and *ku*) of the non-sporulating mycobacterium *Mycobacterium smegmatis* are not sensitive to DSBs induced by IR (ionizing radiation) during exponential growth phase, stationary-phase cells are much more sensitive to such breaks [29], establishing that NHEJ is much more important for the survival of non-dividing cells. Although *M. smegmatis* strains deficient in NHEJ are sensitive to IR-induced damage, terrestrial environments do not produce high doses of such radiation. Significantly, IR-resistant bacteria can be isolated from natural sources by selecting for strains that are resistant to desiccation, suggesting that IR-resistance is simply a result of the adaptation to a common physiological stress, namely desiccation [30] and, notably, NHEJ-deficient *M. smegmatis* strains are very sensitive to desiccation [29].

During transmission within airborne droplets, desiccation may be a real threat to the survival of many bacterial species, including pathogens such as *M. tuberculosis*. NHEJ may confer resistance to desiccation and is likely to be essential for the survival of such organisms. In addition, *M. tuberculosis* can survive for many years in a dormant state inside macrophages, while retaining the ability to initiate infection when the host immunity is compromised. Bacilli residing within macrophages are continually exposed to endogenous genotoxic stresses, such as oxidative damage. It is likely that the primordial NHEJ repair pathway evolved to protect the genomes of quiescent bacteria against the genotoxic damage induced by extreme environmental stresses, where HR-mediated repair is not a viable option [11].

Under conditions of limited nutrients, many prokaryotic species (e.g. *Bacillus*) undergo a programmed cell differentiation process known as sporulation [31]. The resulting spores protect the dormant haploid cell from a wide range of environmental stresses, including UV radiation, freezing, drying and heating. It is essential that genome stability is maintained under conditions of prolonged dormancy so that viable spores can germinate and actively divide once food becomes available. *Bacillus subtilis* spores deficient in NHEJ are highly sensitive to stresses that induce DSBs [7,32,33], therefore a functional NHEJ repair pathway is essential for bacterial spore viability under conditions that give rise to DSBs. Indeed, the expression of NHEJ genes in *B. subtilis* is specifically up-regulated upon induction of sporulation [32], suggesting that NHEJ plays a specific role in maintaining genome stability in spores.

Funding

This work was funded by the Biotechnology and Biological Science Research Council [grant numbers 8/C17246, BB/D522746 and BB/F013795/1].

References

1. Helleday, T., Lo, J., van Gent, D.C. & Engelward, B.P. (2007) DNA double-strand break repair: from mechanistic understanding to cancer treatment. *DNA Repair* **6**, 923–935

2. Mahaney, B.L., Meek, K. & Lees-Miller, S.P. (2009) Repair of ionizing radiation-induced DNA double-strand breaks by non-homologous end-joining. *Biochem. J.* **417**, 639–650

3. Walker, J.R., Corpina, R.A. & Goldberg, J. (2001) Structure of the Ku heterodimer bound to DNA and its implications for double-strand break repair. *Nature* **412**, 607–614

4. Doherty, A.J., Jackson, S.P. & Weller, G.R. (2001) Identification of bacterial homologues of the Ku DNA repair proteins. *FEBS Lett.* **500**, 186–188

5. Aravind, L. & Koonin, E.V. (2001) Prokaryotic homologs of the eukaryotic DNA-end-binding protein Ku, novel domains in the Ku protein and prediction of a prokaryotic double-strand break repair system. *Genome Res.* **11**, 1365–1374

6. Weller, G.R. & Doherty, A.J. (2001) A family of DNA repair ligases in bacteria? *FEBS Lett.* **505**, 340–342

7. Weller, G.R., Kysela, B., Roy, R., Tonkin, L.M., Scanlan, E., Della, M., Devine, S.K., Day, J.P., Wilkinson, A., di Fagagna, F.D. et al. (2002) Identification of a DNA non homologous end-joining complex in bacteria. *Science* **297**, 1686–1689

8. Della, M., Palmbos, P.L., Tseng, H.M., Tonkin, L.M., Daley, J.M., Topper, L.M., Pitcher, R.S., Tomkinson, A.E., Wilson, T.E. & Doherty, A.J. (2004) Mycobacterial Ku and ligase proteins constitute a two-component NHEJ repair machine. *Science* **306**, 683–685

9. Pitcher, R.S., Brissett, N.C. & Doherty, A.J. (2007) Nonhomologous end joining in bacteria: a microbial perspective. *Annu. Rev. Microbiol.* **61**, 259–282

10. Pitcher, R.S., Wilson, T.E. & Doherty, A.J. (2005) New insights into NHEJ repair processes in prokaryotes. *Cell Cycle* **4**, 675–678

11. Bowater, R. & Doherty, A.J. (2006) Making ends meet: repairing breaks in bacterial DNA by non-homologous end-joining. *PLoS Genet.* **2**, 93–99

12. Pitcher, R.S., Tonkin, L.M., Green, A.J. & Doherty, A.J. (2005) Domain structure of a NHEJ DNA repair ligase from *Mycobacterium tuberculosis*. *J. Mol. Biol.* **351**, 531–544

13. Pitcher, R.S., Brissett, N.C., Picher, A.J., Andrade, P., Juarez, R., Thompson, D., Fox, G.C., Blanco, L. & Doherty, A.J. (2007) Structure and function of a mycobacterial NHEJ DNA repair polymerase. *J. Mol. Biol.* **366**, 391–405

14. Zhu, H. & Shuman, S. (2005) A primer-dependent polymerase function of *Pseudomonas aeruginosa* ATP-dependent DNA ligase (LigD). *J. Biol. Chem.* **280**, 418–427

15. Zhu, H., Wang, L.K. & Shuman, S. (2005) Essential constituents of the 3′-phosphoesterase domain of bacterial DNA ligase D, a nonhomologous end-joining enzyme. *J. Biol. Chem.* **280**, 33707–33715

16. Zhu, H. & Shuman, S. (2006) Substrate specificity and structure– function analysis of the 3′-phosphoesterase component of the bacterial NHEJ protein, DNA ligase D. *J. Biol. Chem.* **281**, 13873–13881

17. Iyer, L.M., Koonin, E.V., Leipe, D.D. & Aravind, L. (2005) Origin and evolution of the archaeo-eukaryotic primase superfamily and related palm-domain proteins: structural insights and new members. *Nucleic Acids Res.* **33**, 3875–3896

18. Frick, D.N. & Richardson, C.C. (2001) DNA primases. *Annu. Rev. Biochem.* **70**, 39–80

19. Zhu, H., Nandakumar, J., Aniukwu, J., Wang, L.K., Glickman, M.S., Lima, C.D. & Shuman, S. (2006) Atomic structure and nonhomologous end-joining function of the polymerase component of bacterial DNA ligase D. *Proc. Natl. Acad. Sci. U.S.A.* **103**, 1711–1716

20. Arezi, B. & Kuchta, R.D. (2000) Eukaryotic DNA primase. *Trends Biochem. Sci.* **25**, 572–576

21. Augustin, M.A., Huber, R. & Kaiser, J.T. (2001) Crystal structure of a DNA-dependent RNA polymerase (DNA primase). *Nat. Struct. Biol.* **8**, 57–61

22. Rydberg, B. & Game, J. (2002) Excision of misincorporated ribonucleotides in DNA by RNase H (type 2) and FEN-1 in cell-free extracts. *Proc. Natl. Acad. Sci. U.S.A.* **99**, 16654–16659

23. Garcia-Diaz, M., Bebenek, K., Krahn, J.M., Blanco, L., Kunkel, T.A. & Pedersen, L.C. (2004) A structural solution for the DNA polymerase λ-dependent repair of DNA gaps with minimal homology. *Mol. Cell* **13**, 561–572

24. Moon, A.F., Garcia-Diaz, M., Bebenek, K., Davis, B.J., Zhong, X., Ramsden, D.A., Kunkel, T.A. & Pedersen, L.C. (2007) Structural insight into the substrate specificity of DNA polymerase μ. *Nat. Struct. Mol. Biol.* **14**, 45–53

25. Brissett, N.C., Pitcher, R.S., Juarez, R., Picher, A.J., Green, A.J., Dafforn, T.R., Fox, G.C., Blanco, L. & Doherty, A.J. (2007) Structure of a NHEJ polymerase-mediated DNA synaptic complex. *Science* **318**, 456–459

26. McElhinny, S.A.N., Havener, J.M., Garcia-Diaz, M., Juarez, R., Bebenek, K., Kee, B.L., Blanco, L., Kunkel, T.A. & Ramsden, D.A. (2005) A gradient of template dependence defines distinct biological roles for family X polymerases in non homologous end-joining. *Mol. Cell* **19**, 357–366

27. Juarez, R., Ruiz, J.F., McElhinny, S.A., Ramsden, D. & Blanco, L. (2006) A specific loop in human DNA polymerase mu allows switching between creative and DNA-instructed synthesis. *Nucleic Acids Res.* **34**, 4572–4582

28. Gong, C.L., Bongiorno, P., Martins, A., Stephanou, N.C., Zhu, H., Shuman, S. & Glickman, M.S. (2005) Mechanism of nonhomologous end-joining in mycobacteria: a low-fidelity repair system driven by Ku, ligase D and ligase C. *Nat. Struct. Mol. Biol.* **12**, 304–312

29. Pitcher, R.S., Green, A.J., Brzostek, A., Korycka-Machala, M., Dziadek, J. & Doherty, A.J. (2007) NHEJ protects mycobacteria in stationary phase against the harmful effects of desiccation. *DNA Repair* **6**, 1271–1276

30. Sanders, S.W. & Maxcy, R.B. (1979) Isolation of radiation-resistant bacteria without exposure to irradiation. *Appl. Environ. Microbiol.* **38**, 436–439

31. Errington, J. (2003) Regulation of endospore formation in *Bacillus subtilis. Nat. Rev. Microbiol.* **1**, 117–126

32. Wang, S.T., Setlow, B., Conlon, E.M., Lyon, J.L., Imamura, D., Sato, T., Setlow, P., Losick, R. & Eichenberger, P. (2006) The forespore line of gene expression in *Bacillus subtilis. J. Mol. Biol.* **358**, 16–37

33. Moeller, R., Stackebrandt, E., Reitz, G., Berger, T., Rettberg, P., Doherty, A.J., Horneck, G. & Nicholson, W.L. (2007) Role of DNA repair by non-homologous end joining (NHEJ) in *Bacillus subtilis* spore resistance to extreme dryness, mono- and polychromatic UV and ionizing radiation. *J. Bacteriol.* **189**, 3306–3311

Biochem. Soc. Symp. 76
Citation reference: Biochem. Soc. Trans. (2009) **37**, 547–551.
© The Authors. Journal compilation © 2009 The Biochemical Society

4

Structure, function and evolution of the **XPD** family of iron–sulfur-containing 5′→3′ DNA helicases

Malcolm F. White[1]

Centre for Biomolecular Sciences, University of St Andrews, North Haugh, St Andrews, Fife KY16 9ST, U.K.

Abstract

The XPD (xeroderma pigmentosum complementation group D) helicase family comprises a number of superfamily 2 DNA helicases with members found in all three domains of life. The founding member, the XPD helicase, is conserved in archaea and eukaryotes, whereas the closest homologue in bacteria is the DinG (damage-inducible G) helicase. Three XPD paralogues, FancJ (Fanconi's anaemia complementation group J), RTEL (regulator of telomere length) and Chl1, have evolved in eukaryotes and function in a variety of DNA recombination and repair pathways. All family members are believed to be 5′→3′ DNA helicases with a structure that includes an essential iron–sulfur-cluster-binding domain. Recent structural, mutational and biophysical studies have provided a molecular framework for the mechanism of the XPD helicase and help to explain the phenotypes of a considerable number of mutations in the *XPD* gene that can cause three different genetic conditions: xeroderma pigmentosum, trichothiodystrophy and Cockayne's syndrome. Crystal structures of XPD from three archaeal organisms reveal

[1]*email mfw2@st-andrews.ac.uk*

a four-domain structure with two canonical motor domains and two unique domains, termed the Arch and iron–sulfur-cluster-binding domains. The latter two domains probably collaborate to separate duplex DNA during helicase action. The role of the iron–sulfur cluster and the evolution of the XPD helicase family are discussed.

Eukaryotic XPD (xeroderma pigmentosum complementation group D)

The XPD/Rad3 helicase family comprises a group of related superfamily 2 DNA helicases with a $5' \rightarrow 3'$ directionality. Family members are found in all domains of life, including bacteria, archaea and eukaryotes. In eukaryotes, XPD (Rad3 in *Saccheromyces cerevisiae*) functions as part of the TFIIH (transcription factor IIH) complex. The ten-subunit TFIIH complex has a dual role in transcription initiation and NER (nucleotide excision repair). In the former, TFIIH opens the DNA around the promoter site, whereas, in the latter, it opens the DNA around a site of DNA damage. XPD is an essential structural component of TFIIH and acts as a bridging subunit between the core TFIIH subunits and the CAK [CDK (cyclin-dependent kinase)-activating kinase] complex [1]. The helicase activity of XPD is essential for NER, but is not required for transcription initiation. A second helicase in TFIIH, XPB (xeroderma pigmentosum complementation group B), has the opposite polarity to TFIIH. Although XPB is a very weak helicase, its ATPase activity is essential for both NER and transcription initiation [1,2].

Mutations in the *XPD* gene give rise to three different genetic conditions in humans: XP (xeroderma pigmentosum), TTD (trichothiodystrophy) and CS (Cockayne's syndrome). XP is characterized by extreme light sensitivity, inability to remove UV photoproducts from DNA and highly elevated rates of skin cancer (reviewed in [3]). These characteristics are consistent with a loss of the helicase activity of XPD and therefore lack of NER activity. In contrast, TTD mutations cause developmental and growth abnormalities, as well as reduced DNA-repair activity, but typically do not result in elevated cancer rates. These symptoms are thought to arise due to defects in both NER and transcription arising from the relevant XPD mutations [3]. Defective transcription probably prevents cells becoming cancerous, explaining the apparent discrepancy between XP and TTD. CS is a rare disease where both transcription and repair are defective and is characterized by segmental progeria (premature aging) [3].

Archaeal XPD: discovery of the iron–sulfur cluster

Most archaea contain a clear homologue of eukaryotic XPD. The function of this protein in archaea is still unclear, although a role in an NER-type pathway has been predicted [4]. The protein is not part of a TFIIH-type complex and apparently functions as a monomer. When the XPD homologue from

Sulfolobus acidocaldarius was cloned and overexpressed in *Escherichia coli*, it was immediately apparent that the protein was an iron–sulfur protein owing to its yellow–green colour [5]. The likely iron–sulfur-cluster-binding site was identified as a set of four conserved cysteine residues close to the Walker B motif, and this was confirmed by site-directed mutagenesis. It was shown that the iron–sulfur domain was not essential for stability or the enzyme's ability to bind to ssDNA (single-stranded DNA) or its ATPase activity, but was essential for the helicase activity of the protein. It also became clear that the four cysteine residues were conserved in eukaryotic XPD, suggesting that the iron–sulfur domain was present. This was confirmed by genetic experiments in *S. cerevisiae*, which showed that the abolition of iron–sulfur cluster binding by mutagenesis of a conserved cysteine resulted in a severe UV-sensitive phenotype in yeast, consistent with a loss of activity of Rad3 *in vivo* [5]. Furthermore, the four cysteine residues were also conserved in the other eukaryotic XPD paralogues: FancJ (Fanconi's anaemia complementation group J), RTEL (regulator of telomere length) and Chl1, suggesting a general role for the cluster in this broad family of helicases.

DinG (damage-inducible G): the bacterial XPD

Most bacteria also contain a homologue of XPD. This was originally identified as a gene induced in the SOS response in *E. coli*: DinG [6]. However, the function of DinG in bacteria is not well defined, as knockouts have little discernible phenotype. *In vitro*, the DinG enzyme has activity very like that of archaeal XPD, and the protein is not thought to exist in a complex [7]. When the iron–sulfur cluster was identified in archaeal XPD, it was noted that the four conserved cysteine ligands were also present in most DinG sequences at a similar location. This evidence was taken to suggest that DinG was also an iron–sulfur-cluster-binding protein [5]. Subsequent biochemical data confirmed this prediction [7].

Although most bacterial DinG sequences have four conserved cysteine residues, a minority have no cysteine residues in this region (e.g. *Staphylococcus aureus* DinG) and therefore presumably cannot bind an iron–sulfur cluster [8]. Furthermore, some DinG sequences have an N-terminal exonuclease 1 domain, suggesting a fusion of a helicase activity with a $3' \rightarrow 5'$ ssDNA exonuclease. This could result in a protein that unwinds DNA and degrades the displaced strand, similar to the Werner protein in eukaryotes [9]. However, there are currently no biochemical data to support this idea.

Eukaryotic paralogues of the XPD helicase

In eukaryotic genomes up to three paralogues of XPD have been identified. All share the four conserved cysteine residues and are therefore likely to be iron–sulfur proteins. The best characterized is the helicase FancJ {also known as BACH1/BRIP1 [BRCA1 (breast cancer 1 early-onset)-interacting protein

C-terminal helicase 1]} which plays a role in a DNA cross-link repair pathway that is mutated in Fanconi's anaemia patients (reviewed in [10]). FancJ interacts with the breast cancer-susceptibility protein BRCA1 and may also have a role in double-strand break repair [11]. Recently, a role for FancJ in the unwinding of G4 quadruplex structures during DNA replication has been proposed [12,13]. One mutation of human FancJ that results in Fanconi's anaemia is targeted to Ala[349], which is mutated to a proline residue. This residue is not conserved in the XPD family, but is positioned next to the fourth conserved cysteine ligand in human FancJ. Mutation of the equivalent residue in archaeal XPD (F136P) resulted in the destabilization of the iron–sulfur cluster and consequently a loss of helicase activity [5]. This suggests that the A349P mutation of FancJ in humans probably causes Fanconi's anaemia by disrupting the iron–sulfur clusterbinding domain and thus inactivating the FancJ helicase [5].

A second paralogue is RTEL. *Rtel*-knockout mice die during gestation with multiple developmental defects, genomic instability and telomere loss [14]. RTEL has also been suggested to be a functional equivalent of yeast Srs2 which antagonizes homologous recombination by dissociating D-loops in metazoa [15]. Thirdly, the Chl1 protein is found in yeast and some metazoa. It also contains the four conserved cysteine residues and is therefore probably an iron–sulfur-dependent helicase. In yeast, Chl1 is important for chromosome segregation [16]. Human ChlR1 interacts with the cohesin complex, and deletion of the mouse gene is lethal and has defects in chromosome segregation [17,18].

Crystal structures of XPD

Crystal structures of archaeal XPDs have been reported recently by three groups [8,19,20]. All three structures reveal a four-domain organization, with the iron–sulfur-cluster-binding domain and an Arch domain arising from the first of two canonical helicase motor domains. Together, the Arch and iron–sulfur domains form a channel through which ssDNA is dragged by the action of the motor domains in a cyclical ATP-dependent reaction (Figure 1). This is consistent with a role for the iron–sulfur domain in breaking the DNA duplex, in other words acting as the 'ploughshare' seen in many DNA helicases [21], and data from fluorescently labelled DNA species support the idea that the DNA duplex is broken near the iron–sulfur-binding domain [22]. However, it is not yet clear which specific part of the protein is utilized to separate the DNA strands, and it remains a formal possibility that the DNA helix is broken at the other side of the protein on motor domain 2, as suggested by Wolski et al. [19]. Further work will be required to resolve these issues.

The crystal structures and accompanying biochemical data shed light on the *in vivo* consequences of the mutations seen in human XP, TTD and CS. XP mutations are clustered in two main areas: around the ATP-binding site, and along the path of the ssDNA along the top of the two motor domains. XP residues tend to be highly conserved from archaea through to humans. These

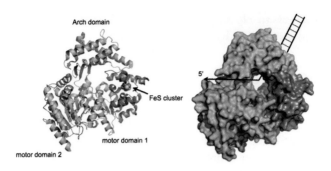

Figure 1. Structure of XPD from *Thermoplasma acidophilum*
Left-hand panel: cartoon of the XPD structure from *T. acidophilum* [19] with the four major domains labelled and the iron–sulfur-cluster-binding domain highlighted in blue. Right-hand panel: the protein is shown as a space-filling representation, emphasizing the narrow pore formed between the Arch and iron–sulfur cluster domains that is wide enough to accommodate ssDNA. A schematic representation of the likely path of DNA emphasizes the possibility that the DNA duplex is separated at the constriction formed by these two domains, and that the single strand is dragged across the top of the motor domains from right to left in this depiction.

observations suggest a role in DNA binding and catalysis. Mutations causing XP are thought to inactivate XPD helicase without perturbing the overall structure of the enzyme. This has the consequence of knocking out NER activity while preserving the role of TFIIH in transcription initiation where the helicase activity is not required [23]. Site-directed mutagenesis of XP-targeted residues in the archaeal enzyme system confirm this hypothesis, as the resulting mutations deactivate the helicase and/or ATPase activity of the enzyme without disrupting the structure [5,8,20].

In contrast, TTD-causing mutations tend to be in less conserved residues. Several are located on the surface of the archaeal enzyme well away from the ssDNA-binding and active sites, or deep in the hydrophobic core of the Arch domain. Mutation of these residues does not always knock out the helicase activity of the archaeal enzyme [8]. The prediction here is that TTD mutations destabilize the structure of TFIIH by either destabilizing XPD directly or by weakening its interaction with other subunits of TFIIH. One example of direct destabilization is seen for the human mutation C259Y. In the crystal structure, the side chain of the cysteine residue points into the core of the Arch domain and there is no room to accommodate a bulky tyrosine side chain. The equivalent mutation in archaeal XPD, A204Y, results in an active helicase that is temperature-sensitive, suggesting a decrease in overall protein stability [8]. Another class of TTD mutations target non-conserved residues on the surface of the XPD protein, and some of these mutations have no effect on either the stability or activity of the archaeal enzyme. In human XPD, these mutations probably weaken the interactions between XPD and the other proteins in the TFIIH complex. Since XPD is only functional in the context of TFIIH, this destabilization leads to a loss of NER activity, despite the fact that no important functional residues of XPD have been altered [8,20].

The role of the iron–sulfur cluster

The discovery of an iron–sulfur cluster domain in XPD was unexpected, and the role of the cluster has been the subject of considerable speculation. Iron–sulfur clusters are comparatively rare in DNA-repair proteins; the only other example being the cluster found in certain members of the DNA glycosylase family [24]. Here, the cluster has been postulated to have a structural role, but also potentially a role in the detection of DNA damage. The Barton group has suggested that glycosylases with an iron–sulfur cluster might pass an electron on to DNA as a mechanism to test for the presence of DNA damage [25]. Since XPD has also been predicted to play a role in the detection of DNA damage during NER, this has prompted speculation that the iron–sulfur cluster might play an active role in the detection of DNA damage, such as photoproducts. However, although this is superficially an attractive hypothesis, the observation that four human helicases with different functions in the cell each have an iron–sulfur cluster leads to the obvious conclusion that the cluster cannot have such a specific function.

A second possibility is that the cluster confers a redox-sensing function on the protein. In this scenario, the activity of an enzyme such as XPD could be controlled by the oxidation state of the iron–sulfur cluster, specifically by inactivating the protein under conditions of oxidative stress by decomposing the cluster. However, it seems counterintuitive that a DNA-repair enzyme required for the removal of DNA lesions caused by oxidative stress should be deactivated when it is most needed.

Instead, it is more likely that the iron–sulfur cluster has a purely structural role in stabilizing the small domain that, with the Arch domain, separates the DNA duplex during helicase function. Iron–sulfur clusters have recently been discovered in several other proteins, including DNA primase [26], RNA polymerase [27], and the bacterial AddAB and eukaryotic Dna2 enzymes [28]. It is possible that iron–sulfur clusters are a type of 'molecular fossil' that predates the advent of aerobic lifestyles. Iron–sulfur clusters may have been replaced by redox-insensitive zinc domains in most situations, but have persisted in some proteins owing to the quirks of evolution. Bear in mind that the machinery for iron–sulfur cluster biosynthesis, although complex, is essential anyway for the assembly of redox proteins. There is therefore presumably no great cost in maintaining iron–sulfur clusters as a structural feature in proteins where the cluster is relatively redox insensitive. For both AddAB and DinG, some bacterial lineages where iron is particularly toxic or in short supply appear to have overcome the requirement for an iron–sulfur-cluster-binding domain [28]. Again, this suggests a structural rather than functional/sensing role for the iron–sulfur cluster in these proteins.

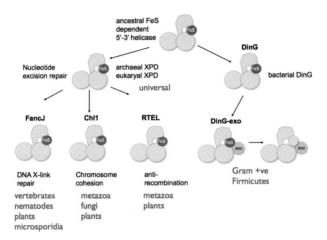

Figure 2. Proposed evolution of XPD family
An ancestral 5′→3′ helicase with an essential iron–sulfur-cluster-binding domain has given rise to the XPD family in archaea and eukaryotes, with successive gene duplication and specialization in the latter generating the RTEL, FancJ and Chl1 helicases. In Gram-positive bacteria, the DinG helicase has acquired an N-terminal exonuclease (exo) domain of unknown function and has subsequently lost the iron–sulfur-cluster-binding domain.

Evolution of the XPD family

The ubiquitous nature of the XPD family across all three domains of life suggests that the ancestral helicase including the iron–sulfur-binding domain is an ancient protein that was present in the last common ancestor. The closer similarity of eukaryotic and archaeal XPD compared with the much more distant bacterial DinG protein mirrors the situation for many proteins that are involved in information processing. In particular, proteins involved in DNA replication and recombination, transcription and translation are all more highly similar in eukaryotes/archaea and more divergent or even unrelated in bacteria [29,30]. The observation that archaeal XPD is most similar to the eukaryotic XPD (rather than any of the paralogues) and the ubiquitous nature of XPD across all of the eukaryotic phyla suggest that XPD is the founding member of the family. The same argument suggests that archaeal XPD may have a role to play in an archaeal NER-like pathway, though this remains to be proved.

The XPD paralogues FancJ, RTEL and Chl1 probably arose during the evolution and diversification of the eukaryotic domain as new DNA-repair pathways evolved. In bacteria, the role of DinG is also still unclear, but it is also likely to function in a repair pathway of some description. The lack of phenotype of a *DinG* knockout may be explained by the existence of a second repair pathway with overlapping specificity. As shown in Figure 2, DinG in Gram-positive bacteria acquired a further function with the fusion of an exonuclease III-type domain at the N-terminus. This nuclease–helicase fusion is reminiscent of the Werner's syndrome helicase. In most sequenced Gram-positive bacteria, the iron–sulfur-cluster domain seems to have been lost subsequent to the fusion of the exonuclease domain. It is not yet clear whether these proteins are active helicases, or whether the protein has assumed a new role in this lineage and uses the helicase part of the protein as a structure or DNA-binding feature as seen, for example, in the eukaryotic XPF (xeroderma pigmentosum complementation group F) nuclease [31].

Acknowledgements

Thanks to Jana Rudolf, Anne-Marie McRobbie, Christophe Rouillon and all members of the Scottish Structural Proteomics Facility for their contributions to this research.

Funding

This work was funded by Cancer Research UK.

References

1. Coin, F., Oksenych, V. & Egly, J.M. (2007) Distinct roles for the XPB/p52 and XPD/p44 subcomplexes of TFIIH in damaged DNA opening during nucleotide excision repair. Mol. Cell **26**, 245–256
2. Tirode, F., Busso, D., Coin, F. & Egly, J.M. (1999) Reconstitution of the transcription factor TFIIH: assignment of functions for the three enzymatic subunits, XPB, XPD, and cdk7. Mol. Cell **3**, 87–95
3. Lehmann, A.R. (2003) DNA repair-deficient diseases, xeroderma pigmentosum, Cockayne syndrome and trichothiodystrophy. Biochimie **85**, 1101–1111
4. White, M.F. (2003) Archaeal DNA repair: paradigms and puzzles. Biochem. Soc. Trans. **31**, 690–693
5. Rudolf, J., Makrantoni, V., Ingledew, W.J., Stark, M.J. & White, M.F. (2006) The DNA repair helicases XPD and FancJ have essential iron–sulfur domains. Mol. Cell **23**, 801–808
6. Voloshin, O.N., Vanevski, F., Khil, P.P. & Camerini-Otero, R.D. (2003) Characterization of the DNA damage-inducible helicase DinG from Escherichia coli. J. Biol. Chem. **278**, 28284–28293
7. Voloshin, O.N. & Camerini-Otero, R.D. (2007) The DinG protein from Escherichia coli is a structure-specific helicase. J. Biol. Chem. **282**, 18437–18447
8. Liu, H., Rudolf, J., Johnson, K.A., McMahon, S.A., Oke, M., Carter, L., McRobbie, A.M., Brown, S.E., Naismith, J.H. & White, M.F. (2008) Structure of the DNA repair helicase XPD. Cell **133**, 801–812
9. Bukowy, Z., Harrigan, J.A., Ramsden, D.A., Tudek, B., Bohr, V.A. & Stevnsner, T. (2008) WRN exonuclease activity is blocked by specific oxidatively induced base lesions positioned in either DNA strand. Nucleic Acids Res. **36**, 4975–4987
10. Wu, Y., Suhasini, A.N. & Brosh, R.M. (2009) Welcome the family of FANCJ-like helicases to the block of genome stability maintenance proteins. Cell. Mol. Life Sci. **66**, 1209–1222
11. Cantor, S.B., Bell, D.W., Ganesan, S., Kass, E.M., Drapkin, R., Grossman, S., Wahrer, D.C., Sgroi, D.C., Lane, W.S., Haber, D.A. & Livingston, D.M. (2001) BACH1, a novel helicase-like protein, interacts directly with BRCA1 and contributes to its DNA repair function. Cell **105**, 149–160
12. London, T.B., Barber, L.J., Mosedale, G., Kelly, G.P., Balasubramanian, S., Hickson, I.D., Boulton, S.J. & Hiom, K. (2008) FANCJ is a structure-specific DNA helicase associated with the maintenance of genomic G/C tracts. J. Biol. Chem. **283**, 36132–36139
13. Wu, Y., Shin-ya, K. & Brosh, Jr, R.M. (2008) FANCJ helicase defective in Fanconia anemia and breast cancer unwinds G-quadruplex DNA to defend genomic stability. Mol. Cell. Biol. **28**, 4116–4128
14. Ding, H., Schertzer, M., Wu, X., Gertsenstein, M., Selig, S., Kammori, M., Pourvali, R., Poon, S., Vulto, I., Chavez, E. et al. (2004) Regulation of murine telomere length by Rtel: an essential gene encoding a helicase-like protein. Cell **117**, 873–886

15. Barber, L.J., Youds, J.L., Ward, J.D., McIlwraith, M.J., O'Neil, N.J., Petalcorin, M.I., Martin, J.S., Collis, S.J., Cantor, S.B., Auclair, M. et al. (2008) RTEL1 maintains genomic stability by suppressing homologous recombination. *Cell* **135**, 261–271

16. Skibbens, R.V. (2004) Chl1p, a DNA helicase-like protein in budding yeast, functions in sister-chromatid cohesion. *Genetics* **166**, 33–42

17. Farina, A., Shin, J.H., Kim, D.H., Bermudez, V.P., Kelman, Z., Seo, Y.S. & Hurwitz, J. (2008) Studies with the human cohesin establishment factor, ChlR1: association of ChlR1 with Ctf18-RFC and Fen1. *J. Biol. Chem.* **283**, 20925–20936

18. Inoue, A., Li, T., Roby, S.K., Valentine, M.B., Inoue, M., Boyd, K., Kidd, V.J. & Lahti, J.M. (2007) Loss of ChlR1 helicase in mouse causes lethality due to the accumulation of aneuploid cells generated by cohesion defects and placental malformation. *Cell Cycle* **6**, 1646–1654

19. Wolski, S.C., Kuper, J., Hanzelmann, P., Truglio, J.J., Croteau, D.L., Van Houten, B. & Kisker, C. (2008) Crystal structure of the FeS cluster-containing nucleotide excision repair helicase XPD. *PLoS Biol.* **6**, e149

20. Fan, L., Fuss, J.O., Cheng, Q.J., Arvai, A.S., Hammel, M., Roberts, V.A., Cooper, P.K. & Tainer, J.A. (2008) XPD helicase structures and activities: insights into the cancer and aging phenotypes from XPD mutations. *Cell* **133**, 789–800

21. Singleton, M.R., Dillingham, M.S. & Wigley, D.B. (2007) Structure and mechanism of helicases and nucleic acid translocases. *Annu. Rev. Biochem.* **76**, 23–50

22. Pugh, R.A., Honda, M., Leesley, H., Thomas, A., Lin, Y., Nilges, M.J., Cann, I.K. & Spies, M. (2008) The iron-containing domain is essential in Rad3 helicases for coupling of ATP hydrolysis to DNA translocation and for targeting the helicase to the single-stranded DNA-double-stranded DNA junction. *J. Biol. Chem.* **283**, 1732–1743

23. Dubaele, S., Proietti De Santis, L., Bienstock, R.J., Keriel, A., Stefanini, M., Van Houten, B. & Egly, J.M. (2003) Basal transcription defect discriminates between xeroderma pigmentosum and trichothiodystrophy in XPD patients. *Mol. Cell* **11**, 1635–1646

24. Hinks, J.A., Evans, M.C., De Miguel, Y., Sartori, A.A., Jiricny, J. & Pearl, L.H. (2002) An iron–sulfur cluster in the family 4 uracil–DNA glycosylases. *J. Biol. Chem.* **277**, 16936–16940

25. Boal, A.K., Yavin, E., Lukianova, O.A., O'Shea, V.L., David, S.S. & Barton, J.K. (2005) DNA-bound redox activity of DNA repair glycosylases containing [4Fe–4S] clusters. *Biochemistry* **44**, 8397–8407

26. Klinge, S., Hirst, J., Maman, J.D., Krude, T. & Pellegrini, L. (2007) An iron–sulfur domain of the eukaryotic primase is essential for RNA primer synthesis. *Nat. Struct. Mol. Biol.* **14**, 875–877

27. Hirata, A., Klein, B.J. & Murakami, K.S. (2008) The X-ray crystal structure of RNA polymerase from Archaea. *Nature* **451**, 851–854

28. Yeeles, J.T., Cammack, R. & Dillingham, M.S. (2009) An iron–sulfur cluster is essential for the binding of broken DNA by AddAB-type helicase–nucleases. J. Biol. Chem. **284**, 7746–7755

29. Bell, S.D. & Jackson, S.P. (1998) Transcription and translation in Archaea: a mosaic of eukaryal and bacterial features. *Trends Microbiol.* **6**, 222–228

30. Kelman, Z. & White, M.F. (2005) Archaeal DNA replication and repair. *Curr. Opin. Microbiol.* **8**, 669–676

31. Ciccia, A., McDonald, N. & West, S.C. (2008) Structural and functional relationships of the XPF/MUS81 family of proteins. *Annu. Rev. Biochem.* **77**, 259–287

Biochem. Soc. Symp. 76
Citation reference: Biochem. Soc. Trans. (2009) **37**, 553–559.
© The Authors. Journal compilation © 2009 The Biochemical Society

5

Genomic instability and cancer: lessons from analysis of Bloom's syndrome

Miranda Payne and Ian D. Hickson[1]

Weatherall Institute of Molecular Medicine, University of Oxford, John Radcliffe Hospital, Oxford OX3 9DS, U.K.

Abstract

Bloom's syndrome (BS) is a rare autosomal recessive disorder characterized by genomic instability and cancer predisposition. The underlying genetic defect is mutation of the *BLM* gene, producing deficiency in the RecQ helicase BLM (Bloom's syndrome protein). The present article begins by introducing BLM and its binding partners before reviewing its known biochemical activities and its potential roles both as a pro-recombinase and as a suppressor of homologous recombination. Finally, the evidence for an emerging role in mitotic chromosome segregation is examined.

Introduction to BLM and Bloom's syndrome

Bloom's syndrome (BS) is a rare autosomal recessive disorder characterized by proportional dwarfism, immunodeficiency, hypersensitivity to sunlight, subfertility and cancer predisposition [1,2]. It is caused by mutation in the BS gene, *BLM*, which encodes Bloom's syndrome protein. BLM belongs to the RecQ family of DNA helicases, of which human cells express five members [RecQ1, RecQ4, RecQ5, BLM and WRN (Werner's syndrome protein)] [2,3].

[1] *To whom correspondence should be addressed (email ian.hickson@imm.ox.ac.uk).*

Germline mutations in any of three of the human RecQ family result in diseases associated with premature aging, cancer predisposition or both [2]. It is this clear relationship with human disease that has led to the extensive study of this family of helicases.

The classical hallmark of BS cells is their high frequency of SCEs (sister-chromatid exchanges) [4], which are reciprocol exchanges that arise predominantly as part of HR (homologous recombination) events occurring during repair of DNA damage in the S- or G_2-phases of the cell cycle. However, the inherent genomic instability of BS cells and their inability to respond appropriately to replicative stresses is reflected in the range of other cellular abnormalities observed. These include elevated frequencies of several types of chromosomal aberration, including breaks, quadriradials and translocations [3,5], hypersensitivity to certain DNA-damaging agents, such as hydroxyurea, and an increased number of micronuclei [6].

BLM and its binding partners

The RecQ family, of which BLM is a member, is evolutionarily conserved from bacteria to humans. This conservation is most striking in the centrally located helicase domain, which contains the seven characteristic consensus motifs typifying Superfamily II helicases. BLM contains two additional domains, conserved in both *Escherichia coli* RecQ and the *Saccharomyces cerevisiae* orthologue, Sgs1. The RQC (RecQ C-terminal) domain appears to be important for ATPase activity, DNA-binding and helicase function [7]. It includes a Zn^{2+}-binding region containing four conserved cysteine residues, mutation of two of which gives rise to BS [8], as well as a winged-helix motif also found in proteins outside the RecQ helicase family that are known to interact with DNA. The HRDC (helicase and RNaseD C-terminal) domain confers DNA structure specificity and is essential for the ability to bind to and unwind DHJs (double Holliday junctions) [9] (see below). The N-terminal domain of BLM is likely to mediate many of the interactions between BLM and other proteins, as well as being an important regulatory domain. Post-translational modification, including phosphorylation and SUMOylation, affects both the intracellular localization and the function of BLM.

It is known that the physical interaction of BLM with other specific nuclear proteins is required for it to fulfil some of its functions. In mammalian cells, BLM binds directly to the DNA decatenase topoisomerase III [10] and hRMI1 (BLAP75) [11] in a co-operative relationship conserved between homologous proteins in other organisms, including *Schizosaccharomyces pombe* (Rqh1, Top3, Rmi1 proteins) and *S. cerevisiae* (Sgs1, Top3 and Rmi1 proteins) (reviewed in [12]). More recently, a fourth candidate member, RMI2 (BLAP18) has been identified, which appears to play a critical role in complex stability [13,14]. There is close functional interdependency between the components of this BTR (BLM–topoisomerase III–RMI1/2) multiprotein complex. BLM stimulates topoisomerase III to relax negatively supercoiled DNA [15], whereas depletion of hRMI1, using siRNA (short interfering RNA), leads to impaired BLM focus formation at sites of DNA damage, an increase in SCEs and defective cell proliferation [11]. hRMI2 is similarly required for correct BLM localization following replication blockade. In the absence of hRMI2, cells exhibit an increase in spontaneous chromosome breaks [14]. It is likely that BLM fulfils the majority of its roles within the context of these binding partners. However, it seems that there are also circumstances in which BLM can act independently. For instance, camptothecin-induced replication arrest is followed by disruption of the BTR complex and dissociation of BLM from topoisomerase III [16]. BLM is also known to interact with the recombinase Rad51 [17] and can bind to the ssDNA (single-stranded DNA)-binding protein RPA (replication protein A), in a reaction that efficiently stimulates BLM helicase activity [18].

Multiple enzymatic properties of BLM have been demonstrated *in vitro*. In common with many RecQ helicases, the $3'{\rightarrow}5'$ helicase activity of BLM is Mg^{2+}- and ATP-dependent and DNA-structure-specific. Although it can unwind a wide variety of structures, its efficiency is greatest when unwinding certain complex or forked DNA structures, including D-loops (displacement loops), duplexes with internal 'bubbles' and G-quadruplexes [19,20], suggesting that it is these which form its preferred physiological substrate. RecQ helicases, including BLM, also possess the ability to catalyse the reverse reaction to that of a helicase, promoting the annealing of complementary single strands of DNA in an Mg^{2+}-independent reaction that is dependent on the C-terminal domain and is inhibited by ssDNA-binding proteins [21]. The ATPase activity of BLM is strongly dependent on the presence of ssDNA [22], reminiscent of yeast Srs2 [23].

Determining the *in vivo* roles of BLM is proving more complex. Mutations in BLM cause a hyper-recombination phenotype [1], implying that BLM functions to suppress recombination. However, BLM has also been implicated in the promotion of both early and late steps in the process of HR-mediated replication fork repair. These apparently conflicting roles appear to coexist. A priority must be to establish which of the many potential functions of BLM are critical in suppressing chromosomal instability and which can be undertaken either by other members of the RecQ helicase family or, indeed, by other DNA helicases, such as those belonging to the UvrD/Srs2/Fbh1 family.

Below, we summarize the putative pro-recombinogenic and anti-recombinogenic roles for BLM before focusing in more detail on the emerging role for BLM in mitotic chromosome segregation.

Pro-recombinogenic roles of BLM

The HR-mediated repair of a DSB (double-strand break) is initiated by $5'{\rightarrow}3'$ resection of the DSB ends, to produce a region of ssDNA, followed by the Rad51-dependent invasion of the 3'-end of the DSB into an intact homologous

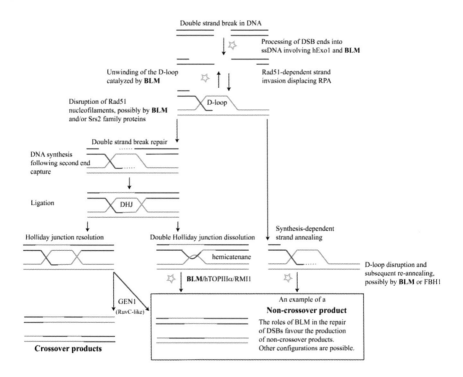

Figure 1. BLM favours the formation of non-crossover products
Schematic representation for the potential roles of BLM in the repair of a DSB by HR including the processing of DHJs by Holliday junction dissolution. The roles of BLM favour the formation of non-crossover products and hence minimize LOH. Steps in the various pathways where BLM might act are indicated by green stars. FBH1, F-box DNA helicase 1; hExo1, human exonuclease 1; hTOPIIIα, human topoisomerase IIIα.

duplex (usually the sister chromatid) to form a D-loop (Figure 1). BLM appears to promote resection and can stimulate the nucleolytic activity of hExo1 (human exonuclease 1), a double-stranded exonuclease probably responsible for processing the DSB ends into ssDNA in readiness for assembly of the nucleofilament proteins [24,25]. This activity of BLM is mediated independently of its helicase activity and is evidence that BLM has a very early role in the initiation of HR. Generation of regions of ssDNA are also critical for the induction of robust cell-cycle checkpoint signalling, including the recruitment of proteins such as BRCA1 (breast cancer 1 early-onset), NBS1 (Nijmegen breakage syndrome protein 1) and DNA-damage-checkpoint mediators such as 53BP1 (p53-binding protein 1). Protein recruitment to stalled forks is delayed or absent in BS cells following exposure to hydroxyurea [26], a defect which is reversed by expression of a helicase-defective form of BLM [26].

The ATPase activity of RecQ helicases becomes critical in intra-S-phase checkpoint functions, including the stabilization and subsequent HR-dependent restart of arrested replication forks [27]. It has been suggested that BLM has a role in the processing of stalled forks to produce a configuration that permits restart of replication, potentially by promoting fork regression [28]. This process uses 'template switching' in which the nascent lagging strand is used as a template to extend the leading strand past the site of damage. A one-ended DSB is generated that can be processed to facilitate HR-mediated replication restart. This possible role for BLM is supported by the fact that BLM helicase activity is essential for maintaining arrested forks in a state competent for replication restart following transient exposure to aphidicolin [29] and is consistent with the requirement for the helicase activity of the *S. cerevisiae* RecQ helicase for the continued association of DNA polymerases and with arrested replication forks [30]. Although HR-independent pathways exist for circumventing lesions that have induced stalled replication forks, collapsed replication forks resulting from the collision of a fork with a single-strand break in the template are totally dependent on HR for their recovery. Hence BLM has a critical role in maintaining the fidelity of HR early in the process.

It is established that BLM also has a role in the terminal stages of HR. This is suggested by the accumulation of HR-dependent recombination intermediates resembling Holliday junctions in Sgs1-deficient *S. cerevisiae* [31]. Holliday junctions must be processed to permit chromosome segregation and this can be achieved by at least two pathways (Figure 1). The classical pathway of Holliday junction resolution involves the symmetrical nicking of one of the pairs of identical strands of the same polarity at the crossover point of a Holliday junction. *E. coli* RuvC was the first cellular nuclease identified as acting as a Holliday junction resolvase capable of promoting this process. The RuvC-like pathway of Holliday junction resolution allows the nicked duplex DNA to be ligated with no need for additional processing. Resolution products can be either crossover or non-crossover, depending on which pair of strands is nicked. Recently, it has been proposed that the human nuclease GEN1 and its *S. cerevisiae* orthologue Yen1 fulfil the role of Holliday junction resolvases in their respective species [32].

An alternative terminal mechanism in HR is Holliday junction dissolution, which occurs only when a DHJ structure is generated. Within the context of the BTR complex, BLM is able to mediate the convergence and subsequent collapse of the two Holliday junctions into a hemicatenane structure (Figure 1) [33,34] in a process that is dependent on the HRDC domain [9]. The DNA single-strand passage activity of hTopoIII (human topoisomerase III) decatenates the structure, assisted by hRMI1 [35,34]. Work in *Drosophila* on the orthologous proteins suggests that RPA may additionally stimulate the helicase activity of BLM [36]. This novel mechanism of processing Holliday junctions has the significant advantage that the products generated are exclusively non-crossover [33]. Dissolution provides BLM with a potential role late in HR for suppressing crossing-over, which would minimize LOH (loss of heterozygosity) and prevent unwanted genomic rearrangements. In the absence of BLM, processing of DHJs must proceed by the classical RuvC-like resolution pathway, giving rise to the crossovers [37] and elevated SCEs seen in BS cells [4]. The catalysis of dissolution is highly specific for BLM, which cannot be replaced by other RecQ helicases [9]. Consistent with this is the fact that hypomorphic BLM-mediated knockout mice cells show LOH [38]. In most HR reactions, the sequence homology between sister chromatids ensures that sequence alteration is avoided and crossovers have minimal physiological significance. However, when non-sisters or non-allelic loci are used as the template for repair, the consequent genomic rearrangements risk the stability of the genome. It is in this situation that the promotion of alternative pathways of repair by BLM that produce non-crossover products, such as synthesis-dependent strand annealing and Holliday junction dissolution, have a critical role in preserving chromosomal integrity.

Anti-recombinogenic roles

D-loop destruction

The D-loop structure represents the initial strand-invasion step of HR (Figure 1) and is a common intermediate in most models for recombination-mediated DNA-repair processes. BLM possesses the ability to disrupt D-loops generated by the RecA recombinase, with the invading strand being displaced from the duplex with high efficiency [19,39]. This may represent a mechanism for the suppression of HR by BLM [19], potentially to avoid inappropriate template usage and may be facilitated *in vivo* by the physical association of BLM and Rad51 [17].

Alternatively, it has been proposed that BLM-mediated D-loop dissociation after primer extension by DNA polymerase might be a necessary step before re-annealing of two ends of the broken DNA molecule during DSB repair [22,40]. This would place BLM in the position of promoting HR via synthesis-dependent strand annealing, a pathway that prevents the formation of crossovers and hence SCEs [41] (Figure 1). Co-ordination between these roles may be achieved by the fact that BLM cannot dissociate D-loops when hRad51 is present in an active ATP-bound conformation in the presence of Ca^{2+} [22], minimizing the risk of premature disruption of D-loops before completion of the primer extension by DNA polymerase. In the absence of sufficient DNA polymerase, D-loop dissociation would require conversion of the hRad51 filament into an inactive ADP-bound form.

Disruption of Rad51 nucleofilaments

Disruption of the Rad51–ssDNA filament offers an appealing potential mechanism for the early suppression of inappropriate HR. Filament disruption results in inhibition of DNA-strand exchange. Low concentrations of BLM helicase can efficiently disrupt the nucleofilament by displacing hRad51 protein from ssDNA in an ATPase-dependent manner [22], in a manner reminiscent of other DNA helicases, including RecQL5 [42] and the yeast DNA helicase Srs2 [23]. Consistent with the notion of functional redundancy is the fact that overexpression of the sole yeast RecQ orthologue Sgs1 can suppress recombination defects observed in *S. cerevisiae* Srs2-deletion mutants [43,44]. Regulation of this role for BLM may be achieved by a similar mechanism to the regulation of D-loop dissociation. BLM can only disrupt an inactive filament in its inactive ADP-bound form. Hence the nucleofilament remains susceptible to BLM dissociation until the cell is fully prepared for HR.

Mitotic roles

It is well established that even during an apparently unperturbed cell cycle, *sgs1*, *rqh1* and *top3* mutant cells display defects in chromosome segregation (reviewed in [12]). In mammalian cells, the presence of anaphase bridges can be used as a cytological marker of chromosome mis-segregation. These represent incompletely segregated chromosomal DNA connecting the daughter nuclei, and may give rise to the generation of micronuclei as a consequence of the breakage of the bridge by mitotic spindle forces [45]. BS cells have an elevated frequency of micronuclei [6], and it has been proposed that both anaphase bridges and micronuclei may contribute to the cancer predisposition observed in BS via the creation of gene dosage imbalances. Recently, there has been considerable focus on whether BLM has a role in the maintenance of faithful chromosome segregation at mitosis. It has been shown that loss of BLM function causes impairment in mitotic chromosome segregation and that BLM both localizes to anaphase bridges and is associated with lagging chromatin during the later stages of mitosis [46]. It may be that failure by BTR to complete Holliday junction dissolution before anaphase results in bridge formation due to persistent interlinking of the DNA molecules. Alternatively, BLM may play a role in the resolution of intertwined DNA structures arising during replication. Centromeric loci are preferentially associated with BLM-associated bridges, and this supports the proposal that at least some of the bridges represent aberrant replication structures, as does the fact that inhibition of topoisomerase II exacerbates chromosome mis-segregation defects in BS cells. Hence anaphase bridges may arise during replication either as fully replicated catenanes or partially replicated hemicatenated DNA arising at sites of converging replication forks [12].

DNA bridges in anaphase are more prevalent than previously thought. A new class of UFBs (ultrafine bridges) has been reported that stain neither with conventional DNA dyes, e.g. DAPI (4′,6-diamidino-2-phenylindole), nor with antibodies against histones. These UFBs have been observed independently in the context of staining for BLM protein [46] and the SNF2-family ATPase PICH [Plk1 (Polo-like kinase 1)-interacting checkpoint helicase] [47]. PICH is an essential component of the spindle assembly checkpoint, localizes to kinetochores and inner centromeres, and associates with ultrafine anaphase threads [47], which are identical with the BLM–DNA bridges observed by Chan et al. [46]. These UFBs have been found with such high frequency in all cultured cell types examined so far that it has been postulated that they may represent a physiological rather than pathological process [48].

BLM, along with its binding partners, also localizes to UFBs. These bridges persist in up to 30% of late-anaphase cells, the proportion of which can be increased by pre-treatment with a topoisomerase II inhibitor [46]. The high frequency of UFBs found even in normal untreated cells supports the proposal that bridge formation is part of a physiological regulatory mechanism. Certainly, as cells progress through anaphase, a progressive reduction in the percentage of cells exhibiting bridges is observed, suggesting successful resolution before cytokinesis [46].

The origin of UFBs is unclear. Indeed, they may not represent a uniform population. Many bridges connect sister kinetochores and probably evolve directly from catenated centromeric chromatin. Later in anaphase, longer bridges are evident and some of these may represent incompletely replicated DNA or unresolved recombination intermediates [46]. The role of BLM on these bridges is also unclear. Cells lacking BLM show a higher frequency of these bridges than do isogenic cells corrected by expression of BLM [46]. BLM-deficient cells also exhibit UFBs that persist longer into anaphase than in cells expressing BLM. Although this may suggest a role for BLM in the resolution of bridges, it cannot represent the only resolution mechanism, because the bridges eventually disappear even in the absence of BLM. If BLM does play a role, it seems likely that it achieves this via its usual association with topoisomerase III and RMI1/2. This model for BLM in bridge resolution is supported by the fact that PICH staining on UFBs can be observed from metaphase [47]. However, BLM associates only from the start of anaphase [46]. Following replication, BLM and binding partners may be recruited to persistent sites of catenated DNA to facilitate faithful sister-chromatid disjunction, although most decatenation of fully replicated DNA is probably co-ordinated by topoisomerase II [47,48]. This model for the role of BLM on the bridges is attractive because it represents an extension of the proposed role for BLM in the resolution of recombination intermediates.

Fragile sites are hotspots for anaphase bridging

FA (Fanconi's anaemia) proteins represent a group of 13 proteins that, if any are defective, give rise to the clinical syndrome of FA. In common with BS, FA is associated with chromosomal instability. BLM and the FA proteins associate in a multienzyme complex called BRAFT (BLM–RPA–FA–topoisomerase IIIα) [49], although the functional relevance of this association is unclear. Recently, the FA proteins FANCD2 and FANCI (FA complementation group D2 and I respectively) were shown to associate with specific genomic loci in metaphase chromosomes with one focus of protein located on each sister locus (K.L. Chan, T. Palmai-Pallag, S. Ying and I.D. Hickson, unpublished work). These so-called sister foci were non-randomly distributed, being associated primarily with fragile-site loci, particularly FRA16D (K.L. Chan, T. Palmai-Pallag, S. Ying and

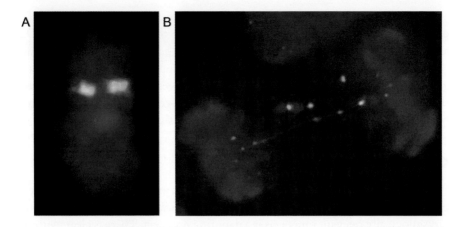

Figure 2. Role of BLM in mitosis
(**A**) FANCD2 foci localize to fragile sites on metaphase chromosomes. Co-localization of FANCD2 sister foci (green) with a FRA16D probe (red) on a metaphase chromosome 16. FANCD2 and FANCI have been shown to associate with common fragile-site loci, such as the one on chromosome 16. Paired foci can be observed as early in the cell cycle as G_2-phase and persist throughout prophase and metaphase before segregating symmetrically. DNA is shown in blue. (**B**) BLM localizes to UFBs in anaphase. BLM (red) localizes to DAPI-negative UFBs in late anaphase even in normal, unperturbed, cells. Some of these show co-localization with FANCD2 foci at the bridge termini (green). These FANCD2-associated bridges are those that arise from fragile-site loci. Most of the non-FANCD2-associated bridges arise from centromeric DNA. DNA is shown in blue.

I.D. Hickson, unpublished work) (Figure 2A). Moreover, these loci have been shown to be linked by BLM-associated UFBs on some occasions (K.L. Chan, T. Palmai-Pallag, S. Ying and I.D. Hickson, unpublished work) (Figure 2B). Indeed, FANCD2 can form a focus at each terminus of a subset of the bridges ([46], and K.L. Chan, T. Palmai-Pallag, S. Ying and I.D. Hickson, unpublished work). However, this association is preserved even in the absence of BLM, where FANCD2 can be observed staining the extremities of bridges visualized using an antibody to detect PICH (K.L. Chan, T. Palmai-Pallag, S. Ying and I.D. Hickson, unpublished work). Fragile-site expression is known to be induced by partial inhibition of DNA replication and it now seems that fragile-site bridging follows a similar pattern of induction (K.L. Chan, T. Palmai-Pallag, S. Ying and I.D. Hickson, unpublished work). Fragile-site loci are, by definition, sites with intrinsic replication difficulties. Replicative stress may cause interlinking of sister chromatids by replication intermediates, with a preference for vulnerable genetic locations.

The role of FANCD2 in localizing to the termini of UFBs remains unknown, as does the contribution of BLM. FANCD2 possibly flags regions of the genome inadequately processed during the S/G_2-phases of the cell cycle, which then generate UFBs in mitosis. Certainly, FANCD2 sister foci can be observed as early in the cell cycle as G_2-phase, and these then persist throughout prophase and metaphase.

Replication inhibitors, such as aphidicolin, increase not only the percentage of cells containing UFBs in anaphase but also the number of FANCD2-associated UFBs. It may be that the absence of BLM permits aberrant bridge resolution and hence the gradual loss of tumour-suppressor function for those genes coinciding with fragile sites. The resultant genomic rearrangements and the generation of aneuploidy would be an alternative mechanism by which lack of BLM would result in a greater risk of oncogenesis.

Conclusion

BLM has many potential roles in the pathways of DNA repair and replication. Establishing which of its many biochemical properties translate into physiologically relevant functions is a daunting prospect. There is clear evidence to support a role for BLM both as a pro-recombinase and in the suppression of HR. It seems most of these conflicting roles are united in the common aim of minimizing the generation of crossover products during recombination and hence preserving genomic stability. Certainly BLM deficiency, as seen in BS, is characterized by a hyper-recombinant cellular phenotype that causes greater generation of crossover products following DSB repair and consequent loss of heterozygosity. This provides one mechanism for the cancer predisposition that is characteristic of BS. More recently, a role for BLM in mitosis was proposed on the basis of the discovery that BLM localizes both to bulky anaphase bridges and to previously undiscovered UFBs. These bridges also link sister chromatids in anaphase, and BLM may contribute to their timely resolution before cytokinesis. A role for BLM in mitotic chromosome segregation would represent a logical extension from its proven activity resolving recombination intermediates and provides an alternative mechanism for the tumorigenesis observed in BS. Chromosome mis-segregation due to inefficient resolution of anaphase bridges would potentially increase cellular aneuploidy and gene-dosage imbalances and hence increase the potential for malignant transformation.

In summary, BLM functions in multiple intracellular processes related to DNA recombination and repair, many of which remain to be clarified. The cellular and patient phenotypes observed in BS arise from the complex interplay between these roles.

Acknowledgements

We thank Dr Kok-Lung Chan for providing Figures and members of the Hickson laboratory for helpful discussions.

Funding

We thank Cancer Research UK for financial support.

References

1. German, J. (1993) Bloom syndrome: a Mendelian prototype of somatic mutational disease. *Medicine* **72**, 393–406

2. Hickson, I.D. (2003) RecQ helicases: caretakers of the genome. *Nat. Rev. Cancer* **3**, 169–178

3. Bachrati, C.Z. & Hickson, I.D. (2008) RecQ helicases: guardian angels of the DNA replication fork. *Chromosoma* **117**, 219–233

4. Chaganti, R.S., Schonberg, S. & German, J. (1974) A manyfold increase in sister chromatid exchanges in Bloom's syndrome lymphocytes. *Proc. Natl. Acad. Sci. U.S.A.* **71**, 4508–4512

5. German, J. (1995) Bloom's syndrome. *Dermatol. Clin.* **13**, 7–18

6. Rosin, M.P. & German, J. (1985) Evidence for chromosome instability *in vivo* in Bloom syndrome: increased numbers of micronuclei in exfoliated cells. *Hum. Genet.* **71**, 187–191

7. Guo, R.B., Rigolet, P., Zargarian, L., Fermandjian, S. & Xi, X.G. (2005) Structural and functional characterizations reveal the importance of a zinc binding domain in Bloom's syndrome helicase. *Nucleic Acids Res.* **33**, 3109–3124

8. Ellis, N.A., Groden, J., Ye, T.Z., Straughen, J., Lennon, D.J., Ciocci, S., Proytcheva, M. & German, J. (1995) The Bloom's syndrome gene product is homologous to RecQ helicases. *Cell* **83**, 655–666

9. Wu, L., Chan, K.L., Ralf, C., Bernstein, D.A., Garcia, P.L., Bohr, V.A., Vindigni, A., Janscak, P., Keck, J.L. & Hickson, I.D. (2005) The HRDC domain of BLM is required for the dissolution of double Holliday junctions. *EMBO J.* **24**, 2679–2687

10. Wu, L., Davies, S.L., North, P.S., Goulaouic, H., Riou, J.F., Turley, H., Gatter, K.C. & Hickson, I.D. (2000) The Bloom's syndrome gene product interacts with topoisomerase III. *J. Biol. Chem.* **275**, 9636–9644

11. Yin, J., Sobeck, A., Xu, C., Meetei, A.R., Hoatlin, M., Li, L. & Wang, W. (2005) BLAP75, an essential component of Bloom's syndrome protein complexes that maintain genome integrity. *EMBO J.* **24**, 1465–1476

12. Mankouri, H.W. & Hickson, I.D. (2007) The RecQ helicase–topoisomerase III–Rmi1 complex: a DNA structure-specific 'dissolvasome'? *Trends Biochem. Sci.* **32**, 538–546

13. Xu, D., Guo, R., Sobeck, A., Bachrati, C.Z., Yang, J., Enomoto, T., Brown, G.W., Hoatlin, M.E., Hickson, I.D. & Wang, W. (2008) RMI, a new OB-fold complex essential for Bloom syndrome protein to maintain genome stability. *Genes Dev.* **22**, 2843–2855

14. Singh, T.R., Ali, A.M., Busygina, V., Raynard, S., Fan, Q., Du, C.H., Andreassen, P.R., Sung, P. & Meetei, A.R. (2008) BLAP18/RMI2, a novel OB-fold-containing protein, is an essential component of the Bloom helicase–double Holliday junction dissolvasome. *Genes Dev.* **22**, 2856–2868

15. Wu, L. & Hickson, I.D. (2002) The Bloom's syndrome helicase stimulates the activity of human topoisomerase IIIα. *Nucleic Acids Res.* **30**, 4823–4829

16. Rao, V.A., Fan, A.M., Meng, L., Doe, C.F., North, P.S., Hickson, I.D. & Pommier, Y. (2005) Phosphorylation of BLM, dissociation from topoisomerase IIIα, and colocalization with γ-H2AX after topoisomerase I-induced replication damage. *Mol. Cell. Biol.* **25**, 8925–8937

17. Wu, L., Davies, S.L., Levitt, N.C. & Hickson, I.D. (2001) Potential role for the BLM helicase in recombinational repair via a conserved interaction with RAD51. *J. Biol. Chem.* **276**, 19375–19381

18. Brosh, Jr, R.M., Li, J.L., Kenny, M.K., Karow, J.K., Cooper, M.P., Kureekattil, R.P., Hickson, I.D. & Bohr, V.A. (2000) Replication protein A physically interacts with the Bloom's syndrome protein and stimulates its helicase activity. *J. Biol. Chem.* **275**, 23500–23508

19. Bachrati, C.Z., Borts, R.H. & Hickson, I.D. (2006) Mobile D-loops are a preferred substrate for the Bloom's syndrome helicase. *Nucleic Acids Res.* **34**, 2269–2279

20. Mohaghegh, P., Karow, J.K., Brosh, Jr, R.M., Bohr, V.A. & Hickson, I.D. (2001) The Bloom's and Werner's syndrome proteins are DNA structure-specific helicases. *Nucleic Acids Res.* **29**, 2843–2849

21. Cheok, C.F., Wu, L., Garcia, P.L., Janscak, P. & Hickson, I.D. (2005) The Bloom's syndrome helicase promotes the annealing of complementary single-stranded DNA. *Nucleic Acids Res.* **33**, 3932–3941

22.   Bugreev, D.V., Yu, X., Egelman, E.H. & Mazin, A.V. (2007) Novel pro- and anti-recombination activities of the Bloom's syndrome helicase. *Genes Dev.* **21**, 3085–3094

23.   Krejci, L., Van Komen, S., Li, Y., Villemain, J., Reddy, M.S., Klein, H., Ellenberger, T. & Sung, P. (2003) DNA helicase Srs2 disrupts the Rad51 presynaptic filament. *Nature* **423**, 305–309

24.   Gravel, S., Chapman, J.R., Magill, C. & Jackson, S.P. (2008) DNA helicases Sgs1 and BLM promote DNA double-strand break resection. *Genes Dev.* **22**, 2767–2772

25.   Nimonkar, A.V., Ozsoy, A.Z., Genschel, J., Modrich, P. & Kowalczykowski, S.C. (2008) Human exonuclease 1 and BLM helicase interact to resect DNA and initiate DNA repair. *Proc. Natl. Acad. Sci. U.S.A.* **105**, 16906–16911

26.   Davalos, A.R. & Campisi, J. (2003) Bloom syndrome cells undergo p53-dependent apoptosis and delayed assembly of BRCA1 and NBS1 repair complexes at stalled replication forks. *J. Cell Biol.* **162**, 1197–1209

27.   Lopes, M., Cotta-Ramusino, C., Pellicioli, A., Liberi, G., Plevani, P., Muzi-Falconi, M., Newlon, C.S. & Foiani, M. (2001) The DNA replication checkpoint response stabilizes stalled replication forks. *Nature* **412**, 557–561

28.   Ralf, C., Hickson, I.D. & Wu, L. (2006) The Bloom's syndrome helicase can promote the regression of a model replication fork. *J. Biol. Chem.* **281**, 22839–22846

29.   Davies, S.L., North, P.S. & Hickson, I.D. (2007) Role for BLM in replication-fork restart and suppression of origin firing after replicative stress. *Nat. Struct. Mol. Biol.* **14**, 677–679

30.   Cobb, J.A., Bjergbaek, L., Shimada, K., Frei, C. & Gasser, S.M. (2003) DNA polymerase stabilization at stalled replication forks requires Mec1 and the RecQ helicase Sgs1. *EMBO J.* **22**, 4325–4336

31.   Liberi, G., Maffioletti, G., Lucca, C., Chiolo, I., Baryshnikova, A., Cotta-Ramusino, C., Lopes, M., Pellicioli, A., Haber, J.E. & Foiani, M. (2005) Rad51-dependent DNA structures accumulate at damaged replication forks in sgs1 mutants defective in the yeast ortholog of BLM RecQ helicase. *Genes Dev.* **19**, 339–350

32.   Ip, S.C., Rass, U., Blanco, M.G., Flynn, H.R., Skehel, J.M. & West, S.C. (2008) Identification of Holliday junction resolvases from humans and yeast. *Nature* **456**, 357–361

33.   Wu, L. & Hickson, I.D. (2003) The Bloom's syndrome helicase suppresses crossing over during homologous recombination. *Nature* **426**, 870–874

34.   Wu, L., Bachrati, C.Z., Ou, J., Xu, C., Yin, J., Chang, M., Wang, W., Li, L., Brown, G.W. & Hickson, I.D. (2006) BLAP75/RMI1 promotes the BLM-dependent dissolution of homologous recombination intermediates. *Proc. Natl. Acad. Sci. U.S.A.* **103**, 4068–4073

35.   Raynard, S., Bussen, W. & Sung, P. (2006) A double Holliday junction dissolvasome comprising BLM, topoisomerase IIIα, and BLAP75. *J. Biol. Chem.* **281**, 13861–13864

36.   Plank, J.L., Wu, J. & Hsieh, T.S. (2006) Topoisomerase IIIα and Bloom's helicase can resolve a mobile double Holliday junction substrate through convergent branch migration. *Proc. Natl. Acad. Sci. U.S.A.* **103**, 11118–11123

37.   Constantinou, A., Chen, X.B., McGowan, C.H. & West, S.C. (2002) Holliday junction resolution in human cells: two junction endonucleases with distinct substrate specificities. *EMBO J.* **21**, 5577–5585

38.   Luo, G., Santoro, I.M., McDaniel, L.D., Nishijima, I., Mills, M., Youssoufian, H., Vogel, H., Schultz, R.A. & Bradley, A. (2000) Cancer predisposition caused by elevated mitotic recombination in Bloom mice. *Nat. Genet.* **26**, 424–429

39.   van Brabant, A.J., Ye, T., Sanz, M., German, III, J.L., Ellis, N.A. & Holloman, W.K. (2000) Binding and melting of D-loops by the Bloom syndrome helicase. *Biochemistry* **39**, 14617–14625

40.   McVey, M., Larocque, J.R., Adams, M.D. & Sekelsky, J.J. (2004) Formation of deletions during double-strand break repair in *Drosophila* DmBlm mutants occurs after strand invasion. *Proc. Natl. Acad. Sci. U.S.A.* **101**, 15694–15699

41.   Adams, M.D., McVey, M. & Sekelsky, J.J. (2003) *Drosophila* BLM in double-strand break repair by synthesis-dependent strand annealing. *Science* **299**, 265–267

42. Hu, Y., Raynard, S., Sehorn, M.G., Lu, X., Bussen, W., Zheng, L., Stark, J.M., Barnes, E.L., Chi, P.,
     Janscak, P. et al. (2007) RECQL5/Recql5 helicase regulates homologous recombination and
     suppresses tumor formation via disruption of Rad51 presynaptic filaments. *Genes Dev.* **21**,
     3073–3084

43. Mankouri, H.W., Craig, T.J. & Morgan, A. (2002) SGS1 is a multicopy suppressor of srs2: functional
     overlap between DNA helicases. *Nucleic Acids Res.* **30**, 1103–1113

44. Ira, G., Malkova, A., Liberi, G., Foiani, M. & Haber, J.E. (2003) Srs2 and Sgs1-Top3 suppress
     crossovers during double-strand break repair in yeast. *Cell* **115**, 401–411

45. Hoffelder, D.R., Luo, L., Burke, N.A., Watkins, S.C., Gollin, S.M. & Saunders, W.S. (2004)
     Resolution of anaphase bridges in cancer cells. *Chromosoma* **112**, 389–397

46. Chan, K.L., North, P.S. & Hickson, I.D. (2007) BLM is required for faithful chromosome segregation
     and its localization defines a class of ultrafine anaphase bridges. *EMBO J.* **26**, 3397–3409

47. Baumann, C., Korner, R., Hofmann, K. & Nigg, E.A. (2007) PICH, a centromere-associated SNF2
     family ATPase, is regulated by Plk1 and required for the spindle checkpoint. *Cell* **128**, 101–114

48. Wang, L.H., Schwarzbraun, T., Speicher, M.R. & Nigg, E.A. (2008) Persistence of DNA threads in
     human anaphase cells suggests late completion of sister chromatid decatenation. *Chromosoma* **117**,
     123–135

49. Meetei, A.R., Sechi, S., Wallisch, M., Yang, D., Young, M.K., Joenje, H., Hoatlin, M.E. & Wang, W.
     (2003) A multiprotein nuclear complex connects Fanconi anemia and Bloom syndrome. *Mol. Cell.
     Biol.* **23**, 3417–3426

Biochem. Soc. Symp. 76
Citation reference: Biochem. Soc. Trans. (2009) **37**, 561–568.

6

Regulation of activation-induced cytidine deaminase DNA deamination activity in B-cells by Ser[38] phosphorylation

Uttiya Basu*†‡, Andrew Franklin*†‡, Bjoern Schwer*†‡, Hwei-Ling Cheng*†‡, Jayanta Chaudhuri§ and Frederick W. Alt*†‡[1]

*Howard Hughes Medical Institute, Children's Hospital Boston, 300 Longwood Avenue, Boston, MA 02115, U.S.A., †Department of Genetics, Harvard Medical School, 77 Avenue Louis Pasteur, NRB 0330, Boston, MA 02115, U.S.A., ‡Immune Disease Institute, 800 Huntington Avenue, Boston, MA 02115, U.S.A., and §Memorial Sloan Kettering Cancer Center, Immunology Program, New York, NY 10021, U.S.A.

Abstract

Human and mouse Ig genes are diversified in mature B-cells by distinct processes known as Ig heavy-chain CSR (class switch recombination) and Ig variable-region exon SHM (somatic hypermutation). These DNA-modification processes are initiated by AID (activation-induced cytidine deaminase), a DNA cytidine deaminase predominantly expressed in activated B-cells. AID is post-transcriptionally regulated via multiple mechanisms, including microRNA

[1] To whom correspondence should be addressed
(email alt@enders.tch.harvard.edu).

regulation, nucleocytoplasmic shuttling, ubiquitination and phosphorylation. Among these regulatory processes, AID phosphorylation at Ser[38] has been a focus of particularly intense study and debate. In the present paper, we discuss recent biochemical and mouse genetic studies that begin to elucidate the functional significance of AID Ser[38] phosphorylation in the context of the evolution of this mode of AID regulation and the potential roles that it may play in activated B-cells during a normal immune response.

Introduction

Antibodies comprise IgH (Ig heavy chain) and IgL (Ig light chain). The N-terminal V (variable) region of IgH and IgL comprise the antigen-binding portion of antibody molecules, whereas the C-terminal constant region of IgH determines effector functions of the molecule, such as where it goes in the body and which downstream pathways it activates to eliminate antigen. There are three somatic DNA alteration events that enable mammalian B-cells to generate an antibody repertoire with enormous diversity and an array of effector functions. Developing B-cells undergo V(D)J recombination to assemble exons encoding the IgH and IgL V regions from a large set of germline-encoded V, D and J gene segments. The V(D)J exon is assembled just upstream of the IgH Cμ constant region exons, leading to expression of Ig μ heavy chains. Following the productive assembly of an IgL V-region exon, the μ heavy chain and IgL associate to produce IgM, which is expressed as a receptor on the surface of the newly generated B-cell. Thereafter, the B-cells migrate to secondary lymphoid organs, where, upon encountering cognate antigen, they can be activated to undergo two additional genetic alterations of their Ig genes, namely IgH and IgL V-region exon SHM (somatic hypermutation), which diversifies the V(D)J exon further, and IgH CSR (class switch recombination), which allows expression of different IgH constant regions (C$_H$ regions) and hence different classes of antibody [1,2]. Although two distinct processes, CSR and SHM absolutely require both transcription through the relevant Ig loci and AID (activation-induced cytidine deaminase) [3–5]. AID is a ssDNA (single-stranded DNA)-specific cytidine deaminase, expressed primarily in activated B-cells [6–10]. Most evidence indicates that AID initiates CSR and SHM by deaminating cytidines to uracils in DNA, although there are other views (see [11] for a review). The present article focuses on the post-translational regulation of AID by phosphorylation during CSR and SHM in B-cells.

Class switch recombination

The IgH V(D)J exon is assembled upstream of the Cμ constant region exons, leading to generation of μ heavy chains. Additional sets of C$_H$ exons (Cγ, Cα and Cε) are located 100–200 kb downstream of Cμ. All of the different sets of C$_H$ exons that undergo CSR are flanked upstream by large (1–10 kb), repetitive

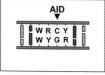 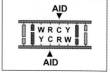

5'-WRCY-3' /5'-RGYW-3'
TGCT/AGCA
AACT/AGTT
TACT/AGTA
TGCC/GGCA
AGCC/GGCT
AACC/GGTT
TACC/GGTA

5'-WRCY-3'/5'-WRCY-3'
AGCT/AGCT

The palindromic AGCT motif conforms to WRCY
and RGYW definition in both directions.
AGCT motifs are more prevalent at Ig switch
region than Ig variable region sequences.

Figure 1. Schematic representation of AID target preferences
In vitro, AID preferentially deaminates C residues in DNA to uracil in the context of a WRCY sequence motif (the target of AID within the motif is underlined) [20–21]. Seven of the eight possible tetranucleotide permutations of this motif conform to the 5'-WRCY-3'/5'-RGYW-3' sequence structure in dsDNA (left); in this context, a single AID-mediated deamination event is possible within each double-stranded motif (as indicated). The palindromic sequence AGCT is unique in that it conforms to the 5'-WRCY-3'/5'-WRCY-3' sequence structure in dsDNA (right); in this context, AID-mediated deamination events are potentially possible on both strands of the DNA duplex within the same double-stranded motif (as indicated). S regions contain a higher density of AGCT motifs than V regions; AGCT motifs are often tandemly repeated within core switch sequences. AID-mediated deamination of C residues at S and V regions *in vivo* co-opts the activities of the BER and MMR pathways [28]. The BER pathway is apparently the dominant pathway during CSR *in vivo*; it is thought that uracil-DNA glycosylase removes AID-generated U lesions, leading to subsequent endonuclease cleavage of the phosphodiester bond 5' of the resultant abasic site [29]. AID-mediated deamination of cytosine residues on both DNA strands within the same or neighbouring 5'-AGCT-3'/5'-AGCT-3' motifs and processing of the resultant U lesions via activity of the BER pathway theoretically could lead to the efficient formation of the DSBs that are required for CSR.

S ('switch') regions, which contain an abundance of so-called SHM motifs (see Figure 1 and below). CSR involves the introduction of DNA DSBs (double-strand breaks) into the 'donor' $S\mu$ region and into a downstream 'acceptor' S region, followed by joining of the donor and acceptor S regions. This CSR process juxtaposes a new downstream set of C_H exons in place of the $C\mu$ exons, allowing expression of the V(D)J exon with a different set of C_H exons. An activator- and cytokine-specific promoter precedes each S region. Activation of these 'germline' promoters and transcription through the corresponding S region is required to target CSR [11]. Such transcription directs the activity of AID to the targeted S region, which is essential for initiating the DSB-inducing process ([12,13], but see [13a]). In this context, mice with targeted deletion of the AID gene or human patients harbouring loss-of-function AID mutations are unable to undergo CSR and express higher levels of IgM antibodies [3,5]. AID initiates CSR by deaminating cytidine residues in transcribed S regions, leading to the generation of uracil lesions in DNA. The resulting U/G mismatches appear to be converted into DSBs through the co-opted activities of the BER (base excision repair) and MMR (mismatch repair) pathways [14,15]. Once DSBs have been generated in two separated S regions, they are synapsed, apparently in large part by general cellular mechanisms [16], and joined, predominantly by the non-homologous end-joining pathway, but also by an alternative end-joining pathway [17].

Somatic hypermutation

During an immune response, the SHM process can introduce substitution mutations at a very high rate (estimated to be $\sim 10^{-3}$–10^{-4}/bp/generation) [18] into the IgH and IgL V-region exons of activated B-cells, ultimately allowing selection of B-cells with increased affinity for antigen [19]. SHM at C/G pairs occurs preferentially at RGYW and WRCY DNA motifs (the mutated position is underlined), which are particularly abundant in the DNA sequences that encode the V-region complementarity-determining regions, the site of the majority of the antigen contact residues. Biochemical studies suggest that the WRCY motif is a preferential target for AID (Figure 1) [20–23]. In this context, CSR regions are also particularly rich in such motifs, most notably the AGCT sequence. SHM requires transcription, with mutations starting from approx. 100–200 bp downstream of the V exon promoter and extending 1.5–2 kb downstream, generally sparing the C_H exons. SHM also occurs at significant levels in S regions and their immediate flanking sequences during CSR, presumably as a by-product of AID generating S region DSBs [24]. In addition, SHM occurs in certain non-Ig genes, although at much lower levels than in S region and V(D)J exon targets during CSR and SHM [25–27]. The mechanisms that lead to such precise targeting of AID are still under investigation, although some mechanisms that may help to contribute to this specificity will be a topic of this review. Mice and human patients with loss-of-function mutations of AID fail to undergo SHM, indicating an essential role for AID in this process as well as in CSR [3,5]. SHM also appears to be initiated by C to U deamination in DNA [2,11]. AID-generated U lesions in the DNA template transition hypermutations at C/G pairs and also co-opt activities of the BER and MMR pathways (resulting in the generation of the complete spectrum of hypermutations at C/G and A/T pairs) [28,29].

Potential mechanisms for AID access to duplexed DNA during CSR and SHM

Several potential mechanisms have been elucidated for transcription-dependent AID access to dsDNA (double-stranded DNA) [30–33]. In the present review, we focus on just two potential mechanisms that have been the focus of studies in our laboratories: one mechanism involves R-loops and the other involves RPA (replication protein A). Other potential mechanisms are mentioned in the last section of the present paper.

    mAID (mouse AID) has been shown to be a ssDNA-specific cytidine deaminase which deaminates ssDNA substrates *in vitro*, but does not deaminate dsDNA substrates, except under certain conditions [6,33]. Several mechanisms have been implicated in AID access to duplex V(D)J exons and S regions *in vivo*. Because of their high G/C content and G-richness on the non-template strand, mammalian S regions generate ssDNA within R-loops transcribed in the physiological direction [34–36]. *In vitro* purified mAID deaminates the non-template strand of T7 RNA polymerase-transcribed dsDNA sequences that form R-loops (e.g. S regions in sense orientation), but not transcribed dsDNA sequences that do not form R-loops [6,33]. Moreover, gene-targeting experiments showed that optimal S region function *in vivo* depends on transcriptional orientation, supporting the notion that S region transcription might allow AID access to ssDNA in S regions via R-loop formation. Thus R-loop-forming ability may have evolved in mammalian S regions to enhance AID access during CSR [35].

Variable region exons do not form R-loops [33]. *In vitro* assays led to the identification of RPA, a trimeric ssDNA-binding protein involved in replication and repair, as a factor that allowed purified B-cell mAID to deaminate transcribed SHM substrates, which contained repeated AGCT motifs, but which did not form R-loops [33]. The 32-kDa subunit of RPA interacts with purified B-cell mAID, and the AID–RPA complex binds to transcribed WRCY/RGYW-containing DNA *in vitro*, apparently promoting AID deamination of the substrates predominantly within or near SHM motifs. It has been proposed that the AID–RPA complex may bind to and stabilize ssDNA within transcription bubbles to allow AID to access ssDNA substrates [33]. These overall findings led to the proposal that AID may access transcribed V regions, in the absence of R-loops, via an RPA-dependent mechanism [11,33].

Both AID and Ig gene SHM occur in bony fish [37–39]. However, CSR first occurs evolutionarily in amphibians, leading to the suggestion that CSR may have evolved after SHM [40–42]. XSμ (*Xenopus* Sμ) is A/T-rich and does not form R-loops when transcribed *in vitro* [23,40]. Yet, XSμ can replace mouse Sγ1 to promote substantial CSR in mouse B-cells [23]. CSR junctions within XSμ in mice occurred in a region of densely packed AGCT sequences in the 5′ portion of XSμ; when this sequence was inverted *in vivo*, CSR junctions tracked with the AGCT motifs. Likewise, the AGCT repeat region was the predominant site of deamination by mAID–RPA in the context of an *in vitro* transcription-dependent deamination assay, regardless of orientation [23]. On the basis of these findings, it was suggested that CSR evolved from SHM with the early S regions in amphibians being sequences with a high density of SHM motifs that facilitated AID access via an RPA-dependent mechanism. Given that mammalian S regions are also dense in SHM motifs (notably AGCT motifs), these findings further raised the possibility that AID may access mammalian S regions via an RPA-dependent mechanism and that R-loop-based mechanisms of access may have arisen later in evolution to facilitate targeting of AID activity further [23]. Because the high density of AID-preferred AGCT motifs appears to target DSBs in XSμ, it seems possible that the higher density of these motifs

	CDA^{ssDNA}	RPA-binding	CDA^{dsDNA**}	%CSR	%SHM	References
mAID^{WT}	+++++	+++++	+++++	+++++	+++++	43, 44, 45, 51
mAID^{S38A}	+++++	-	-	+	++	43, 44, 45, 51
mAID^{S38A,T40D}	+++++	++++	++++++	++++	nd	52
zAID^{WT}	+++++	+++++	+++++	+++++	nd	52
zAID^{D44A}	+++++	-	-	++	nd	52
zAID^{G42S,D44A}	+++++	++++	++	+++++	nd	52

**ACTIVITY MEASURED IN TRANSCRIPTION AND RPA DEPENDENT ASSAY

Figure 2. Schematic representation of different *in vitro* and *in vivo* activities of AID mutant proteins

The *in vitro* biochemical activities of each of the proteins presented are its cytidine deaminase activity on ssDNA (CDA^{ssDNA}) or on transcribed RGYW-rich dsDNA (CDA^{dsDNA}). The ability of each protein to bind to RPA *in vitro* is also represented (RPA-binding). The CSR or SHM *in vivo* activities of each protein represents data obtained from retroviral complementation assays or from knockin mouse models. nd, not done.

in IgH S regions compared with Ig V-region exons may contribute to the DSB formation (and hence CSR) or SHM outcome of AID deamination at these sites respectively [11].

Post-translational modification of AID by phosphorylation

Mammalian AID is phosphorylated on multiple residues. Purified B-cell mAID is phosphorylated at Ser[38], Tyr[184] and Thr[140] [43–45]. To date, only the functional significance of Ser[38] phosphorylation has been elucidated in detail. The ability of AID to interact with RPA and function in transcription-dependent dsDNA deamination assays depends on phosphorylation at Ser[38] [33,43]. The Ser[38] residue exists in a PKA (protein kinase A) consensus motif; accordingly, mAID can be phosphorylated *in vitro* on Ser[38] by PKA. In addition, a variety of evidence suggests that PKA also phosphorylates mAID on Ser[38] in cells, including activated B-cells [43,46]. Mouse AID that is not phosphorylated on Ser[38] does not bind RPA and does not mediate dsDNA deamination of transcribed AGCT-rich substrates *in vitro* [43], with both activities, however, being restored by *in vitro* PKA phosphorylation of non-phosphorylated mAID [43]. Correspondingly, a mutant form of mAID in which the Ser[38] residue was changed to alanine (mAID^{S38A}) retains ssDNA-deamination activity, but lacks the ability to be phosphorylated by PKA and fails to interact with RPA or function in transcription-dependent dsDNA deamination assays [43]. Mouse AID^{S38A} also had reduced CSR activity (15–30% of wild-type activity) in activated AID-deficient B-cells when ectopically introduced via a retroviral expression vector (Figure 2) [43,44,46,47]. Likewise, drug-induced PKA inhibition decreased CSR, and PKA activation via deletion of the PKA negative regulatory subunit increased CSR *in vivo* [46]. Together, these studies supported a model that proposed that mammalian AID phosphorylation at Ser[38] is a mechanism for augmenting the ability of AID to access S region

DNA and initiate CSR. In this context, a similar *ex vivo* system to test AID SHM activity in mouse B-cells does not exist, but AID[S38A] was found to have reduced capacity to mediate SHM in substrates introduced into mouse non-lymphoid cells and in Ig genes in chicken DT40 cells [44,48].

Despite the strong circumstantial evidence outlined above which points to a potential role for AID phosphorylation during CSR and SHM, this form of AID regulation has been the subject of significant debate. A major argument against this form of AID regulation came from a study that reported that retrovirally driven expression of the AID[S38A] mutant protein in AID-deficient B-cells restored CSR to nearly wild-type levels [49]. However, given that the AID[S38A] protein is a hypomorphic mutant with full ssDNA-deamination activity, these apparently discrepant findings might have resulted from overexpression levels that allowed the mutant to 'catch-up' with wild-type activity [43,44,46,47]. In another study, the AID[S38A] protein purified from insect cell lines appeared to have a similar activity to wild-type AID protein in a transcription-dependent DNA deamination assay [50]. However, in this case, the substrate sequences employed had a high GC content which could generate R-loops upon transcription and allow RPA-independent access via the R-loop mechanism [6,35]. Another point used to question the role of AID Ser[38] phoshorylation was based on the observation that zAID (zebrafish AID), which lacks a PKA consensus motif and an Ser[38] equivalent residue at the corresponding position to mAID, is able to catalyse robust CSR in mouse B-cells [48,49]. In this case, however, it was noted that such activity might be provided by a nearby aspartate residue (Asp[44]), which theoretically could allow zAID to mimic Ser[38]-phosphorylated mAID (Figure 3). Finally, it was noted that a putative molecular mimic of AID phosphorylated on Ser[38] (replacement of Ser[38] with aspartate to generate AID[S38D]) fails to undergo CSR at substantial levels (Figure 3) [44,49]. However, it remained possible that this substitution might not fully mimic Ser[38]-phosphorylated AID or might have other unrelated effects on the protein. As discussed in detail in the following sections, each of these questions regarding the physiological role of AID Ser[38] phosphorylation has been addressed recently by either gene-targeted mutation studies [45,51] or by studying zAID activity in more depth [52].

Analysis of CSR and SHM in AID[S38A]-knockin mutant mice

To address the physiological significance of AID phosphorylation at Ser[38], analysis of a mouse model (in which AID[S38A] is expressed at physiological levels utilizing its endogenous control elements) was required. Two recent studies reported the generation and analysis of mice expressing only the AID[S38A] mutant protein, which occurred at levels quite comparable with those of wild-type mAID expression in activated B-cells, from their endogenous AID alleles [45,51]. In addition, one of these studies also demonstrated that the AID[S38A] protein expressed from the endogenous AID allele failed to associate with

AMPHIBIANS, BIRDS, MAMMALS (SHM AND CSR)

```
                ▼ ▼
kgrretylcyvvkrrdsatsfsl  Human
kgrretylcyvvkrrdsatsfsl  Chimpanzee
kgrhetylcyvvkrrdsatscsl  Mouse

kgrhetylcyivkrryssvscal  Frog
kgrretylcyvvkrrdsatscsl  Chicken
```

BONY FISH (SHM ONLY)

```
                ▼ ▼
rgrhetylcfvvkrrigpdslsf  Zebrafish
rgrhetylcfvvkrrvgpdtltf  Pufferfish
rgrnetylcfvvkkrnspdslsf  Catfish
```

Figure 3. Conservation of AID phosphorylation site Ser³⁸ in different species
The PKA phosphorylation site of AID at Ser³⁸ is present in all organisms that undergo CSR (mammals, amphibians and birds), but is absent from organisms that undergo SHM only (bony fish). The PKA consensus site is represented by 'rrx$^s/_t$'. All bony fish AID amino acid sequences contain an aspartate residue, which is absent in the AID amino acid sequences of organisms that undergo CSR.

RPA *in vivo* [51]. Both studies found that mice homozygous for the AID^{S38A} (AID$^{S38A/S38A}$) mutation have quite severe CSR defects, demonstrating clearly that the apparently normal levels of CSR reported for this mutant form of AID by others [49] probably resulted from overexpression of the mutant protein as proposed in [47].

Activation of AID$^{S38A/S38A}$ B-cells with αCD40 and IL-4 (interleukin 4) for 3 days (to induce CSR of Cγ1) resulted in IgG1 CSR levels that were only 5% of those of wild-type levels, with wild-type levels essentially reaching their maximum values by that day of activation [51]. After 4.5 days of αCD40 and IL-4 treatment, the level of CSR of AID$^{S38A/S38A}$ B-cells reached 40–50% of the wild-type levels, probably reflecting the fact that wild-type B-cells reached their maximum plateau values by day 3.5 and that the AID$^{S38A/S38A}$ hypomorphic mutant B-cells were able to partially 'catch-up' in the intervening 1.5 days of activation [45,51]. On the other hand, activation of AID$^{S38A/S38A}$ B-cells with bacterial LPS (lipopolysacharride) plus anti-δ-dextran for 3 days (to induce CSR of Cγ3) led to barely detectable CSR of IgG3 at any of the measured time-points (less than 1% of wild-type levels) [51]. Thus AID$^{S38A/S38A}$ mutant B-cells appear even more severely impaired for CSR of IgG3 than to IgG1. The more severe CSR defect for CSR of IgG3 might reflect several factors, including a lower level of AID expression following LPS plus anti-δ-dextran stimulation [51] (see below for discussion of effects of AID levels on CSR) and/or the smaller size and different sequence of the Sγ3 target region compared with the $S\gamma 1$ region, which theoretically could make $S\gamma 3$ a poorer AID target [51].

AID expression has been found to demonstrate haploinsufficiency, with $AID^{+/-}$ B-cells having only about half the level of AID expression as $AID^{+/+}$ wild-type B-cells [45,51,53,54]. In this context, $AID^{+/-}$ mice also tend to show proportionately reduced CSR [45,51]; although in our experiments, we observed this reduction to be more marked for CSR of IgG3 than for CSR of IgG1 [45,51] (see below). Remarkably, this haploinsufficiency effect was greatly magnified in the context of the AID^{S38A} mutation. Thus $AID^{S38A/-}$ B-cells had dramatically reduced CSR of both IgG1 and IgG3, compared with levels of $AID^{+/-}$ B-cells after 3 or 4.5 days of stimulation for switching either to IgG1 or to IgG3 [45,51]. In this case, IgG1 CSR of the $AID^{S38A/-}$ B-cells did not exceed 5% of control levels, and CSR of $AID^{S38A/-}$ B-cells to IgG3 were at background $AID^{-/-}$ B-cell levels [45,51]. The potential significance of the haploinsufficiency phenotype is discussed further below.

The activity of mAID in the transcription-coupled SHM assay *in vitro* is dependent on phosphorylation at Ser^{38} and RPA association and was abrogated by the S38A mutation [43,52]. It was therefore hypothesized initially that the AID^{S38A} mutation might have a more severe effect on SHM than on CSR, in which AID might still access S region DNA via an R-loop mechanism [11,33]. However, as mentioned above, no system existed to analyse the effect of the $mAID^{S38A}$ mutation on SHM in B-cells before the generation of $AID^{S38A/S38A}$ mutant mice. Thus the only previous assays to examine the effects of the AID^{S38A} mutation on SHM were performed via the introduction of artificial substrates into fibroblast cells [44]. In contrast with expectations based on the *in vitro* transcription-dependent deamination assays, analyses of SHM just downstream of the rearranged V(D)J allele in the IgH locus (a standard assay for studying SHM *in vivo*) revealed that, whereas B-cells from $AID^{S38A/S38A}$ mice had significantly decreased SHM, substantial residual levels (30% of wild-type levels) remained [44]. Therefore, at least on the basis of this particular SHM assay, CSR appears to be more severely impaired in $AID^{S38A/S38A}$ mice than does SHM. However, as observed for CSR in $AID^{S38A/-}$ mutant mice, SHM levels in $AID^{S38A/-}$ were found to be close to background levels and were thus dramatically decreased compared with those of wild-type mice (which were only down approx. 50%) [45]. The latter finding suggests the possibility that, as observed with IgH CSR, SHM levels may also be closely titrated to AID levels in appropriately activated B-cells. If so, by analogy to CSR, more severe effects of the AID^{S38A} mutation might be observed during SHM in particular physiological contexts in which AID induction levels are not as high as in others or in a substrate-dependent manner (e.g. similar to the potentially differing effects of the AID^{S38A} on CSR of $S\gamma 1$ compared with $S\gamma 3$; see above). Of course, it is also possible that there are additional mechanisms that promote AID access, or downstream functions during SHM that are not dependent on Ser^{38} phosphorylation (see below for further discussion).

Evolution of AID phosphorylation at Ser[38]

Bony fish undergo SHM but do not undergo CSR, potentially because they lack the CSR target sequences (e.g. S regions and different sets of C_H exons). In this context, AID from bony fish (e.g. zebrafish and pufferfish) lacks a PKA phosphorylation site corresponding to Ser[38], but still catalyses CSR following ectopic expression in AID-deficient mouse B-cells [38,39]. These findings led some to conclude that AID phosphorylation at Ser[38] is not likely to be of physiological relevance [38,39,49]. However, AID from all species of bony fish analysed has been found to contain an aspartate residue at position 44 (Asp[44]) [38,39]. Biochemical studies revealed that zAID Asp[44] acts as a mimic of the phosphorylated mAID Ser[38] residue with respect to RPA binding and function in the transcription-dependent dsDNA deamination assay [52]. Likewise, the integrity of the AID Asp[44] residue is required for normal CSR; a zAID[D44A] mutant shows greatly reduced CSR activity, which correlates with loss of ability to bind RPA and loss of activity in the transcription-coupled dsDNA-deamination assay (Figure 2) [52].

These observations led to the hypothesis that bony fish AID represents a 'constitutively active' mimic of Ser[38] phosphorylated AID from higher organisms. Notably, increases in AID activity beyond its physiological levels seem to affect its off-target activities (e.g. initiation of translocations) more dramatically than its on-target activities (e.g. CSR and SHM of Ig genes) [55–58]. This property may have led to the evolution of precise mechanisms to titrate the level of active AID to better control its physiological activity. Such regulatory mechanisms appear to include a variety of different post-transcriptional modes of control [43,47,52,58–61]. Notably, amphibians, in which CSR first evolved, as well as higher vertebrates, all express AID that appears to be capable of regulation via Ser[38] phosphorylation. In this context, one speculation is that the evolution of CSR, which involves large numbers of dangerous DNA DSBs, also led to the evolution of more stringent AID control mechanisms, including Ser[38] phosphorylation.

A standard method to mimic a phosphorylated serine residue is to convert it into an aspartate residue. In this regard, several groups generated an AID[S38D] mutant protein and found it to still be impaired with respect to promoting CSR following introduction into AID-deficient activated B-cells [44], which again has been cited as evidence that Ser[38] phosphorylation has no physiological relevance [49]. However, any amino acid substitution might have adverse negative effects on activity via a variety of different mechanisms (so such an argument is not necessarily valid). On the other hand, if one could indeed make a relevant second site mutation that simultaneously reversed all of the negative biochemical and *in vivo* CSR effects of the AID[S38A] mutation, it would be strong evidence in support of the proposed mechanism. Taking a clue from zAID, an aspartate residue was incorporated into the mAID[S38A] polypeptide at the same relative position (in place of the threonine residue at position 40) as the zAID Asp[44] residue to generate the mAID$^{S38A/T40D}$ double-mutant protein [52]. Remarkably, the AID T40D mutation substantially reversed the negative biochemical effects of the S38A mutation (Figure 2). Thus the mAID$^{S38A/T40D}$ protein now showed an ability to bind RPA constitutively and thereby catalyse RPA-dependent deamination of a transcribed dsDNA substrate in a PKA-phosphorylation-independent fashion. In addition, the mAID$^{S38A/T40D}$ double-mutant protein had significantly increased CSR activity compared with the AID^{S38A} mutant protein. These observations demonstrate that the AID$^{S38A/T40D}$ protein acts like a mimic of AID phosphorylated at Ser[38] both with respect to known biochemical activities and *in vivo* CSR activity (Figure 2) [52]. This linkage of the various biochemical and CSR activities with this second site mutation provides the most compelling evidence to date for the physiological relevance of AID phosphorylation at Ser[38] and resulting RPA interaction. A remaining question, potentially of significant mechanistic interest, is why the AID^{S38D} mutant protein does not regain CSR activity.

Perspective

The clear defects in CSR and, to a lesser extent, SHM of the AID$^{S38A/S38A}$ mutant mice, coupled with the generation of a 'Ser[38] phosphomimetic' form of the mAID protein provide strong evidence in support of a significant physiological role of AID phosphorylation at Ser[38]. Likewise, these studies also strongly support the physiological significance of Ser[38]-phosphorylated AID interaction with RPA to augment AID access to transcribed target DNA sequences. Yet, there are many important unanswered questions regarding this mechanism. One major question is the precise role of Ser[38] phosphorylation in AID regulation. The bulk of AID in activated B-cells is found in the cytoplasm with only a fraction of AID being found in the nucleus [43,62]. On the other hand, most of the Ser[38]-phosphorylated AID in activated B-cells is found in the nucleus, probably in association with the chromatin fraction of cellular DNA [44]. In this context, it remains to be determined where the PKA phosphorylation of AID occurs within activated B-cells and how it is regulated. In any case, PKA-phosphorylated AID may be preferentially accumulated in the nucleus, perhaps in the context of binding to target DNA via its RPA association. Likewise, the precise role for the evolution of the regulation of AID interaction with RPA via Ser[38] phosphorylation remains to be determined. As outlined above, it appears that the pool of functionally active AID in activated B-cells is quite strictly titrated. Moreover, the effect of small decreases in the level of AID that cannot be phosphorylated on Ser[38] appear disproportionately greater than similar decreases in wild-type AID levels, suggesting that Ser[38] phosphorylation might have a significant role in determining the level of 'active' AID in the cells. It has been speculated that such a level of regulation may be critical to maintain the balance between on-target AID in the context of SHM and CSR compared with off-target activities that could lead to mutations and/or DSBs in other cellular genes that might contribute to transformation [27,55,56,63,64]. The availability of a mutant AID that appears to behave like a 'constitutively Ser^{38}-phosphorylated mimetic' should now allow these notions to be addressed by gene-targeted knockin mutational strategies that will facilitate evaluation of the effects of having all of the endogenous AID in an 'activated' form.

IgH CSR appears to be dramatically impaired in AID$^{S38A/S38A}$ mutant B-cells. Residual IgH CSR activity (generally less than 5% of wild-type levels) could be provided by the R-loop mechanism for AID access. However, this raises the question of why R-loops do not provide greater access. Among the possibilities is that the Ser^{38} phosphorylation/RPA mode of AID access is important for accessing the template strand (which is hybridized to the germline transcript in a R-loop). Another would be that the RPA bound to S region DNA in the context of the AID–RPA complex has additional functions in recruitment of factors downstream of AID deamination [11,33]. The relatively high levels of residual SHM in AID$^{S38A/S38A}$ mice raises various questions. First, the SHM levels observed in AID$^{S38A/S38A}$ represent steady-state levels in B-cells that have probably undergone significant selection following the germinal centre response in which SHM occurs. Thus it still remains possible that the actual rate of SHM might be lower than indicated by the steady-state levels. In this regard, we note that, on the basis of kinetics of induction, the actual rate of CSR in AID$^{S38A/S38A}$ activated B-cells appears much less than the steady-state levels observed in activated AID$^{S38A/S38A}$ compared with wild-type B-cells following 4.5 days of induction (see above). On the other hand, there well may be additional mechanisms by which AID accesses transcribed V-region exons in the context of SHM. Studies of genetically modified yeast and DT40 cells have suggested the existence of a R-loop-related mechanism of AID access that relies on factors involved in the processing of nascent RNA transcripts and their release from the DNA template [65–67]. In addition, other potential modes of generation of ssDNA substrates, including generation of negative supercoiling of transcribed DNA, have been shown to provide AID access to DNA substrates in biochemical assays [30–32]. Clearly, there is much to be done to elucidate further the mechanisms that target AID to its appropriate substrates and protect other cellular DNA sequences from its highly mutagenic activities. In this regard, none of the postulated mechanisms for AID access appears sufficient to provide the remarkable specificity of AID access to Ig gene SHM and CSR substrates compared with other cellular DNA sequences.

Acknowledgements

U.B. is a fellow of the Leukemia and Lymphoma Society of America. F.W.A. is an Investigator of the Howard Hughes Medical Institute.

Funding

J.C. is supported by grants from the Damon-Runyon Scholars Fund and the Bressler Foundation. This work was supported by National Institutes of Health [grant numbers A1077595 and A1077595 to F.W.A.].

References

1. Chaudhuri, J. & Alt, F.W. (2004) Class-switch recombination: interplay of transcription, DNA deamination and DNA repair. *Nat. Rev. Immunol.* **4**, 541–552
2. Honjo, T., Kinoshita, K. & Muramatsu, M. (2002) Molecular mechanism of class switch recombination: linkage with somatic hypermutation. *Annu. Rev. Immunol.* **20**, 165–196
3. Muramatsu, M., Kinoshita, K., Fagarasan, S., Yamada, S., Shinkai, Y. & Honjo, T. (2000) Class switch recombination and hypermutation require activation-induced cytidine deaminase (AID), a potential RNA editing enzyme. *Cell* **102**, 553–563
4. Muramatsu, M., Sankaranand, V.S., Anant, S., Sugai, M., Kinoshita, K., Davidson, N.O. & Honjo, T. (1999) Specific expression of activation-induced cytidine deaminase (AID), a novel member of the RNA-editing deaminase family in germinal center B cells. *J. Biol. Chem.* **274**, 18470–18476
5. Revy, P., Muto, T., Levy, Y., Geissmann, F., Plebani, A., Sanal, O., Catalan, N., Forveille, M., Dufourcq-Labelouse, R., Gennery, A. et al. (2000) Activation-induced cytidine deaminase (AID) deficiency causes the autosomal recessive form of the hyper-IgM syndrome (HIGM2). *Cell* **102**, 565–575
6. Chaudhuri, J., Tian, M., Khuong, C., Chua, K., Pinaud, E. & Alt, F.W. (2003) Transcription-targeted DNA deamination by the AID antibody diversification enzyme. *Nature* **422**, 726–730
7. Ramiro, A.R., Stavropoulos, P., Jankovic, M. & Nussenzweig, M.C. (2003) Transcription enhances AID-mediated cytidine deamination by exposing single-stranded DNA on the nontemplate strand. *Nat. Immunol.* **4**, 452–456.
8. Dickerson, S.K., Market, E., Besmer, E. & Papavasiliou, F.N. (2003) AID mediates hypermutation by deaminating single stranded DNA. *J. Exp. Med.* **197**, 1291–1296
9. Sohail, A., Klapacz, J., Samaranayake, M., Ullah, A. & Bhagwat, A.S. (2003) Human activation-induced cytidine deaminase causes transcription-dependent, strand-biased C to U deaminations. *Nucleic Acids Res.* **31**, 2990–2994
10. Petersen-Mahrt, S.K., Harris, R.S. & Neuberger, M.S. (2002) AID mutates *E. coli* suggesting a DNA deamination mechanism for antibody diversification. *Nature* **418**, 99–103
11. Chaudhuri, J., Basu, U., Zarrin, A., Yan, C., Franco, S., Perlot, T., Vuong, B., Wang, J., Phan, R.T., Datta, A. et al. (2007) Evolution of the immunoglobulin heavy chain class switch recombination mechanism. *Adv. Immunol.* **94**, 157–214
12. Lutzker, S., Rothman, P., Pollock, R., Coffman, R. & Alt, F.W. (1988) Mitogen- and IL-4-regulated expression of germ-line Igγ2b transcripts: evidence for directed heavy chain class switching. *Cell* **53**, 177–184
13. Lutzker, S. & Alt, F.W. (1988) Structure and expression of germ line immunoglobulin γ2b transcripts. *Mol. Cell. Biol.* **8**, 1849–1852
13a. Erratum (1988) *Mol. Cell. Biol.* **8**, 4585
14. Neuberger, M.S., Harris, R.S., Di Noia, J. & Petersen-Mahrt, S.K. (2003) Immunity through DNA deamination. *Trends Biochem. Sci.* **28**, 305–312
15. Di Noia, J. & Neuberger, M.S. (2002) Altering the pathway of immunoglobulin hypermutation by inhibiting uracil-DNA glycosylase. *Nature* **419**, 43–48
16. Zarrin, A.A., Del Vecchio, C., Tseng, E., Gleason, M., Zarin, P., Tian, M. & Alt, F.W. (2007) Antibody class switching mediated by yeast endonuclease-generated DNA breaks. *Science* **315**, 377–381

17. Yan, C.T., Boboila, C., Souza, E.K., Franco, S., Hickernell, T.R., Murphy, M., Gumaste, S., Geyer, M., Zarrin, A.A., Manis, J.P. et al. (2007) IgH class switching and translocations use a robust non-classical end-joining pathway. Nature 449, 478–482

18. McKean, D., Huppi, K., Bell, M., Staudt, L., Gerhard, W. & Weigert, M. (1984) Generation of antibody diversity in the immune response of BALB/c mice to influenza virus hemagglutinin. Proc. Natl. Acad. Sci. U.S.A. 81, 3180–3184

19. Liu, Y.J., Joshua, D.E., Williams, G.T., Smith, C.A., Gordon, J. & MacLennan, I.C. (1989) Mechanism of antigen-driven selection in germinal centres. Nature 342, 929–931

20. Pham, P., Bransteitter, R., Petruska, J. & Goodman, M.F. (2003) Processive AID-catalysed cytosine deamination on single-stranded DNA simulates somatic hypermutation. Nature 424, 103–107

21. Yu, K., Huang, F.T. & Lieber, M.R. (2004) DNA substrate length and surrounding sequence affect the activation-induced deaminase activity at cytidine. J. Biol. Chem. 279, 6496–6500

22. Beale, R.C., Petersen-Mahrt, S.K., Watt, I.N., Harris, R.S., Rada, C. & Neuberger, M.S. (2004) Comparison of the differential context-dependence of DNA deamination by APOBEC enzymes: correlation with mutation spectra in vivo. J. Mol. Biol. 337, 585–596

23. Zarrin, A.A., Alt, F.W., Chaudhuri, J., Stokes, N., Kaushal, D., Du Pasquier, L. & Tian, M. (2004) An evolutionarily conserved target motif for immunoglobulin class-switch recombination. Nat. Immunol. 5, 1275–1281

24. Xue, K., Rada, C. & Neuberger, M.S. (2006) The in vivo pattern of AID targeting to immunoglobulin switch regions deduced from mutation spectra in $msh2^{-/-}$ $ung^{-/-}$ mice. J. Exp. Med. 203, 2085–2094

25. Shen, H.M., Peters, A., Baron, B., Zhu, X. & Storb, U. (1998) Mutation of BCL-6 gene in normal B cells by the process of somatic hypermutation of Ig genes. Science 280, 1750–1752

26. Pasqualucci, L., Neumeister, P., Goossens, T., Nanjangud, G., Chaganti, R.S., Kuppers, R. & Dalla-Favera, R. (2001) Hypermutation of multiple proto-oncogenes in B-cell diffuse large-cell lymphomas. Nature 412, 341–346

27. Liu, M., Duke, J.L., Richter, D.J., Vinuesa, C.G., Goodnow, C.C., Kleinstein, S.H. & Schatz, D.G. (2008) Two levels of protection for the B cell genome during somatic hypermutation. Nature 451, 841–845

28. Rada, C., Di Noia, J.M. & Neuberger, M.S. (2004) Mismatch recognition and uracil excision provide complementary paths to both Ig switching and the A/T-focused phase of somatic mutation. Mol. Cell 16, 163–171

29. Rada, C., Williams, G.T., Nilsen, H., Barnes, D.E., Lindahl, T. & Neuberger, M.S. (2002) Immunoglobulin isotype switching is inhibited and somatic hypermutation perturbed in UNG-deficient mice. Curr. Biol. 12, 1748–1755

30. Besmer, E., Market, E. & Papavasiliou, F.N. (2006) The transcription elongation complex directs activation-induced cytidine deaminase-mediated DNA deamination. Mol. Cell. Biol. 26, 4378–4385

31. Shen, H.M., Ratnam, S. & Storb, U. (2005) Targeting of the activation-induced cytosine deaminase is strongly influenced by the sequence and structure of the targeted DNA. Mol. Cell. Biol. 25, 10815–10821

32. Shen, H.M. & Storb, U. (2004) Activation-induced cytidine deaminase (AID) can target both DNA strands when the DNA is supercoiled. Proc. Natl. Acad. Sci. U.S.A. 101, 12997–13002

33. Chaudhuri, J., Khuong, C. & Alt, F.W. (2004) Replication protein A interacts with AID to promote deamination of somatic hypermutation targets. Nature 430, 992–998

34. Tian, M. & Alt, F.W. (2000) Transcription-induced cleavage of immunoglobulin switch regions by nucleotide excision repair nucleases in vitro. J. Biol. Chem. 275, 24163–24172

35. Shinkura, R., Tian, M., Smith, M., Chua, K., Fujiwara, Y. & Alt, F.W. (2003) The influence of transcriptional orientation on endogenous switch region function. Nat. Immunol. 4, 435–441

36. Yu, K., Chedin, F., Hsieh, C.L., Wilson, T.E. & Lieber, M.R. (2003) R-loops at immunoglobulin class switch regions in the chromosomes of stimulated B cells. Nat. Immunol. 4, 442–451

37. Diaz, M., Flajnik, M.F. & Klinman, N. (2001) Evolution and the molecular basis of somatic hypermutation of antigen receptor genes. Philos. Trans. R. Soc. London Ser. B 356, 67–72

38. Wakae, K., Magor, B.G., Saunders, H., Nagaoka, H., Kawamura, A., Kinoshita, K., Honjo, T. & Muramatsu, M. (2006) Evolution of class switch recombination function in fish activation-induced cytidine deaminase, AID. *Int. Immunol.* **18**, 41–47

39. Barreto, V.M., Pan-Hammarstrom, Q., Zhao, Y., Hammarstrom, L., Misulovin, Z. & Nussenzweig, M.C. (2005) AID from bony fish catalyzes class switch recombination. *J. Exp. Med.* **202**, 733–738

40. Du Pasquier, L., Robert, J., Courtet, M. & Mussmann, R. (2000) B-cell development in the amphibian *Xenopus*. *Immunol. Rev.* **175**, 201–213

41. Flajnik, M.F. (2002) Comparative analyses of immunoglobulin genes: surprises and portents. *Nat. Rev. Immunol.* **2**, 688–698

42. Stavnezer, J. & Amemiya, C.T. (2004) Evolution of isotype switching. *Semin. Immunol.* **16**, 257–275

43. Basu, U., Chaudhuri, J., Alpert, C., Dutt, S., Ranganath, S., Li, G., Schrum, J.P., Manis, J.P. & Alt, F.W. (2005) The AID antibody diversification enzyme is regulated by protein kinase A phosphorylation. *Nature* **438**, 508–511

44. McBride, K.M., Gazumyan, A., Woo, E.M., Barreto, V.M., Robbiani, D.F., Chait, B.T. & Nussenzweig, M.C. (2006) Regulation of hypermutation by activation-induced cytidine deaminase phosphorylation. *Proc. Natl. Acad. Sci. U.S.A.* **103**, 8798–8803

45. McBride, K.M., Gazumyan, A., Woo, E.M., Schwickert, T.A., Chait, B.T. & Nussenzweig, M.C. (2008) Regulation of class switch recombination and somatic mutation by AID phosphorylation. *J. Exp. Med.* **205**, 2585–2594

46. Pasqualucci, L., Kitaura, Y., Gu, H. & Dalla-Favera, R. (2006) PKA-mediated phosphorylation regulates the function of activation-induced deaminase (AID) in B cells. *Proc. Natl. Acad. Sci. U.S.A.* **103**, 395–400

47. Basu, U., Chaudhuri, J., Phan, R.T., Datta, A. & Alt, F.W. (2007) Regulation of activation induced deaminase via phosphorylation. *Adv. Exp. Med. Biol.* **596**, 129–137

48. Chatterji, M., Unniraman, S., McBride, K.M. & Schatz, D.G. (2007) Role of activation-induced deaminase protein kinase A phosphorylation sites in Ig gene conversion and somatic hypermutation. *J. Immunol.* **179**, 5274–5280

49. Shinkura, R., Okazaki, I.M., Muto, T., Begum, N.A. & Honjo, T. (2007) Regulation of AID function *in vivo. Adv. Exp. Med. Biol.* **596**, 71–81

50. Pham, P., Smolka, M.B., Calabrese, P., Landolph, A., Zhang, K., Zhou, H. & Goodman, M.F. (2008) Impact of phosphorylation and phosphorylation-null mutants on the activity and deamination specificity of activation-induced cytidine deaminase. *J. Biol. Chem.* **283**, 17428–17439

51. Cheng, H.-L., Vuong, B., Basu, U., Franklin, A., Schwer, B., Phan, R., Datta, A., Manis, J., Alt, F.W. & Chaudhuri, J. (2009) Integrity of serine-38 AID phosphorylation site is critical for somatic hypermutation and class switch recombination in mice. Proc. Natl. Acad. Sci. U.S.A. **106**, 2717–2722

52. Basu, U., Wang, Y. & Alt, F.W. (2008) Evolution of phosphorylation-dependent regulation of activation-induced cytidine deaminase. *Mol. Cell.* **32**, 285–291

53. Sernandez, I.V., de Yebenes, V.G., Dorsett, Y. & Ramiro, A.R. (2008) Haploinsufficiency of activation-induced deaminase for antibody diversification and chromosome translocations both *in vitro* and *in vivo. PLoS ONE* **3**, e3927

54. Takizawa, M., Tolarova, H., Li, Z., Dubois, W., Lim, S., Callen, E., Franco, S., Mosaico, M., Feigenbaum, L., Alt, F.W. et al. (2008) AID expression levels determine the extent of cMyc oncogenic translocations and the incidence of B cell tumor development. *J. Exp. Med.* **205**, 1949–1957

55. Ramiro, A., San-Martin, B.R., McBride, K., Jankovic, M., Barreto, V., Nussenzweig, A. & Nussenzweig, M.C. (2007) The role of activation-induced deaminase in antibody diversification and chromosome translocations. *Adv. Immunol.* **94**, 75–107

56. Ramiro, A.R., Jankovic, M., Callen, E., Difilippantonio, S., Chen, H.T., McBride, K.M., Eisenreich, T.R., Chen, J., Dickins, R.A., Lowe, S.W. et al. (2006) Role of genomic instability and p53 in AID-induced c-myc–Igh translocations. *Nature* **440**, 105–109

57. Ramiro, A.R., Nussenzweig, M.C. & Nussenzweig, A. (2006) Switching on chromosomal translocations. *Cancer Res.* **66**, 7837–7839

58. Teng, G., Hakimpour, P., Landgraf, P., Rice, A., Tuschl, T., Casellas, R. & Papavasiliou, F.N. (2008) MicroRNA-155 is a negative regulator of activation-induced cytidine deaminase. *Immunity* **28**, 621–629

59. Basu, U., Franklin, A. & Alt, F.W. (2008) Post-translational regulation of activation-induced cytidine deaminase. *Philos. Trans. R. Soc. London Ser. B* **364**, 667–673

60. Aoufouchi, S., Faili, A., Zober, C., D'Orlando, O., Weller, S., Weill, J.C. & Reynaud, C.A. (2008) Proteasomal degradation restricts the nuclear lifespan of AID. *J. Exp. Med.* **205**, 1357–1368

61. Dorsett, Y., McBride, K.M., Jankovic, M., Gazumyan, A., Thai, T.H., Robbiani, D.F., Di Virgilio, M., San-Martin, B.R., Heidkamp, G., Schwickert, T.A. et al. (2008) MicroRNA-155 suppresses activation-induced cytidine deaminase-mediated Myc–Igh translocation. *Immunity* **28**, 630–638

62. Schrader, C.E., Linehan, E.K., Mochegova, S.N., Woodland, R.T. & Stavnezer, J. (2005) Inducible DNA breaks in Ig S regions are dependent on AID and UNG. *J. Exp. Med.* **202**, 561–568

63. Robbiani, D.F., Bothmer, A., Callen, E., Reina-San-Martin, B., Dorsett, Y., Difilippantonio, S., Bolland, D.J., Chen, H.T., Corcoran, A.E., Nussenzweig, A. & Nussenzweig, M.C. (2008) AID is required for the chromosomal breaks in c-myc that lead to c-myc/IgH translocations. *Cell* **135**, 1028–1038

64. Ramiro, A.R., Jankovic, M., Eisenreich, T., Difilippantonio, S., Chen-Kiang, S., Muramatsu, M., Honjo, T., Nussenzweig, A. & Nussenzweig, M.C. (2004) AID is required for c-myc/IgH chromosome translocations *in vivo*. *Cell* **118**, 431–438

65. Gomez-Gonzalez, B. & Aguilera, A. (2007) Activation-induced cytidine deaminase action is strongly stimulated by mutations of the THO complex. *Proc. Natl. Acad. Sci. U.S.A.* **104**, 8409–8414

66. Li, X. & Manley, J.L. (2006) Cotranscriptional processes and their influence on genome stability. *Genes Dev.* **20**, 1838–1847

67. Li, X. & Manley, J.L. (2005) Inactivation of the SR protein splicing factor ASF/SF2 results in genomic instability. *Cell* **122**, 365–378

Biochem. Soc. Symp. 76
Citation reference: Biochem. Soc. Trans. (2009) 37, 569–576.

7

The impact of heterochromatin on DSB repair

Aaron A. Goodarzi, Angela T. Noon and Penny A. Jeggo[1]

Genome Damage and Stability Centre, University of Sussex, Brighton BN1 9RQ, U.K.

Abstract

DNA NHEJ (non-homologous end-joining) is the major DNA DSB (double-strand break) repair pathway in mammalian cells. Although NHEJ-defective cell lines show marked DSB-repair defects, cells defective in ATM (ataxia telangiectasia mutated) repair most DSBs normally. Thus NHEJ functions independently of ATM signalling. However, ~15% of radiation-induced DSBs are repaired with slow kinetics and require ATM and the nuclease Artemis. DSBs persisting in the presence of an ATM inhibitor, ATMi, localize to heterochromatin, suggesting that ATM is required for repairing DSBs arising within or close to heterochromatin. Consistent with this, we show that siRNA (small interfering RNA) of key heterochromatic proteins, including KAP-1 [KRAB (Krüppel-associated box) domain-associated protein 1], HP1 (heterochromatin protein 1) and HDAC (histone deacetylase) 1/2, relieves the requirement for ATM for DSB repair. Furthermore, ATMi addition to cell lines with genetic alterations that have an impact on heterochromatin, including Suv39H1/2 (suppressor of variegation 3–9 homologue 1/2)-knockout, ICFa (immunodeficiency, centromeric region instability, facial anomalies syndrome

---

[1] To whom correspondence should be addressed (email p.a.jeggo@sussex.ac.uk).

type a) and Hutchinson–Guilford progeria cell lines, fails to have an impact on DSB repair. KAP-1 is a highly dose-dependent, transient and ATM-specific substrate, and mutation of the ATM phosphorylation site on KAP-1 influences DSB repair. Collectively, the findings show that ATM functions to overcome the barrier to DSB repair posed by heterochromatin. However, even in the presence of ATM, γ-H2AX (phosphorylated histone H2AX) foci form on the periphery rather than within heterochromatic centres. Finally, we show that KAP-1's association with heterochromatin is diminished as cells progress through mitosis. We propose that KAP-1 is a critical heterochromatic factor that undergoes specific modifications to promote DSB repair and mitotic progression in a manner that allows localized and transient chromatin relaxation, but precludes significant dismantling of the heterochromatic superstructure.

Introduction

ATM (ataxia telangiectasia mutated) is a PIKK (phosphoinositide 3-kinase-like kinase) that lies at the heart of a signal transduction response to DNA DSBs (double-strand breaks) [1]. The very existence of a highly complex DSB signalling response attests to the significance of DSBs as lesions promoting genomic instability and/or cell death. The dramatic clinical features caused by loss of ATM in A-T (ataxia telangiectasia) patients serves further to demonstrate the importance of an appropriate response to DSB formation [2]. ATM signalling activated by DSB formation promotes cell-cycle-checkpoint arrest, apoptosis and also influences DSB repair. Whereas apoptosis functions to remove damaged cells from the cycling population, cell-cycle-checkpoint arrest can both enhance the opportunity for repair and serve as an alternative to apoptosis to limit the proliferative capacity of damaged cells. DNA NHEJ (non-homologous end-joining) functions as the major DSB-rejoining pathway in mammalian cells [3]. A-T cell lines rejoin the majority of DSBs with normal kinetics, demonstrating that most NHEJ occurs independently of ATM signalling [4,5]. However, the rejoining of ~15% of IR (ionizing radiation)-induced DSBs require ATM and additional proteins that function in the ATM signal transduction process, including γ-H2AX (phosphorylated histone H2AX) and 53BP1 (p53-binding protein 1) [5]. Previous studies have demonstrated that, although the majority of DSBs are repaired with fast kinetics in mammalian cells, a subset of breaks is rejoined with slower kinetics [6]. Strikingly, ATM is required for the slow component of DSB repair, which represents a ~15% subset of X- or γ-ray-induced DSBs [5]. ATM-dependent DSB repair also requires the nuclease Artemis [5]. Artemis nuclease activity has the capacity to cleave hairpin-ended DSBs and to remove 3'- or 5'-single-stranded overhangs following remodelling of the DNA ends by the DNA-PK (DNA-dependent protein kinase) [7,8]. Furthermore, Artemis is an ATM-dependent substrate after radiation [5,9–11]. For this and other reasons, it was suggested that ATM may function to promote Artemis-dependent end processing before rejoining by NHEJ [5].

However, in a more recent study, a closer look at the ATM-dependency for DSB repair following exposure to a range of agents producing DNA ends of differing complexity suggested that there was only a weak correlation between end complexity and ATM-dependent DSB repair [12]. Although the impact of ATM/Artemis in the repair of complex DSBs requires further examination and should not be discounted, we sought additional or alternative explanations for the role of ATM in the repair of X- or γ-ray-induced DSBs. In the present article, we discuss the impact of heterochromatin on DSB repair and the role of ATM in promoting DSBs that are located within or close to heterochromatic DNA.

DSBs that require ATM for their repair are localized to the periphery of heterochromatic DNA regions

Depending upon cell type, approx. 10–25% of mammalian DNA is transcriptionally inactive or 'silenced' and is highly compacted by heterochromatinization. Driven by mounting evidence that chromatin architecture strongly influences repair processes and that ATM signalling modifies chromatin structure, we considered the possibility that ATM may be specifically required for DSB repair within heterochromatic DNA [13,14]. To examine this, we exploited the mouse NIH 3T3 cell line in which pericentric and centromeric heterochromatic regions can be readily visualized as densely staining DAPI (4′,6-diamidino-2-phenylindole) regions, termed chromocentres [12,15]. Initially, we verified that the regions visualized by DAPI staining in mouse NIH 3T3 cells were enriched for heterochromatic factors, including H3K9me3 (histone H3 trimethylated at Lys⁹), KAP-1 [KRAB (Krüppel-associated box) domain-associated protein 1], HP1 (heterochromatin protein 1) and CENP-A (centromeric protein A), and depleted for the known euchromatic markers, HMGB1 (high-mobility group protein B1) and the transcription factor E2F1 (see Figure 2 in [12]). Following exposure of NIH 3T3 cells to IR in the presence of a specific ATMi (ATM inhibitor), KU55933, we examined the localization of γ-H2AX foci present at early and late times. At 0.5 h post-IR, γ-H2AX foci were stochastically distributed throughout the nucleus (Figure 1). Using high-resolution imaging, we estimated that ~20% of the γ-H2AX foci present at 0.5 h co-localized (i.e. overlapped or bordered) with chromocentres. Strikingly, the γ-H2AX foci that remained at 24 h post-IR in the presence of ATMi were predominantly (~70%) localized to the periphery of the chromocentres (Figure 1). We also enumerated the rate of loss of all γ-H2AX foci regardless of localization and those that localized to the periphery of densely DAPI-staining chromocentres, classified as DSBs located within or close to heterochromatic DNA (HC-DSBs) and, by subtraction, estimated the rate of loss of DSBs considered to be located within euchromatic DNA (EC-DSBs). Strikingly, we observed that, in control cells, the EC- and HC-DSBs were repaired with fast and slow kinetics respectively, and that addition of the ATMi specifically had an

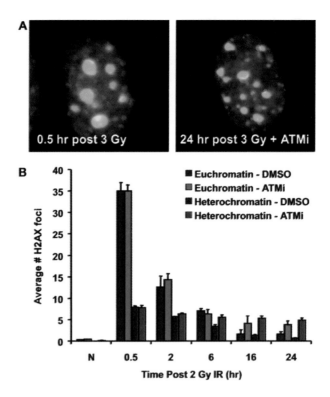

Figure I. DSBs that persist following IR treatment in the absence of ATM kinase activity are localized around the periphery of chromocentres
(**A**) DMSO or 10 μM KU55933 ATMi was added to confluent NIH 3T3 cells. After 30 min, cells were irradiated with 2 Gy of IR and harvested 0.5 or 24 h after IR treatment, as indicated. Cells were fixed and immunostained for γ-H2AX (red) and DAPI (green). Images shown are representative of the total cell population. At 0.5 h after IR treatment, ~20% of DSBs overlap or touch chromocentres. In contrast, by 24 h, ~70% of DSBs are in contact with the periphery of chromocentres. (**B**) NIH 3T3 cells were treated with or without ATMi as in (**A**) and irradiated with 2 Gy of IR. Cells were fixed at the times indicated and immunostained as in (**A**). Total γ-H2AX foci and γ-H2AX foci overlapping with the periphery of heterochromatic regions (assessed by DAPI staining) were enumerated. Euchromatic numbers were estimated by subtracting the heterochromatic number of foci from the total number. Results are means ± S.D. for three independent experiments.

impact on the repair of the HC-DSBs (Figure 1B). These findings suggest that the slow component of DSB repair may represent the repair of DSBs located close to or within heterochromatic DNA and that ATM is specifically required for the repair of such DSBs.

Knockdown or loss of heterochromatic building factors relieves the requirement for ATM for DSB repair

The findings above predicted that reducing the heterochromatic DNA content might diminish the requirement for ATM for DSB repair. A range of DNA and histone modifications, as well as the recruitment of specific heterochromatic

Table 1 DSB repair has a diminished dependence on ATM when heterochromatin is impaired

The results show the number of γ-H2AX foci present 24 h after 3 Gy of IR in the absence (first column) or presence (second column) of ATMi. ATMi was added 30 min prior to irradiation. Data are only shown for the 24 h time point. Full analysis is given in [12]. In some instances, there was a high background number of γ-H2AX foci. We assessed whether the number of foci was elevated relative to this background. Thus, for example, following HDAC1/2 siRNA, there were elevated γ-H2AX foci in the absence of ATMi, but this was not increased further by ATMi addition, and the foci remaining were fewer than observed in cells treated with scrambled siRNA and ATMi. Thus we consider that HDAC1/2 siRNA at least partially alleviates the requirement for ATM for DSB repair.

Treatment or cell line	Number of H2AX foci at 24 h	
	DMSO-treated cells	ATMi-treated cells
Scrambled siRNA	2.1 ± 0.4	10.7 ± 0.8
KAP-1 siRNA	3.2 ± 1.5	3.6 ± 1.0
HP1$\alpha\beta\gamma$ siRNA	2.8 ± 1.5	4.4 ± 0.4
HDAC1/2 siRNA	5.2 ± 1.1	5.8 ± 1.3
SUV39H1/2$^{+/+}$ MEFs	0.8 ± 0.4	8.6 ± 0.4
SUV39H1/2$^{-/-}$ MEFs	1.9 ± 0.2	5.0 ± 0.4
Normal fibroblasts	0.9 ± 0.2	9.3 ± 0.6
HGPS fibroblasts	1.1 ± 0.3	5.0 ± 0.6
ICFa fibroblasts	5.2 ± 2.6	7.5 ± 2.6

building factors, function co-ordinately to create heterochromatic DNA [16,17]. DNA methylation by DNA methyltransferases is the most significant DNA modification, whereas histone H3 acetylation promotes a more open chromatin conformation and histone H3 methylation at Lys[9] (H3K9me) confers a more closed conformation. The HDACs (histone deacetylases) HDAC1, HDAC2 and HDAC3 are important in removing heterochromatin-inhibiting histone H3 acetylation, whereas Suv39H1/2 (suppressor of variegation 3–9 homologue 1/2) are important SET (suppressor of variation 3–9, enhancer of zeste, trithorax)-domain histone methyltransferases. Additionally, HP1 and the co-repressor, KAP-1, are critical heterochromatic building proteins [18]. Heterochromatin building occurs in an interwoven manner with loss of any component adversely affecting compaction similar to the demise of a carefully stacked pack of cards following the removal of any single card. We therefore examined the impact of a range of critical heterochromatic components on the ATM-dependency for DSB repair. Strikingly, we observed that knockdown or loss of any one of several heterochromatic factors relieved or reduced the DSB-repair defect imparted by the addition of ATMi [12] (summarized in Table 1). Thus, following KAP-1 siRNA (small interfering RNA), DSBs were repaired at a similar rate to that observed in control cells with or without addition of ATMi. Similar results were obtained following HDAC1/2 siRNA or HP1 siRNA. Furthermore, mouse embryonic fibroblasts knocked out for the Suv39H1/2 histone methyltransferases, which show reduced HP1 localization within pericentric heterochromatin, also showed a diminished DSB-repair defect following ATMi addition, reflecting a reduced dependency on ATM [19]. We also examined cells from ICFa (immunodeficiency, centromeric region instability, facial anomalies syndrome type a) and HGPS (Hutchinson–Gilford progeria syndrome), both of which show progressive heterochromatin disorganization, and, in both cases, observed a diminished DSB repair defect 24 h after ATMi addition compared with normal human cell lines. Collectively, these results suggest that the manipulation of essential heterochromatic building factors, although not affecting the normal rate of DSB repair as such, has an impact on the requirement for ATM for DSB repair, consolidating the notion that ATM is specifically needed for repair of DSBs located within or close to heterochromatic DNA.

KAP-1 is a highly DSB dose-dependent and specific ATM substrate

KAP-1 harbours the motif LSSQE, which encompasses the consensus ATM-phosphorylation motif (S/TQ). We raised antibodies that recognize KAP-1 phosphorylated at the predicted ATM-phosphorylation site (Ser^{824}). Western blotting using these anti-pSer^{824}-KAP-1 (pKAP-1) antibodies confirmed that, although there was no detectable signal in undamaged cells, they recognize an IR-inducible substrate that has the mobility of KAP-1 (Figure 2). Moreover, KAP-1 phosphorylation was almost entirely ATM-dependent, with no detectable signal observed in an ATM$^{-/-}$ lymphoblastoid cell line (LBL) and no significant reduction being found in an ATR (ATM-and Rad3-related)-deficient LBL (ATR-SS cells) following treatment with IR or etoposide, an agent that induced DSBs following topoisomerase II inhibition (Figure 2). Furthermore, we did not detect any evidence of pKAP-1 following exposure to hydroxyurea or UV, agents which do not directly induce DSBs. These findings strongly suggest that KAP-1 is an unusually specific ATM substrate that is only induced by direct DSB induction. Additionally, pKAP-1 was observed at early times post-IR (10–30 min, depending on dose), its magnitude was highly dose-dependent and was relatively transient with its rate of decay being dose-dependent, largely disappearing by 6 h post-physiological exposure levels.

Importantly, ectopic expression of S824A KAP-1 in cells that were knocked down for endogenous KAP-1 showed a similar DSB-repair defect to that observed in A-T cell lines, whereas expression of S824D KAP-1 conferred repair kinetics that were similar to wild-type and unaffected by ATMi addition [12]. Collectively, these findings argue that Ser^{824} is a critical phosphorylation site on KAP-1, which is regulated by ATM-dependent phosphorylation and is required for ATM-dependent DSB repair.

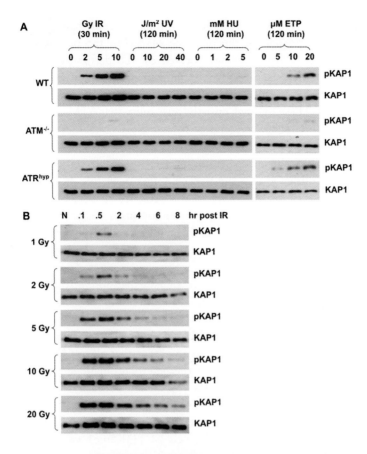

Figure 2. KAP-1 is an efficient and specific ATM phosphorylation substrate
(**A**) GM02188 [WT (wild-type)], GM03189D (A-T) and DK0064 [hypomorphic ATR-SS (ATR^hyp)] were irradiated with 0, 2, 5 or 10 Gy of IR and harvested 30 min later, irradiated with 0, 10, 20 or 40 J/m^2 UVC (UV) radiation and harvested 120 min later, treated with 1, 2 or 5 mM hydroxyurea (HU) and harvested 120 min later or treated with 5, 10 or 20 μM etoposide (ETP) and harvested 120 min later. KAP-1 was immunoblotted as in Figure 1. Then, 40 μg of whole-cell extract (prepared as described previously [12]), was immunoblotted for either pSer^824 KAP-1 (pKAP1) or total KAP-1. (**B**) GM02188 (WT) cells were exposed to the indicated doses of IR and examined from 0.1 to 8 h post-IR for levels of phosphorylated KAP-1 (pKAP1) and total KAP-1 as descibed in (**A**).

Heterochromatin is a barrier to DSB repair and signalling which ATM partially relieves

The findings above, taken together with additional published observations [12], strongly suggest that ATM is specifically required to repair DSBs that arise within or proximal to heterochromatin, which is achieved by phosphorylation of KAP-1, a co-repressor that interacts with HP1. The finding that ATM is specifically required for the slow component of DSB repair and that DSBs associated with heterochromatin are repaired with slower kinetics compared with DSBs located within euchromatin [12], suggest that heterochromatin poses a barrier to the DSB repair that is relieved, at least in part, by ATM. We aimed to evaluate how KAP-1 phosphorylation impacts upon heterochromatin. In Figure 1, we show that, in the presence of ATMi, the persisting γ-H2AX foci at 24 h after 3 Gy of IR are located on the periphery of the densely DAPI-staining chromocentres. It is striking that, although the γ-H2AX foci partially encroach into the densely DAPI-staining regions, complete overlap is rarely observed. These findings raise the possibility that ATM-dependent KAP-1 phosphorylation might overcome the barrier to γ-H2AX foci expansion posed by heterochromatin. We therefore examined the relationship between γ-H2AX foci formation and chromocentre location in wild-type cells, where ATM is functional. We observed that the γ-H2AX foci persisting at 0.5 h after 1 Gy of IR were, like those remaining in the presence of ATMi, predominantly located around the periphery of the chromocentres (Figure 3). Using high-resolution imaging, we delineated the chromocentre regions (shown in blue), the γ-H2AX foci (green) and the regions of overlap (red). The regions of overlap are predominantly on the edge of the chromocentres, consistent with the notion that heterochromatin poses a barrier to signal expansion. Strikingly, there was only limited encroachment of γ-H2AX formation into the chromocentric mass (Figure 3), similar to our previous observations in cells treated with ATMi [12]. These findings therefore argue that, although ATM phosphorylation events may serve to relax the heterochromatin to an extent that allows DSB repair, they do not result in overt dismantling of the heterochromatic superstructure and do not fully relieve the barrier to foci expansion posed by heterochromatin. In this context, it is also important to note that the densely DAPI-staining chromocentres in KAP-1 siRNA-treated NIH 3T3 cells are clearly detectable albeit with moderately diminished levels of H3K9me3 (see supplementary material in [12]).

The distribution of KAP-1 on chromatin is reorganized during mitosis

The results described above and published findings suggest that ATM's impact on heterochromatin occurs via phosphorylation of KAP-1 on Ser[824], which modifies KAP-1 binding to heterochromatin and triggers heterochromatin relaxation [12,14]. The interaction of HP1 with chromatin during interphase is promoted by H3K9me3. Notably, although H3K9me3 does not alter during mitosis, the binding of HP1 to chromatin has been reported to diminish [20]. Rather than affecting the histone-methylation code, evidence suggests that mitotic cells regulate HP1 chromatin binding via histone H3 Ser[10] phosphorylation by Aurora B kinase [21]. Driven in part by our goal to examine ATM's role in DSB repair in G_2-phase, we examined the localization of KAP-1 during the cell cycle. Immunofluorescence analysis of G_1-phase cells using α-KAP-1 antibodies showed a pronounced enrichment of KAP-1 at the densely DAPI-staining chromocentres, consistent with the substantial evidence that these represent regions of heterochromatin, to which KAP-1 is preferentially localized

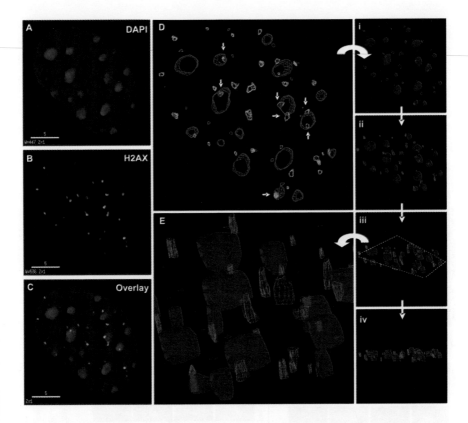

Figure 3. The restriction of heterochromatin on γ-H2AX foci formation is not relieved by the presence of ATM

(A–C) Confluent NIH 3T3 cells were irradiated with 1 Gy of IR and harvested 0.5 h later. Cells were fixed and immunostained for γ-H2AX (green) and DAPI (blue). High-resolution three-dimensional images of deconvolved Z-stacks were obtained, showing DAPI-stained chromocentres (**A**, blue), γ-H2AX foci (**B**, green) and overlayed images (**C**). (**D**) Using softWoRx¨ suite software (Applied Precision), quantitative measurements of densely DAPI-stained chromocentres and γ-H2AX foci were made, and a three-dimensional wireframe model was generated showing regions of blue–green overlap in red (indicated by arrows). The three-dimensional model was rotated along the z-axis (i–iv). (**E**) An enlarged image of the region of the z-axis rotated image shown in (**D**, iii), outlined by the white broken lines. Scale bar, 5 μm.

(Figure 4A). In G_1-phase, these densely staining chromocentres were also enriched for H3K9me3, but were depleted of the euchromatic marker, H3K9ac (histone H3 acetylated at Lys[9]) (Figures 4B and 4C). In contrast, in G_2-phase, the DAPI regions were more diffuse compared with G_1-phase and contained KAP-1, H3K9me3 and H3K9ac, suggesting that these regions no longer uniquely represent heterochromatic chromocentres (Figures 4B and 4C). We monitored KAP1 localization through G_2/M-phase using phospho-H3 staining to delineate cell-cycle positions. Cells with minimal (but detectable) phospho-H3 signal, determined to be at the very beginning of G_2-phase, have similar KAP-1-enriched chromocentres to G_1/S-phase cells. As the levels of phospho-H3 increase and cells progress through G_2-phase towards the mitotic

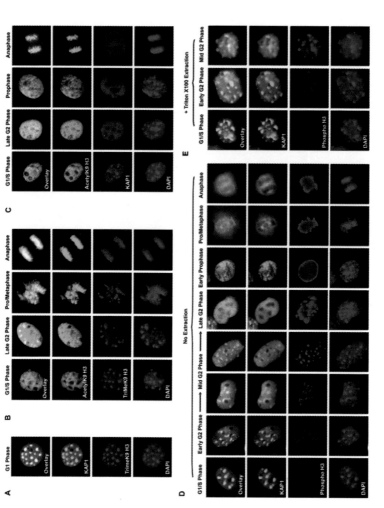

Figure 4. KAP-1 is removed from chromatin during progression through mitosis

(A) Confluent G_0/G_1-phase NIH 3T3 cells were fixed and immunostained with KAP-1 (green), H3K9me3 (TriMeK9 H3, red) and DAPI (blue). (B) Exponential-phase NIH 3T3 cells were fixed and immunostained with H3K9ac (AcetylK9 H3, green), H3K9me3 (TriMeK9 H3, red) and DAPI (blue). (C) Exponential-phase NIH 3T3 cells were fixed and immunostained with KAP-1 (green), H3K9me3 (TriMeK9 H3, red) and DAPI (blue). (D) Exponential-phase NIH 3T3 cells were fixed and immunostained with KAP-1 (green), histone H3 pSer[10] (Phospho H3, red) and DAPI (blue). Progression through G_2/M-phase was assessed by phospho-H3 staining and DAPI morphology. (E) Exponential-phase NIH 3T3 cells were first extracted with 0.1% (v/v) Triton X-100 in PBS for 30 s before being fixed and immunostained as in (D). NB: the specific morphologies of KAP-1, H3K9me3 and H3K9ac during G_2-phase shown in (B) and (C) were ... to localize ... G₂/M-phase marker such as pSer[10] of histone H3 or cyclin B1.

boundary, some (but not all) KAP-1 is redistributed from densely DAPI-stained regions to give pan-nuclear staining, indicating the active reorganization of heterochromatin in preparation for mitotic chromosome hypercondensation (Figure 4D). It was notable that the pan-nuclear KAP-1 localization observed during mid/late-G_2-phase was unaffected by detergent extraction (Figure 4E), suggesting that KAP-1 remains bound to chromatin, but that the densely DAPI-staining regions may less stringently represent 'pure' heterochromatic chromocentres. In further contrast, as cells progressed through mitosis, the localization of KAP-1 was observed to be completely distinct from that of the DAPI staining, indicating the release of KAP-1 from chromatin during progression through mitosis (Figure 4). Thus, although KAP-1 partly co-localized with DAPI staining in very late G_2-phase, in prophase, metaphase and anaphase, there was almost no KAP-1 co-localizing with DAPI staining. Strikingly, in late telophase, KAP-1 rapidly relocalized to chromatin. These findings closely parallel studies of HP1 localization during progression through mitosis [21].

Collectively, these findings suggest that, in G_2-phase, heterochromatic DNA becomes more diffusely organized than in G_1-phase and during transition through mitosis both KAP-1 and HP1 are released from the chromatin.

Discussion

A-T cell lines display dramatic radiosensitivity, which, more than 20 years ago, was proposed to be due to a defect in the repair of chromosomal DSBs [22]. Despite this early observation, consolidation of this notion was slow in surfacing, primarily because the majority of DSBs are repaired normally in A-T cells when assessed by physical methods such as PFGE (pulsed-field gel electrophoresis) [4]. Although DSB-repair defects were detected by PFGE, the modest impact and high doses necessitated by the technique limited the significance of the findings [4]. Later, A-T cells were demonstrated to display cell-cycle-checkpoint defects, and the biological impact of ATM loss was attributed to defective checkpoint function [23]. Only more recently, with the advent of γ-H2AX foci analysis as a sensitive monitor of DSB repair following physiologically relevant doses of IR, was a repair defect in A-T cell lines confirmed and its contribution to A-T radiosensitivity appreciated [5]. However, the mechanistic role that ATM plays in DSB repair has, until recently, remained unclear.

In a recent study and consolidated further here, we have shown that ATM is specifically required for the repair of DSBs located close to or within heterochromatic regions [12]. The organization of heterochromatin in mouse and human cells is distinct due, in part, to the fact that mouse cells have acrocentric chromosomes. Of relevance to our recent work is the exploitation of the mouse NIH 3T3 cell line, in which heterochromatin is organized into readily visualized chromocentres that show dense DAPI staining. Recently, we and others have observed that γ-H2AX foci formation does not occur within chromocentres but rather on their periphery (Figures 1 and 4) [24]. Strikingly, although the γ-H2AX foci that form in A-T cells are smaller than those in control cells, we observed a similar magnitude of γ-H2AX encroachment into the chromocentres in either the presence or absence of ATM kinase activity. Furthermore, the γ-H2AX foci that remain at later times in a control or an A-T cell line are preferentially located at the periphery of chromocentres and show a similar magnitude of overlap with them. This is consistent with our finding that DSBs associated with chromocentres (HC-DSBs) are repaired with slower kinetics than DSBs located within euchromatic DNA and that A-T is specifically defective in the slow component of DSB repair, i.e. in the repair of HC-DSBs. We also show that knockdown or loss of multiple factors that contribute to the heterochromatic superstructure including KAP-1, HDAC1/2, Suv39H1/2 and HP1 can relieve the requirement for ATM for DSB repair. Finally, KAP-1 is a highly sensitive ATM substrate with its phosphorylation being rapidly lost as DSB repair proceeds. We also showed previously that KAP-1 phosphorylation at Ser^{824} is required for its role in ATM-dependent DSB repair [12]. Collectively, these findings strongly suggest that, following the introduction of DSBs, ATM phosphorylates KAP-1, which promotes the repair of DSBs located within or close to heterochromatic DNA. This raises the question of how KAP-1 phosphorylation has an impact on the heterochromatic superstructure. Ziv et al. [14] showed previously that exposure to neocarzinostatin, a radiomimetic DNA-damaging agent, increased the accessibility of micrococcal nuclease to DNA in an ATM-dependent manner. Critically, they showed that KAP-1 siRNA also increased accessibility and that expression of S824A or S824D KAP-1 prevented or enhanced accessibility respectively. Additionally, we showed previously that the presence of KAP-1 in a chromatin fraction enriched for heterochromatic proteins diminished after IR in an ATM-dependent manner. Taken together, these findings suggest that ATM-dependent KAP-1 phosphorylation modifies its chromatin binding, which, in turn, influences heterochromatic structure. However, the precise impact of KAP-1 phosphorylation is unclear and, clearly, the higher-order chromatin structure is not dismantled following IR-induced KAP-1 phosphorylation. We therefore suggest that KAP-1 phosphorylation confers sufficient localized heterochromatic relaxation to allow DSB repair without necessitating significant disassembly of the higher-order chromatin structure. Possibly consistent with this, we observed that the duration and extent of KAP-1 phosphorylation is short and highly dose-dependent. We thus propose that the DSB response restricts the duration, location and extent of KAP-1 phosphorylation to limit the overall impact on higher-order structure, but promotes localized DSB repair. In contrast, we show that KAP-1's distribution and chromatin association is altered dramatically as cells progress through mitosis, similar to the release observed previously for HP1. Global chromatin alterations are required to mediate the dramatic DNA condensation needed for cell division, which coincides with a significant decrease in many nuclear processes (e.g. transcription). In this context, it is perhaps not surprising that the mechanisms of chromatin alteration following DSB formation and mitotic entry are distinct. Finally, we demonstrate that KAP-1 is phosphorylated predominantly by ATM with minimal phosphorylation contributed by ATR following, for example, replication-fork stalling or UV irradiation. It is likely that, since higher-order chromatin structure is dismantled during replication, KAP-1 phosphorylation might be less important for DSB repair during S-phase or at collapsed replication forks, thus eliminating the need for ATR to phosphoryate this substrate. Given the fact that the majority of DSB-response substrates are phosphorylated redundantly by ATM and ATR, the unusual specificity of KAP-1 phosphorylation is noteworthy and potentially important.

In summary, KAP-1 is a strong and functionally critical ATM substrate, whose phosphorylation is highly dose-dependent and transient. Collectively, the emerging data suggest that KAP-1 is a 'keystone' heterochromatic building factor that can become modified after DSB formation as well as during the cell cycle to allow critical, but highly defined, changes to the higher-order structure necessary for DSB repair and potentially for events during mitosis.

Funding

Work in the P.A.J. laboratory is supported by the Medical Research Council, the International Association for Cancer Research, the Wellcome Trust and European Union grant [grant number FIGH-CT-200200207] (DNA Repair).

References

1. Lavin, M.F. (2008) Ataxia-telangiectasia: from a rare disorder to a paradigm for cell signalling and cancer. Nat. Rev. Mol. Cell Biol. **9**, 759–769
2. Chun, H.H. & Gatti, R.A. (2004) Ataxia-telangiectasia, an evolving phenotype. DNA Repair **3**, 1187–1196
3. Wyman, C. & Kanaar, R. (2006) DNA double-strand break repair: all's well that ends well. Annu. Rev. Genet. **40**, 363–383
4. Foray, N., Priestley, A., Alsbeih, G., Badie, C., Capulas, E.P., Arlett, C.F. & Malaise, E.P. (1997) Hypersensitivity of ataxia-telangiectasia fibroblasts to ionizing radiation is associated with a repair deficiency of DNA double-strand breaks. Int. J. Radiat. Biol. **72**, 271–283
5. Riballo, E., Kuhne, M., Rief, N., Doherty, A., Smith, G.C., Recio, M.J., Reis, C., Dahm, K., Fricke, A., Krempler, A. et al. (2004) A pathway of double-strand break rejoining dependent upon ATM, Artemis, and proteins locating to γ-H2AX foci. Mol. Cell **16**, 715–724
6. Metzger, L. & Iliakis, G. (1991) Kinetics of DNA double-strand break repair throughout the cell cycle as assayed by pulsed field gel electrophoresis in CHO cells. Int. J. Radiat. Biol. **59**, 1325–1339
7. Ma, Y., Pannicke, U., Schwarz, K. & Lieber, M.R. (2002) Hairpin opening and overhang processing by an Artemis/DNA-dependent protein kinase complex in nonhomologous end joining and V(D)J recombination. Cell **108**, 781–794
8. Goodarzi, A.A., Yu, Y., Riballo, E., Douglas, P., Walker, S.A., Ye, R., Harer, C., Marchetti, C., Morrice, N., Jeggo, P.A. et al. (2006) DNA-PK autophosphorylation facilitates Artemis endonuclease activity. EMBO J. **25**, 3880–3889

9. Poinsignon, C., de Chasseval, R., Soubeyrand, S., Moshous, D., Fischer, A., Hache, R.J. & de
    Villartay, J.P. (2004) Phosphorylation of Artemis following irradiation-induced DNA damage. *Eur. J.
    Immunol.* **34**, 3146–3155
10. Zhang, X., Succi, J., Feng, Z., Prithivirajsingh, S., Story, M.D. & Legerski, R.J. (2004) Artemis is a
    phosphorylation target of ATM and ATR and is involved in the G_2/M DNA damage checkpoint
    response. *Mol. Cell. Biol.* **24**, 9207–9220
11. Wang, J., Pluth, J.M., Cooper, P.K., Cowan, M.J., Chen, D.J. & Yannone, S.M. (2005) Artemis
    deficiency confers a DNA double-strand break repair defect and Artemis phosphorylation status
    is altered by DNA damage and cell cycle progression. *DNA Repair* **4**, 556–570
12. Goodarzi, A.A., Noon, A.T., Deckbar, D., Ziv, Y., Shiloh, Y., Löbrich, M. & Jeggo, P.A. (2008) ATM
    signaling facilitates repair of DNA double-strand breaks associated with heterochromatin. *Mol. Cell*
    31, 167–177
13. Downs, J.A., Allard, S., Jobin-Robitaille, O., Javaheri, A., Auger, A., Bouchard, N., Kron, S.J.,
    Jackson, S.P. & Cote, J. (2004) Binding of chromatin-modifying activities to phosphorylated histone
    H2A at DNA damage sites. *Mol. Cell* **16**, 979–990
14. Ziv, Y., Bielopolski, D., Galanty, Y., Lukas, C., Taya, Y., Schultz, D.C., Lukas, J., Bekker-Jensen, S.,
    Bartek, J. & Shiloh, Y. (2006) Chromatin relaxation in response to DNA double-strand breaks is
    modulated by a novel ATM- and KAP-1 dependent pathway. *Nat. Cell Biol.* **8**, 870–876
15. Guenatri, M., Bailly, D., Maison, C. & Almouzni, G. (2004) Mouse centric and pericentric satellite
    repeats form distinct functional heterochromatin. *J. Cell Biol.* **166**, 493–505
16. Horn, P.J. & Peterson, C.L. (2006) Heterochromatin assembly: a new twist on an old model.
    Chromosome Res. **14**, 83–94
17. Trojer, P. & Reinberg, D. (2007) Facultative heterochromatin: is there a distinctive molecular
    signature? *Mol. Cell* **28**, 1–13
18. Sripathy, S.P., Stevens, J. & Schultz, D.C. (2006) The KAP1 corepressor functions to coordinate the
    assembly of de novo HP1-demarcated microenvironments of heterochromatin required for KRAB
    zinc finger protein-mediated transcriptional repression. *Mol. Cell. Biol.* **26**, 8623–8638
19. Lehnertz, B., Ueda, Y., Derijck, A.A., Braunschweig, U., Perez-Burgos, L., Kubicek, S., Chen, T., Li,
    E., Jenuwein, T. & Peters, A.H. (2003) Suv39h-mediated histone H3 lysine 9 methylation directs
    DNA methylation to major satellite repeats at pericentric heterochromatin. *Curr. Biol.* **13**,
    1192–1200
20. Schmiedeberg, L., Weisshart, K., Diekmann, S., Meyer Zu Hoerste, G. & Hemmerich, P. (2004)
    High- and low-mobility populations of HP1 in heterochromatin of mammalian cells. *Mol. Biol. Cell*
    15, 2819–2833
21. Fischle, W., Tseng, B.S., Dormann, H.L., Ueberheide, B.M., Garcia, B.A., Shabanowitz, J., Hunt, D.F.,
    Funabiki, H. & Allis, C.D. (2005) Regulation of HP1-chromatin binding by histone H3 methylation
    and phosphorylation. *Nature* **438**, 1116–1122
22. Cornforth, M.N. & Bedford, J.S. (1985) On the nature of a defect in cells from individuals with
    ataxia-telangiectasia. *Science* **227**, 1589–1591
23. Kastan, M.B., Zhan, Q., El-Deiry, W.S., Carrier, F., Jacks, T., Walsh, W.V., Plunkett, B.S., Vogelstein,
    B. & Fornace, A.J. (1992) A mammalian cell cycle checkpoint pathway utilizing p53 and GADD45 is
    defective in ataxia-telangiectasia. *Cell* **71**, 587–597
24. Cowell, I.G., Sunter, N.J., Singh, P.B., Austin, C.A., Durkacz, B.W. & Tilby, M.J. (2007) γH2AX foci
    form preferentially in euchromatin after ionising-radiation. *PLoS ONE* **2**, e1057

Biochem. Soc. Symp. 76
Citation reference: Biochem. Soc. Trans. (2009) **37**, 577–581.

8

Short-patch single-strand break repair in ataxia oculomotor apraxia-1

John J. Reynolds*, Sherif F. El-Khamisy*† and Keith W. Caldecott*[1]

*Genome Damage and Stability Centre, University of Sussex, Science Park Road, Falmer, Brighton BN1 9RQ, U.K., and †Biochemistry Department, Faculty of Pharmacy. Ain Shams University, Cairo, Egypt

Abstract

AOA1 (ataxia oculomotor apraxia-1) results from mutations in aprataxin, a component of DNA strand break repair that removes AMP from 5′-termini. In the present article, we provide an overview of this disease and review recent experiments demonstrating that short-patch repair of oxidative single-strand breaks in AOA1 cell extracts bypasses the point of aprataxin action and stalls at the final step of DNA ligation, resulting in accumulation of adenylated DNA nicks. Strikingly, this defect results from insufficient levels of non-adenylated DNA ligase and short-patch single-strand break repair can be restored in AOA1 extracts, independently of aprataxin, by addition of recombinant DNA ligase.

AOA1 (ataxia oculomotor apraxia-1)

AOA1 is an autosomal recessive spinocerebellar ataxia syndrome that resembles Friedreich's ataxia and A-T (ataxia telangiectasia) neurologically, but which

[1] *To whom correspondence should be addressed*
(email k.w.caldecott@sussex.ac.uk).

lacks extraneurological features such as immunodeficiency and telangiectasia. A recent study of 14 French, Italian and Algerian AOA1 patients from nine families supports the likelihood that, although cerebellar atrophy, ataxia and sensorimotor axonal neuropathy are common to most AOA1 patients, the presence and severity of other features is more variable (~85% of patients in the case of oculomotor apraxia) [1]. Variation in clinical impact and/or severity of AOA1 is suggested further by reported clinical overlap with other neurological diseases/conditions, such as MSA (multiple system atrophy) and ataxia with coenzyme Q10 deficiency [2–4]. AOA1 accounts for 5–10% of all autosomal recessive cerebellar ataxias and has variable age of onset (typically 1–18 years), with a mean of ~5 years [1,5]. Unlike A-T cells, AOA1 cells are only mildly sensitive, if at all, to ionizing radiation and other genotoxins, and exhibit normal cell-cycle-checkpoint control and chromosome stability following ionizing radiation [6]. Consistent with these observations, elevated cancer incidence has not been reported in AOA1 patients. The gene mutated in AOA1 is designated *APTX* [7,8], and the protein product of *APTX* is designated aprataxin.

Aprataxin contains a central HIT (histidine triad) domain and is a member of the HIT domain superfamily of nucleotide hydrolases/transferases. The N-terminus of aprataxin exhibits homology with PNK (polynucleotide kinase) [8], and like PNK encodes a divergent FHA (forkhead-associated) domain [9]. The FHA domains of both aprataxin and PNK facilitate constitutive interactions with protein kinase CK2-phosphorylated XRCC1 (X-ray repair complementing defective repair in Chinese-hamster cells 1) [6,9–14]. It is noteworthy that a third member of this divergent FHA domain family has been identified [denoted APLF (aprataxin- and PNK-like factor)/PALF (PNK and aprataxin-like FHA protein)/Xip1] and shown to bind CK2-phosphorylated XRCC1 [15–17]. In fact, all three FHA domain proteins are also sequestered into the DSBR (double-strand break repair) machinery, via FHA domain-mediated interaction with CK2-phosphorylated XRCC4 [6,15,18]. It is thus highly likely that aprataxin, PNK and APLF play roles both in SSBR (single-strand break repair) and DSBR. Aprataxin also associates with PARP-1 [poly(ADP–ribose) polymerase 1] and p53, and additionally with the nucleolar proteins nucleolin, nucleophosmin and UBF-1 (upstream binding factor 1) [12,19]. The association and partial co-localization of aprataxin with nucleolar proteins is also mediated by the FHA domain, although whether these associations are direct or indirect (e.g. via another protein) remains to be determined. Nevertheless, the association of aprataxin with nucleolar proteins may indicate that SSBR and/or DSBR is particularly important at sites of high transcriptional activity, perhaps to prevent SSBs (single-strand breaks) from blocking gene expression.

Most of the mutations identified in AOA1 to date are located within the HIT domain or just upstream of the C-terminal zinc-finger motif, consistent with a critical requirement for the HIT domain for normal neurological function. Many of these mutations greatly reduce the stability and/or cellular level of aprataxin and may thus be functionally null alleles [12,20,21]. Some mutations appear to be associated with later disease onset and/or milder clinical features [8,22–24], which, in some cases, appear to have less impact on ataxia stability and/or activity [20]. On the basis of sequence comparisons and substrate specificity, ataxia appears to represent a discrete branch of the HIT domain superfamily [25]. Indeed, although ataxia can hydrolyse substrates typical of either the Fhit or Hint branch of HIT domain proteins, releasing AMP from diadenosine tetraphosphate or AMP-lysine respectively, its catalytic activity is very low (k_{cat} <0.03 s^{-1}) [20,25]. Apataxin has also been reported to process two types of damaged 3′-terminus arising at oxidative DNA breaks, 3′-phosphate and 3′-phosphoglycolate termini, raising the possibility that it is an end-processing factor. However, the activity of ataxia on such substrates is also very low (k_{cat} ~0.0003–0.003 s^{-1}). A more likely physiological substrate for ataxia are 5′-AMP termini, at which AMP is covalently linked to 5′-phosphate through a pyrophosphate bond [26,27]. DNA strand breaks in which the 5′-terminus is linked to AMP are normal intermediates of DNA ligation, but if they arise before 3′-DNA end processing has occurred, ligation is inhibited. Apataxin can remove AMP from the 5′-terminus of DNA breaks at such 'abortive' DNA ligation events, effectively 'proofreading' the DNA ligase reaction [26]. In addition to the HIT domain, the C-terminal zinc finger is important for ataxia activity on 5′-AMP, probably to increase the affinity and/or specificity of ataxia for 5′-AMP substrates [27]. Although the ability to process 5′-AMP termini is a very elegant activity, it remains to be determined whether or not this type of terminus arises *in vivo*.

AOA1 and short-patch SSBR

To clarify the nature of the SSBR defect in AOA1, we recently reconstituted AOA1-dependent short-patch SSBR assays *in vitro* with human and rodent cell extracts [26,28]. To measure short-patch SSBR, we employed an oligonucleotide duplex harbouring a 1-bp gap with 3′-phosphate termini, a substrate that mimics one of the commonest types of oxidative SSB arising in cells (Figure 1A). The SSB also possesses a 5′-AMP and is therefore a substrate for ataxia. WT (wild-type) extracts efficiently removed AMP from 5′-termini and repaired the SSBs, as indicated by the respective appearance of ^{32}P-labelled 25-mer and 43-mer (Figure 1A, lanes 6–8). In contrast, however, AOA1 extracts did not (Figure 1A, lanes 3–5). It should be noted that SSBR is proficient in AOA1 extracts if the initial SSB lacks 5′-AMP ([28] and results not shown). A number of truncated oligonucleotide fragments were generated by non-specific nucleolytic activity in these experiments (see asterisks in Figure 1A), which is common in lymphoblastoid extracts, and which represent degradation of the 3′-terminus of the ^{32}P-labelled 25-mer. However, this activity did not account for the short-patch repair defect in AOA1 extracts, which was fully complemented by addition of recombinant ataxia (Figure 1A, lanes 9–11). The appearance of ligated product in these experiments was dependent upon

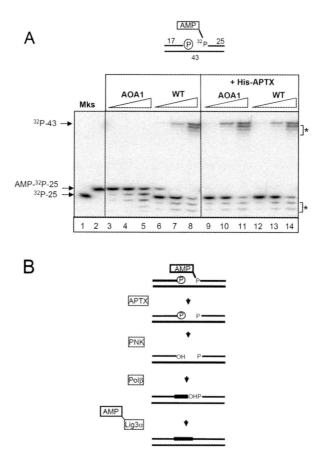

Figure 1. Ataxin-dependent short-patch SSBR of 5′-AMP SSBs in AOA1 lymphoblastoid extracts

(**A**) Defective short-patch SSBR in AOA1 extracts and its complementation by recombinant aprataxin. Upper panel: cartoon of the oligonucleotide duplex employed for these experiments containing a 1-bp gap, 3′-phosphate terminus and 5′-AMP terminus. The 5′-phosphate to which AMP is covalently linked is labelled with ^{32}P. The position of this label restricts the assay to measurements of short-patch repair events only. Numbers denote nucleotide lengths. Lower panel: 0.1, 1.0 or 5.0 μg of either WT (ConR2) or AOA1 (Ap5) extracts were incubated for 60 min at 30°C with ^{32}P-labelled 5′-AMP SSB substrate (25 nM) in the absence (left) or presence (right) of recombinant human aprataxin (APTX) (100 nM). Reaction products were fractionated and detected as described above. ^{32}P-labelled 25-mer containing (AMP-^{32}P-25) or lacking (^{32}P-25) 5′-AMP was fractionated in parallel for size markers (Mks). The position of repaired ^{32}P-labelled 43-mer (^{32}P-43) is also indicated. Non-specific nucleolytic products are indicated by an asterisk. (**B**) Cartoon of aprataxin-dependent short-patch repair of adenylated SSBs in WT cells. Reproduced from Molecular and Cellular Biology (2009), **29**, 1354–1362, doi:10.1128/MCB.01471-08 [28], with permission © 2009 American Society for Microbiology.

the presence of dNTPs, confirming that these experiments measured gap repair rather than ligation across the 1-bp gap (results not shown).

The predicted pathway for short-patch repair of SSBs harbouring 5′-AMP in WT cells is depicted in Figure 1(B). It was considered likely that this pathway

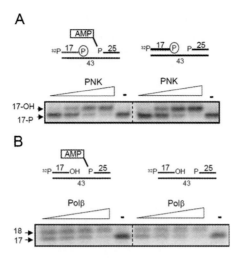

Figure 2. Removal of 5'-AMP by aprataxin is not required for end-processing by PNK or gap-filling by Polβ

(**A**) 5'-AMP does not affect processing of 3'-phosphate termini by PNK. SSB substrate (25 nM) lacking or containing 5'-AMP as indicated (upper panel) was incubated with 25, 50, 125 or 250 nM recombinant human PNK, or without PNK (-), for 1 h at 30 °C. Reaction products were fractionated by denaturing PAGE and detected by phosphorimaging. Note that the 5'-terminus of the 17-mer is labelled with ^{32}P in these experiments to allow detection of 3'-end processing. The position of the 17-mer harbouring the 3'-phosphate (17-P) or 3'-hydroxy group (3'-OH) is indicated. (**B**) 5'-AMP does not affect gap-filling by Polβ. SSB substrate (25 nM) lacking or containing 5'-AMP as indicated (upper panel) was incubated with 5, 15, 30 or 100 nM purified recombinant human Polβ, or without Polβ (-), for 1 h at 30 °C. Reaction products were fractionated by denaturing PAGE and detected by phosphorimaging. The positions of 17-mer and 18-mer are included as markers. Reproduced from Molecular and Cellular Biology (2009), **29**, 1354–1362, doi:10.1128/MCB.01471-08 [28], with permission ©️ 2009 American Society for Microbiology.

arrests in AOA1 extracts at the very beginning, before 3'-DNA end-processing by PNK and/or DNA gap-filling by Polβ (polymerase β), because the presence of AMP at the 5'-terminus might occlude access to the 3'-terminus. Surprisingly, however, the 3'-phosphatase activity of PNK was similar irrespective of whether or not the SSB possessed 5'-AMP, under conditions in which PNK was limiting (Figure 2A). Similar results were observed for DNA gap-filling by Polβ, with similar amounts of ^{32}P-labelled 17-mer converted into ^{32}P-labelled 18-mer, irrespective of the presence or absence of 5'-AMP (Figure 2B). These experiments suggested that neither PNK nor Polβ activity is affected by the presence of 5'-AMP at these time points, and thus short-patch SSBR might fail in AOA1 extracts at the final step of DNA ligation, resulting in the accumulation of adenylated DNA nicks. This was surprising, because adenylated DNA nicks are normal, indeed prerequisite, intermediates of DNA-ligation reactions, requiring only non-adenylated DNA ligase to reseal the breaks. We considered that DNA ligation might fail in AOA1 cell extracts because of insufficient levels of non-adenylated DNA ligase. This would be consistent with the notion that, although DNA ligases exist in both adenylated and non-adenylated states, the former predominates in cells because of the cellular concentration of ATP. This would not be a problem in WT cells, in which ataxin activity ensures that DNA nicks arising during SSBR are not pre-adenylated and are thus substrates for adenylated DNA ligase. However, in AOA1 cells, DNA nicks arise in a pre-adenylated state during SSBR and thus require non-adenylated DNA ligase. We thus suggest that, whereas all cells possess low levels of non-adenylated ligase, because of the rapid adenylation of free ligase molecules by cellular ATP, only in ataxin-defective cells do pre-adenylated nicks arise at a level sufficient to exceed the availability of non-adenylated ligase.

Evidence in support of this hypothesis arose when we compared WT and AOA1 extracts for their ability to ligate adenylated nicks. Whereas adenylated nicks were efficiently ligated by cell extract from WT cells, they remained largely unligated in reactions containing AOA1 cell extract (Figure 3A). To test our hypothesis further, we examined the impact of supplementing short-patch SSBR reactions in AOA1 cell extracts and $Aptx^{-/-}$ mouse neural astrocyte extracts with recombinant DNA ligase. Addition of T4 ligase restored short-patch SSBR efficiency in both AOA1 and $Aptx^{-/-}$ neural cell extract to a level similar to that observed in WT extract (Figure 3B, compare lanes 6 and 10). Importantly, complementation was more efficient in the absence of ATP than in its presence, supporting the notion that it was the non-adenylated subfraction of T4 ligase that was responsible for complementation (Figure 3B, compare lanes 8 and 10). The experiments described above suggested that short-patch repair of some adenylated SSBs can occur independently of ataxin if sufficient non-adenylated DNA ligase is available. To confirm this idea, we also attempted to reconstitute this ataxin-independent SSBR pathway using recombinant proteins. As expected, the repair of adenylated gaps by PNK, Polβ and Lig3α (DNA ligase IIIα) was dependent on ataxin in the presence of ATP, conditions under which Lig3α is largely adenylated (Figure 4). However, in the absence of ATP, short-patch repair of 5′-AMP SSBs occurred independently of ataxin. Taken together, these experiments indicate that short-patch repair arrests in AOA1 cell extracts at the final step of DNA ligation, owing to insufficient levels of non-adenylated DNA ligase.

The finding that adenylated nicks accumulate during short-patch SSBR in AOA1 provides a possible explanation for the normal rate of chromosomal SSBR observed in AOA1. This is because adenylated nicks can be channelled into long-patch SSBR. In this pathway, damaged 5′-termini are displaced as a single-stranded flap during gap-filling from the 3′-terminus and cleaved off by FEN1 (flap endonuclease-1) (reviewed in [29]). This process would not be detected by the short-patch repair assays employed in our recent work [28], because oligonucleotide duplexes of the type employed here are not good substrates for long-patch repair reactions and because cleavage of the single-strand flap would remove the ^{32}P label in our substrates. However, if long-patch repair can compensate for defective short-patch repair in AOA1 cells, then why do ataxin mutations result in disease? One possibility is that

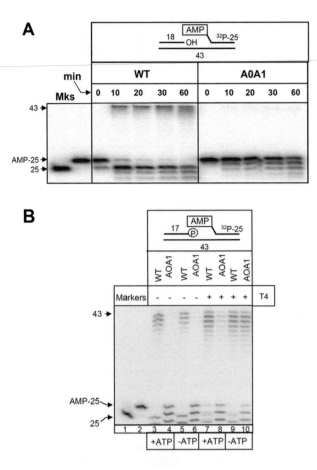

Figure 3. Short-patch SSBR fails in AOA1 due to insufficient levels of non-adenylated DNA ligase

(**A**) AOA1 extracts cannot efficiently ligate adenylated DNA nicks. Total WT (ConR2) or AOA1 (Ap5) lymphoblastoid cell extracts (6.25 μg) were incubated with ^{32}P-labelled adenylated nicked substrate (25 nM) (shown schematically in the upper panel) for the indicated time period at 30 °C. Reaction products were fractionated by denaturing PAGE and detected by phosphorimaging. ^{32}P-labelled 25-mer containing (AMP-25) or lacking (25) 5′-AMP were fractionated for size markers (Mks). The position of 43-mer ligated product (43) is indicated. (**B**) Complementation of the SSBR defect in AOA1 lymphoblastoid extracts by recombinant T4 DNA ligase. Total WT (ConR2) or AOA1 (Ap5) lymphoblastoid cell extracts (5 μg) were incubated with ^{32}P-labelled 5′-AMP SSB substrate (25 nM) (shown schematically in the upper panel) for 1 h at 30°C in the presence or absence of 1 mM ATP and/or 2 units of T4 DNA ligase, as indicated. Reaction products were fractionated by denaturing PAGE and detected by phosphorimaging. The positions of ^{32}P-labelled 43-mer reaction product (43) and ^{32}P-labelled 25-mer containing (AMP-25) or lacking (25) 5′-AMP are indicated. Reproduced from Molecular and Cellular Biology (2009), **29**, 1354–1362, doi:10.1128/MCB.01471-08 [28], with permission © 2009 American Society for Microbiology.

a subset of SSBs arise at which long-patch repair cannot operate. For example, it is possible that aprataxin is also required to repair specific types of damaged 3′-terminus [30]. Long-patch repair would be unable to operate at such breaks, because a 3′-hydroxy primer terminus is not available for DNA gap-filling.

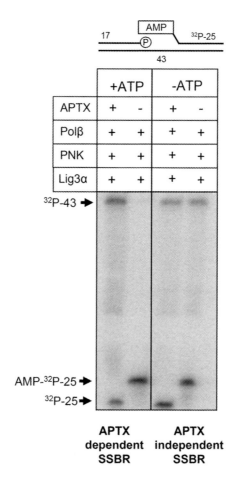

Figure 4. Reconstitution of aprataxin-independent SSBR with recombinant human proteins

Reconstitution of aprataxin-independent SSBR with recombinant human proteins. 5'-AMP SSB substrate (60 nM) (shown schematically above the gel) was incubated with 250 nM recombinant PNK, 100 nM Polβ and 80 nM Lig3α in the presence or absence of 100 nM aprataxin (APTX) and 1 mM ATP, as indicated, for 1 h at 30°C. Reaction products were fractionated by denaturing PAGE and detected by phosphorimaging. Reproduced from Molecular and Cellular Biology (2009), **29**, 1354–1362, doi:10.1128/MCB.01471-08 [28], with permission © 2009 American Society for Microbiology.

Alternatively, since aprataxin is associated with the DSBR machinery [6], it is possible that unrepaired double-strand breaks might account for AOA1. It should be noted, however, that we have so far failed to detect a DSBR defect in AOA1 or *Aptx*$^{-/-}$ cells (S. F. EI-Khamisy and K.W. Caldecott, unpublished work). Finally, it is possible that long-patch repair is not operative or is attenuated in the specific cell types that are affected in AOA1. For example, a number of replication-associated proteins, including several of those implicated in long-patch repair, are down-regulated in certain differentiated cell types [31].

Funding

This work was funded by the Medical Research Council [grant numbers G0600776 and G0400959], the Biotechnology and Biological Sciences Research Council [grant number C516595] and the European Community [Integrated Project DNA repair grant LSHG-CT-2005-512113] (to K.W.C.). S.F.E. was funded partly by the Wellcome Trust [grant number 085284].

References

1. Le Ber, I., Moreira, M.C., Rivaud-Pechoux, S., Chamayou, C., Ochsner, F., Kuntzer, T., Tardieu, M., Said, G., Habert, M.O., Demarquay, G. et al. (2003) Cerebellar ataxia with oculomotor apraxia type 1: clinical and genetic studies. Brain **126**, 2761–2772

2. Baba, Y., Uitti, R.J., Boylan, K.B., Uehara, Y., Yamada, T., Farrer, M.J., Couchon, E., Batish, S.D. & Wszolek, Z.K. (2006) Ataxin (*APTX*) gene mutations resembling multiple system atrophy. Parkinsonism Relat. Disord. **13**, 139–142

3. Quinzii, C.M., Kattah, A.G., Naini, A., Akman, H.O., Mootha, V.K., DiMauro, S. & Hirano, M. (2005) Coenzyme Q deficiency and cerebellar ataxia associated with an aprataxin mutation. Neurology **64**, 539–541

4. Le Ber, I., Dubourg, O., Benoist, J.F., Jardel, C., Mochel, F., Koenig, M., Brice, A., Lombes, A. & Durr, A. (2007) Muscle coenzyme Q10 deficiencies in ataxia with oculomotor apraxia 1. Neurology **68**, 295–297

5. Moreira, M.C., Barbot, C., Tachi, N., Kozuka, N., Mendonca, P., Barros, J., Coutinho, P., Sequeiros, J. & Koenig, M. (2001) Homozygosity mapping of Portuguese and Japanese forms of ataxia-oculomotor apraxia to 9p13, and evidence for genetic heterogeneity. Am. J. Hum. Genet. **68**, 501–508

6. Clements, P.M., Breslin, C., Deeks, E.D., Byrd, P.J., Ju, L., Bieganowski, P., Brenner, C., Moreira, M.C., Taylor, A.M. & Caldecott, K.W. (2004) The ataxia-oculomotor apraxia 1 gene product has a role distinct from ATM and interacts with the DNA strand break repair proteins XRCC1 and XRCC4. DNA Repair **3**, 1493–1502

7. Date, H., Onodera, O., Tanaka, H., Iwabuchi, K., Uekawa, K., Igarashi, S., Koike, R., Hiroi, T., Yuasa, T., Awaya, Y. et al. (2001) Early-onset ataxia with ocular motor apraxia and hypoalbuminemia is caused by mutations in a new HIT superfamily gene. Nat. Genet. **29**, 184–188

8. Moreira, M.C., Barbot, C., Tachi, N., Kozuka, N., Uchida, E., Gibson, T., Mendonca, P., Costa, M., Barros, J., Yanagisawa, T. et al. (2001) The gene mutated in ataxia-ocular apraxia 1 encodes the new HIT/Zn-finger protein aprataxin. Nat. Genet. **29**, 189–193

9. Caldecott, K.W. (2003) DNA single-strand break repair and spinocerebellar ataxia. Cell **112**, 7–10

10. Luo, H., Chan, D.W., Yang, T., Rodriguez, M., Chen, B.P., Leng, M., Mu, J.J., Chen, D., Songyang, Z., Wang, Y. & Qin, J. (2004) A new XRCC1-containing complex and its role in cellular survival of methyl methanesulfonate treatment. Mol. Cell. Biol. **24**, 8356–8365

11. Date, H., Igarashi, S., Sano, Y., Takahashi, T., Takahashi, T., Takano, H., Tsuji, S., Nishizawa, M. & Onodera, O. (2004) The FHA domain of aprataxin interacts with the C-terminal region of XRCC1. Biochem. Biophys. Res. Commun. **325**, 1279–1285

12. Gueven, N., Becherel, O.J., Kijas, A.W., Chen, P., Howe, O., Rudolph, J.H., Gatti, R., Date, H., Onodera, O., Taucher-Scholz, G. & Lavin, M.F. (2004) Aprataxin, a novel protein that protects against genotoxic stress. Hum. Mol. Genet. **13**, 1081–1093

13. Sano, Y., Date, H., Igarashi, S., Onodera, O., Oyake, M., Takahashi, T., Hayashi, S., Morimatsu, M., Takahashi, H., Makifuchi, T. et al. (2004) Aprataxin, the causative protein for EAOH is a nuclear protein with a potential role as a DNA repair protein. Ann. Neurol. **55**, 241–249

14. Loizou, J.I., El-Khamisy, S.F., Zlatanou, A., Moore, D.J., Chan, D.W., Qin, J., Sarno, S., Meggio, F., Pinna, L.A. & Caldecott, K.W. (2004) The protein kinase CK2 facilitates repair of chromosomal DNA single-strand breaks. *Cell* **117**, 17–28

15. Iles, N., Rulten, S., El-Khamisy, S.F. & Caldecott, K.W. (2007) APLF (C2orf13) is a novel human protein involved in the cellular response to chromosomal DNA strand breaks. *Mol. Cell. Biol.* **27**, 3793–3803

16. Kanno, S., Kuzuoka, H., Sasao, S., Hong, Z., Lan, L., Nakajima, S. & Yasui, A. (2007) A novel human AP endonuclease with conserved zinc-finger-like motifs involved in DNA strand break responses. *EMBO J.* **26**, 2094–2103

17. Bekker-Jensen, S., Fugger, K., Danielsen, J.R., Gromova, I., Sehested, M., Celis, J., Bartek, J., Lukas, J. & Mailand, N. (2007) Human Xip1 (C2orf13) is a novel regulator of cellular responses to DNA strand breaks. *J. Biol. Chem.* **282**, 19638–19643

18. Koch, C.A., Agyei, R., Galicia, S., Metalnikov, P., O'Donnell, P., Starostine, A., Weinfeld, M. & Durocher, D. (2004) Xrcc4 physically links DNA end processing by polynucleotide kinase to DNA ligation by DNA ligase IV. *EMBO J.* **23**, 3874–3885

19. Becherel, O.J., Gueven, N., Birrell, G.W., Schreiber, V., Suraweera, A., Jakob, B., Taucher-Scholz, G. & Lavin, M.F. (2006) Nucleolar localization of aprataxin is dependent on interaction with nucleolin and on active ribosomal DNA transcription. *Hum. Mol. Genet.* **15**, 2239–2249

20. Seidle, H.F., Bieganowski, P. & Brenner, C. (2005) Disease-associated mutations inactivate AMP-lysine hydrolase activity of Aprataxin. *J. Biol. Chem.* **280**, 20927–20931

21. Hirano, M., Asai, H., Kiriyama, T., Furiya, Y., Iwamoto, T., Nishiwaki, T., Yamamoto, A., Mori, T. & Ueno, S. (2007) Short half-lives of ataxia-associated aprataxin proteins in neuronal cells. *Neurosci. Lett.* **419**, 184–187

22. Criscuolo, C., Mancini, P., Menchise, V., Sacca, F., De Michele, G., Banfi, S. & Filla, A. (2005) Very late onset in ataxia oculomotor apraxia type I. *Ann. Neurol.* **57**, 777

23. Criscuolo, C., Mancini, P., Sacca, F., De Michele, G., Monticelli, A., Santoro, L., Scarano, V., Banfi, S. & Filla, A. (2004) Ataxia with oculomotor apraxia type 1 in Southern Italy: late onset and variable phenotype. *Neurology* **63**, 2173–2175

24. Tranchant, C., Fleury, M., Moreira, M.C., Koenig, M. & Warter, J.M. (2003) Phenotypic variability of aprataxin gene mutations. *Neurology* **60**, 868–870

25. Kijas, A.W., Harris, J.L., Harris, J.M. & Lavin, M.F. (2006) Aprataxin forms a discrete branch in the HIT (histidine triad) superfamily of proteins with both DNA/RNA binding and nucleotide hydrolase activities. *J. Biol. Chem.* **281**, 13939–13948

26. Ahel, I., Rass, U., El-Khamisy, S.F., Katyal, S., Clements, P.M., McKinnon, P.J., Caldecott, K.W. & West, S.C. (2006) The neurodegenerative disease protein aprataxin resolves abortive DNA ligation intermediates. *Nature* **443**, 713–716

27. Rass, U., Ahel, I. & West, S.C. (2007) Actions of aprataxin in multiple DNA repair pathways. *J. Biol. Chem.* **282**, 9469–9474

28. Reynolds, J.J., El-Khamisy, S.F., Katyal, S., Clements, P., McKinnon, P.J. & Caldecott, K.W. (2009) Defective DNA ligation during short-patch single-strand break repair in ataxia oculomotor apraxia-1. *Mol. Cell. Biol.* **29**, 1354–1362

29. Fortini, P. & Dogliotti, E. (2007) Base damage and single-strand break repair: mechanisms and functional significance of short- and longpatch repair subpathways. *DNA Repair* **6**, 398–409

30. Takahashi, T., Tada, M., Igarashi, S., Koyama, A., Date, H., Yokoseki, A., Shiga, A., Yoshida, Y., Tsuji, S., Nishizawa, M. & Onodera, O. (2007) Aprataxin, causative gene product for EAOH/AOA1, repairs DNA single-strand breaks with damaged 3′-phosphate and 3′-phosphoglycolate ends. *Nucleic Acids Res.* **35**, 3797–3809

31. Narciso, L., Fortini, P., Pajalunga, D., Franchitto, A., Liu, P., Degan, P., Frechet, M., Demple, B., Crescenzi, M. & Dogliotti, E. (2007) Terminally differentiated muscle cells are defective in base excision DNA repair and hypersensitive to oxygen injury. *Proc. Natl. Acad. Sci. U.S.A.* **104**, 17010–17015

Biochem. Soc. Symp. 76
Citation reference: Biochem. Soc. Trans. (2009) **37**, 583–588.

9

A molecular model for drug binding to tandem repeats of telomeric G-quadruplexes

Shozeb M. Haider and Stephen Neidle[1]

CRUK Biomolecular Structure Group, The School of Pharmacy, University of London, 29–39 Brunswick Square, London, WC1N 1AX, U.K.

Abstract

The extreme 3′-ends of human telomeres consist of 150–250 nucleotides of single-stranded DNA sequence together with associated proteins. Small-molecule ligands can compete with these proteins and induce a conformational change in the DNA to a four-stranded quadruplex arrangement, which is also no longer a substrate for the telomerase enzyme. The modified telomere ends provide signals to the DNA-damage-response system and trigger senescence and apoptosis. Experimental structural data are available on such quadruplex complexes comprising up to four telomeric DNA repeats, but not on longer systems that are more directly relevant to the single-stranded overhang in human cells. The present paper reports on a molecular modelling study that uses Molecular Dynamics simulation methods to build dimer and tetramer quadruplex repeats. These incorporate ligand-binding sites and are models for overhang–ligand complexes.

[1] *To whom correspondence should be addressed
(email stephen.neidle@pharmacy.ac.uk).*

Background

Telomeric DNA is the non-coding DNA at the ends of eukaryotic chromosomes that protects the genome from degradation, chromosomal end-to-end fusion and recombination [1]. The inability of DNA polymerase to fully replicate telomeric DNA results in progressive telomere shortening in proliferating somatic cells until a point of critical shortening is reached, when cells enter irreversible growth arrest. Most cancer cells prevent shortening of telomeric DNA by adding hexanucleotide repeats to 3′-ends, utilizing the reverse transcriptase activity of the telomerase enzyme complex [2]. Telomerase expression is a key marker of cellular immortalization and has been observed in 80–85% of cancer cells [3]. The extreme 150–250 nucleotides at the 3′-end of telomeric DNA are single-stranded, and appropriate small-molecule ligands can induce the formation of higher-order folded DNA structures [4–6]. These can inhibit telomerase activity, since elongation and catalysis require a single-stranded DNA substrate for effective hybridization by the RNA subunit of the telomerase complex, leading to telomere shortening and cell death in neoplastic cells. In order to form higher-order DNA, the small molecules compete with the single-strand-binding protein POT1 (protection of telomeres 1) and with the end-capping function of telomerase [7,8]. Their displacement rapidly leads a DNA-damage-response signal, which can be detected, for example by γ-H2AX (phosphorylated histone H2AX) [9]. This in turn activates apoptotic pathways. This approach is currently of interest as a selective therapeutic strategy in human cancer.

Human telomeric DNA comprises tandem repeats of the sequence d(TTAGGG). The formation of higher-order structures in the single-stranded telomeric DNA overhang is a consequence of the ability of a guanine base to form hydrogen-bonding interactions on both its Watson–Crick and Hoogsteen faces [10–12]. This enables guanines to readily self-associate to form a highly stable structural motif involving four guanines held together via eight Hoogsteen hydrogen bonds in a co-planar array, termed a G-quartet. Several G-quartets can stack on top of another, to form a four-stranded G-quadruplex arrangement, with the G-quartets held together by nucleotides from the sequences that occur between each G-tract. Quadruplexes can be formed by the folding of a single contiguous sequence containing multiple G-tracts (unimolecular) or by the association of two or four separate strands (bi- or tetra-molecular). They are stabilized by extensive π–π stacking non-bonded attractive interactions between each G-quartet together with the involvement of alkali metal ions (K^+ and Na^+). These are localized in the central channel of G-quadruplexes and co-ordinate to O6 atoms of the guanines in a bipyramidal prismatic arrangement.

G-quadruplexes can be highly polymorphic, adopting a variety of folds, especially when the loops are 3–4 nt. Several distinct structural topologies of G-quadruplexes have been identified using NMR and X-ray crystallography including those from human telomeric DNA [13–17] and *Oxytricha nova* telomeric DNA [18]. Strand polarity depends in large part upon the nature and length of the loop sequences intervening between the G-tracts. Crystallographic analyses of a human telomeric bimolecular quadruplex and a unimolecular quadruplex have revealed a topology with all strands parallel and propeller-like loops [13]. In contrast, several NMR studies on human telomeric unimolecular quadruplexes have shown distinct topologies involving mixed parallel and antiparallel (3+1) backbone arrangements [14–17]. No structural information is currently available on tandem repeats of quadruplexes (multimers) such as may be formed along the length of the single-stranded telomeric DNA overhang, although several models have been proposed [19,20].

There are only restricted structural data available to date on quadruplex–ligand complexes. Two categories of topologies have been found: (i) the bimolecular diagonal loop crossover topology from O. nova telomeric DNA in complexes with di-substituted acridines [18,21]; and (ii) the parallel-stranded propeller-loop topology from human telomeric DNA, observed in three bimolecular and one unimolecular complexes, with three very different types of ligand [22–24]. This suggests that a parallel topology is an appropriate starting point for models of higher-order quadruplex multimers with bound ligand, which may also provide insight into the structural requirements of the DNA-damage response. No NMR or crystallographic structures relevant to the human four-repeat unimolecular quadruplex have been observed to date with (3+1) structural features.

The starting point for the present study has been the 2.5 Å (1 Å = 0.1 nm) resolution G-quadruplex crystal structure complex with the experimental anticancer drug BRACO-19, a 3,6,9-tri-substituted acridine [8,25–27]. In this structure, the d(TAGGGTTAGGGT) sequence from human telomeric DNA forms a bimolecular, parallel-stranded, propeller-loop topology as observed in the native uni- and bi-molecular structures [13]. The core of the drug complex structure consists of three G-quartets stacked on top of one another. The interspersed TTA loops, which are at the sides of the G-quartet core of the quadruplex, are oriented away from the quartet planes and connect the top of one strand with the bottom of the other, thereby maintaining the continuous parallel arrangement of the G-quadruplex. What differentiates this crystal structure from the native one is that there are two bimolecular quadruplexes in the biological unit. The drug molecule is asymmetrically sandwiched between the two quadruplexes, with one acridine face stacked on to a 5′-TATA tetrad at the interface (formed by the flipping-in of appropriate nucleotides from the ends and the loops). The other face is stacked on to one half of a G-quartet at the 3′-end. The 5′–3′ continuity of the two quadruplexes in the biological unit enables the ready construction of a higher-order model based on the scaffold observed in the crystal structure by means of molecular modelling. This has enabled a unimolecular model of the complex to be built, while retaining all the features present in the original crystal structure, using explicitly-solvated all-atom MD (Molecular Dynamics) simulation methods to obtain low-energy structures and relative free energies estimated using MM-PBSA (Molecular Mechanics and the Poisson–Boltzmann surface area approximation).

The multimer model-building procedure

The crystal structure of the human telomeric DNA bimolecular quadruplex complexed with BRACO-19 [24] was taken from the Protein Data Bank (PDB code 3CE5) and used as a scaffold for further molecular modelling. Since the basic unit is a bimolecular quadruplex, there are only two TTA loops per individual unit. The modelling methodology is analogous to that described previously [19].

The first step was to generate a unimolecular model for both of the units. The crystal structure of human telomeric DNA d[AG$_3$(T$_2$AG$_3$)$_3$] (PDB code 1KF1) was also used and the terminal adenine at the 5′ end of it removed (using the INSIGHT package) to generate a 21-mer. This was then superimposed on the individual units in the 3CE5 structure. The overall RMSD (root mean square deviation) of superimposition of the G-quartets was 0.48 and 0.41 Å for the top and bottom units respectively. The central G-quartets from 3CE5 were deleted and the new G-quartets from 1KF1 were superimposed on the old positions inserted into the units. An additional loop from the 1KF1 structure was also added to the unit. This resulted in one continuous unit consisting of 21 nucleotides. Both units in 3CE5 were replaced in this way. The two units were then joined by a TTA loop that was extracted from the 1KF1 crystal structure, to form a continuous 45-mer, i.e. a dimer of two unimolecular quadruplexes (Figure 1).

MD simulations

The final 45-mer was subjected to several rounds of molecular-mechanics energy minimization to relieve any steric clashes in the structure. K$^+$ ions are required to stabilize quadruplexes and are located between the G-quartets in a vertical alignment along the axis in the electronegative channel within the core. The cations were retained from the BRACO-19 complex crystal structure. One feature of this structure is that the two quadruplex units are offset with respect to each other and are inclined by approx. 30° in two directions [24]. As a result of this offset, the ion channel is discontinuous. This is, however, compensated for by the positively charged nitrogen atom at the centre of the acridine group in the ligand which is positioned on top of the channel (Figure 1b). The system was subjected to 10 ns of explicitly solvated MD using the Amber ff99sb and parmBsc0 force-fields for nucleic acids, as outlined previously [19]. Free energies were estimated employing the MM-PBSA method.

In order to retain the structural features of the 3CE5 crystal structure, modifications were carried out to the loops. This was based on previous observations that the TTA loops are highly flexible and can adopt several

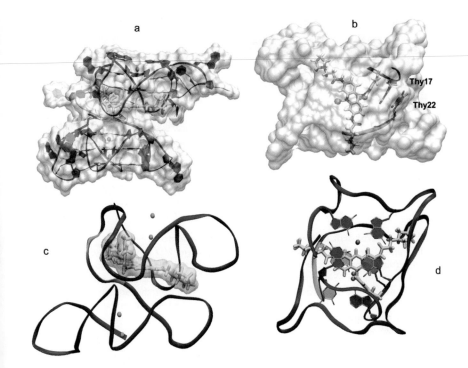

Figure 1. Four views of the model for a complex between the drug BRACO-19 and two contiguous G-quadruplexes

(**A**) Backbone representation of the overall structure. Backbone atoms contributed by guanines are coloured blue, bases from the loops are coloured red, and the connecting loop is coloured green. The ligand (BRACO-19) is coloured yellow, and the ions present in the central electronegative channel within the structure are shown as green balls. (**B**) Stacking arrangement in the 45-mer modelled structure. Thy[17] makes π-stacking interactions in the crystal structure, which is retained within the model and the free Thy[22] base is modelled to stack on top of Thy[17]. The ions are represented as orange balls, highlighting the discontinuous ion channel ending in the positively charged nitrogen group in the central acridine chromophore of the BRACO-19 molecule. The ion channel extends on the other side beginning from the positively charged nitrogen group at the 9 position of the ligand. (**C**) Snapshot of the 45-mer structure at the end of a 10 ns MD run. The structure is remarkably stable while retaining most of the features from the crystal structure. (**D**) Stacking arrangement of the ligand on the TATA tetrad and G-quartet at the interface between the two component quadruplexes. The guanines are coloured blue, bases from the loops are coloured red and those from the connector loop (residues 22–24) are coloured green. The BRACO-19 ligand is coloured yellow, and the ions in the structure are coloured orange.

conformations [19]. First, modifications were carried out to the first TTA loop (residues 4–6). The first thymine (Thy[4]) from the TTA loop flips back into the ligand-binding site and interacts with the ligand, making hydrogen bonds with the central nitrogen in the acridine chromophore and the amide nitrogen in one side chain. This arrangement has also been observed in the *O. nova* antiparallel bimolecular quadruplex crystal structures in complexes with di-substituted acridine ligands [18,21], where it functions to position the ligands in their binding site. As a result of this base flipping and thymine stacking

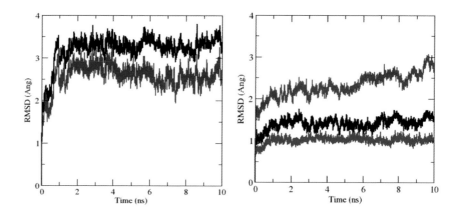

Figure 2. Structural drift observed during the MD simulation
Left: RMSD plot showing the stability of the model during the MD run. RMSD values calculated for all atoms (black) and backbone-only atoms (red) are plotted. Right: RMSD plot comparing the different segments in the 45-mer model. The G-quartets (blue) form the most stable segments in the model. The backbone-only atoms (black) and all atoms (red) from the loops are also illustrated. It is evident that the higher RMSD values observed for the model arise from the wobble exhibited by the free bases in the loops. Ang = Å

in the binding site, the loop connecting to the top of the next guanine run is now reduced to two bases (TA). The second loop is a conventional loop from the crystal structure with no modification to its conformation (TTA, residues 10–12). The first thymine (Thy^{16}) in the third loop is involved in the TATA tetrad. The second thymine (Thy^{17}) loops back in to form a π-stack with the anilino substituent group in the ligand. This structural feature was also retained from the crystal structure. The backbone atoms of Thy^{18} and Ade^{19} in this loop connect to the top of the G-quartet. The next TTA loop (residues 22–24) or the connector loop connects the top quadruplex unit (residues 1–21) to the bottom unit (residues 25–45). The first thymine (Thy^{22}) base in this connector loop forms π-stacking interactions with Thy^{17} (Figure 1b). The two following bases (Thy^{23} and Ade^{24}) contribute towards the TATA tetrad, while their backbone atoms link the two quadruplex units together. There are no modifications in the next loop (TTA, residues 28–30). Adenine from the next loop (Ade^{36}) is modified to stack and form the fourth base in the TATA tetrad (Thy^{16}–Ade^{36}–Thy^{23}–Ade^{24}).

Structural stability of the model

The conformational stability of the model can be assessed by measuring the RMSD over the course of an MD simulation. An unstable model with incorrect geometries, simulated at 300 K, loses its structural integrity. The overall RMSD for the all-atom model (black) and backbone-only atoms (red) are illustrated in Figure 2 (left-hand panel). An initial jump in RMSD value is observed within the first 1 ns of the simulation. This corresponds to the relaxation of

Table 1 RMSD values [for all-atoms and backbone (bb) calculations] and numbers of atoms in the simulated structures

		Environment			
Model	Timescale (ns)	DNA (bb)	Waters	RMSD (all) (Å)	RMSD (bb) (Å)
45-mer (+BRACO-19)	10	1463 (269) (+90)	23256	3.20	2.49
45-mer* (+BSU6039)	15	1463 (269) (+70)	22961	3.68	2.90

*Data from [19].

the starting model. The trajectory is eventually stabilized over the course of the simulation with relatively small fluctuations. The RMSD plot in Figure 2 (right-hand panel) highlights different segments in the model. The co-planar arrangement of guanines in a G-quartet (blue), held together by hydrogen bonds is the most stable segment of the model. There are very few differences in the RMSD values observed between an all-atom model and a backbone-only model for the G-quartets. The all-atom RMSD for the loops (red) is quite high; however, the backbone (black) RMSD of the loops are relatively stable. This clearly suggests that the higher RMSD is a result of the wobbling effect of the nucleotide bases. This correlates with our earlier study that suggested that the loops can rearrange to adopt multiple conformations [19]. Comparison has also been made with the model containing a ligand in its pseudo-intercalation site. The overall RMSD value is lower in the current model compared with the model containing the di-substituted acridine (Table 1). In the current model, thymine (Thy^4) from the first loop flips back and enters the binding site, making strong interactions with BRACO-19. The average Thy^4(O4)-BRA(N21) distance is 3.0 Å and Thy^4(N3)-BRA(N7) is 3.4 Å. These hydrogen-bonding interactions are maintained throughout the course of the simulation, and serve to position and hold the ligand tightly in the binding site, allowing it only limited movement. As a result of this, the ligand stacks on one half of the G-quartet and makes π-stacking interactions with a guanine tetrad on one face and a TATA tetrad on the other (Figure 1d). Both of these stacking platforms are extremely stable with RMSDs of 1.1 and 1.3 Å respectively. The hydrogen-bonding pattern in the TATA tetrad is also maintained with donor–acceptor distances averaging 3.1 Å over the course of the simulation. The TTA linker loop (residues 22–24) is highly stable. This is because two residues from this linker loop take part in the TATA tetrad formation. The other thymine (Thy^{22}) forms π-stacking interactions with Thy^{17}.

The G-quartets

The G-quartets in the 45-mer are extremely stable, with their hydrogen-bonding networks preserved throughout the course of the simulation. There are minor differences in hydrogen-bonding distances. The average N1–O6 distance is 3.00 Å and N2–N7 distance is 2.97 Å. This has increased by 0.14 and 0.15 Å respectively compared with those in the crystal structures. The G-quartet-stacking geometry in terms of rise and twist is also retained in the model. The individual quadruplex units have a quasi-helical repeat of 12 G-quartets per turn, similar to that present in the crystal structure [24].

Conformations of the TTA loops

Previous studies on quadruplex multimers [19] confirmed that TTA loops are the most flexible part of a quadruplex structure. The TTA propeller loops in a parallel-stranded topology are arranged externally, directed away from the G-quartets. They have been previously shown to be highly mobile and can readily adopt several distinct conformations [19]. In the current model, some of the TTA loops contribute towards the structural features within the core of the model, including π-stacking and formation of the TATA tetrad. One thymine base, Thy[4] in the first loop, is flipped back to interact with the ligand. This interaction is important in positioning the ligand in its binding site and is maintained throughout the course of the simulation. The backbone of the remaining two bases in the loop (Thy[5] and Ade[6]) connects the stacked Thy[4] to the guanines. The second loop has no structural modifications and exhibits dynamics similar to that observed in our previous quadruplex modelling studies [19], where stabilization of the loop coming from hydrogen-binding interactions of the central thymine with adjacent adenine and thymine. The first thymine in the third loop (Thy[16]) contributes to the TATA tetrad. The second thymine in this loop (Thy[17]) is arranged such that the base forms a π-stack with the anilino group in the side chain of BRACO-19, a feature observed in the crystal structure and is retained in the model. This structural arrangement is lost after approx. 2.2 ns, and the thymine base no longer makes stacking interactions with the anilino side chain of the ligand. Similarly to loop 1, the backbone atoms in thymine/adenine link the stacked thymine to the top of the next guanine run.

The next loop is the connector loop (residues 22–24) that joins the two individual quadruplex units together. Thy[22], which stacks on Thy[17], also loses its π-stacking arrangement at approx. 2 ns and does not contribute towards any interactions for the remainder of the simulation. The loss of π-stacking interactions between Thy[17], Thy[22] and the anilino group can be attributed to the flexibility of the anilino side chain at the 9 position in the ligand combined with the restraints on the bases set while constructing the model. The next loop in the next quadruplex unit (TTA, residues 28–30) was added to the model without any modifications. However, during the course of the simulation, it adopts a conformation which is reminiscent of those seen in our previous work, where the loops extend outwards away from the quartets [19]. Similar dynamics behaviour is also observed for the two thymines (Thy[34] and Thy[35]) in the next

Table 2 RMSD values and relative energies (kcal/mol, where 1 kcal = 4.184 kJ) for the backbone atoms in the loops

Segment (residues)	RMSD (Å)	Relative energy (kcal/mol)
Loop 1 (4–6)	2.12 (1.04)	− 369.30
Loop 2 (10–12)	2.41 (1.67)	− 359.51
Loop 3 (16–18)	2.28 (1.28)	− 362.83
Connecting loop (22–24)	2.47 (1.36)	− 358.49
Loop 4 (28–30)	2.17 (1.04)	− 368.76
Loop 5 (34–36)	2.10 (1.04)	− 368.91
Loop 6 (40–42)	1.84 (0.95)	− 372.75
TATA tetrad (16,23,24,36)	1.33 (1.10)	− 452.14
GGGG stacking quartet (3,9,15,21)	1.10 (1.31)	− 710.67

loop (TTA, residues 34–36), where they stack on top of one another during the simulation. Ade[35] is stacked to complete the TATA tetrad. The last loop (TTA, residues 40–42) adopts a conformation similar to that observed in the original crystal structure.

Estimated energies can provide relative semi-quantitative indications of the stability of the model and its components. Models with lower energies are expected to be more stable than those with higher values. We have calculated free energies of the TATA tetrad, GGGG stacking tetrad and the loops to identify the individual contributions of these segments. The values are summarized in Table 2, and demonstrate that there are some differences in the stability of the loops, with the connecting loop having the highest energy of the seven loops in the structure. The energies correlate well with RSMD values.

Conclusions

Molecular modelling has shown that a stereochemically plausible and stable structure can be readily constructed for two parallel-topology G-quadruplexes with a drug-binding site at the interface between them. The process has been straightforwardly extended to form a structure with four quadruplexes (Figure 3). In this, the two central quadruplexes do not have a bound drug at their interface, so the channel of K$^+$ ions is continuous. The pattern of external TTA loops is evident along the length of this gently writhing superhelix. It is tempting to suggest that these loops can act as recognition features and play a role in the quadruplex recognition of telomere-associated proteins such as poly(ADP-ribose) polymerase-1 [28] and in the DNA-damage response to the loss of telomere-capping proteins [9].

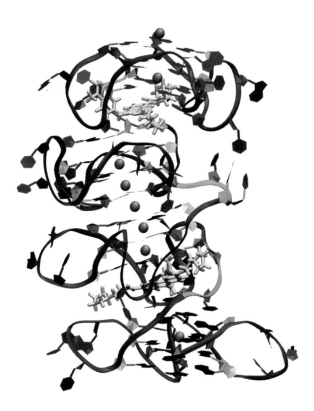

Figure 3. A 93-mer model comprising four quadruplex units and two bound BRACO-19 molecules, constructed from two 45-mer units

Funding

This work was supported by Cancer Research UK [programme grant C129/A4489].

References

1. Cech, T.R. (2000) Life at the end of the chromosome: telomeres and telomerase. *Angew. Chem. Int. Ed.* **39**, 34–43
2. Oganesian, L. & Bryan, T.M. (2007) Physiological relevance of telomeric G-quadruplex formation: a potential drug target. *BioEssays* **29**, 155–165
3. de Cian, A., Lacroix, L., Douarre, C., Temime-Smaali, N., Trentesaux, C., Riou, J.-F. & Mergny, J.-L. (2008) Targeting telomeres and telomerase. *Biochimie* **90**, 131–155
4. Sun, D., Thompson, B., Cathers, B.E., Salazar, M., Kerwin, S.M., Trent, J.O., Jenkins, T.C., Neidle, S. & Hurley, L.H. (1997) Inhibition of human telomerase by a G-quadruplex-interactive compound. *J. Med. Chem.* **40**, 2113–2116
5. Monchaud, D. & Teulade-Fichou, M.P. (2008) A hitchhiker's guide to G-quadruplex ligands. *Org. Biomol. Chem.* **6**, 627–636
6. Ou, T., Lu, Y., Tan, J., Huang, Z., Wong, K. & Gu, L. (2008) G-quadruplexes: targets in anticancer drug design. *ChemMedChem* **3**, 690–713

7.   Gomez, D., O'Donohue, M.F., Wenner, T., Douarre, C., Macadré, J., Koebel, P., Giraud-Panis, M.J., Kaplan, H., Kolkes, A., Shin-ya, K. & Riou, J.-F. (2006) The G-quadruplex ligand telomestatin inhibits pot1 binding to telomeric sequences *in vitro* and induces GFP–POT1 dissociation from telomeres in human cells. *Cancer Res.* **66**, 6908–6912

8.   Gunaratnam, M., Greciano, O., Martins, C., Reszka, A.P., Schultes, C.M., Morjani, H., Riou, J.-F. & Neidle, S. (2007) Mechanism of acridine-based telomerase inhibition and telomere shortening. *Biochem. Pharmacol.* **74**, 679–689

9.   Rodriquez, R., Müller, S., Yeoman, J.A., Trentesaux, C., Riou, J.-F. & Balasubramanian, S. (2008) A novel small molecule that alters shelterin integrity and triggers a DNA-damage response at telomeres. *J. Am. Chem. Soc.* **130**, 15758–15759

10. Davies, J.T. (2004) G-quartets 40 years later: from 5′-GMP to molecular biology and supramolecular chemistry. *Angew. Chem. Int. Ed.* **43**, 668–698

11. Burge, S.E., Parkinson, G.N., Hazel, P., Todd, A.K. & Neidle, S. (2006) Quadruplex DNA: sequence, topology and structure. *Nucleic Acids Res.* **34**, 5402–5415

12. Patel, D.J., Phan, A.T. & Kuryavyi, V. (2007) Human telomere, oncogenic promoter and 5′-UTR G-quadruplexes: diverse higher order DNA and RNA targets for cancer therapeutics. *Nucleic Acids Res.* **35**, 7429–7455

13. Parkinson, G.N., Lee, M.P.H. & Neidle, S. (2002) Crystal structure of parallel quadruplexes from human telomeric DNA. *Nature* **417**, 876–880

14. Phan, A.T., Luu, K.N. & Patel, D.J. (2006) Different loop arrangements of intramolecular human telomeric (3+1) G-quadruplexes in K$^+$ solution. *Nucleic Acids Res.* **34**, 5715–5719

15. Phan, A.T., Kuryavyi, V., Luu, K.N. & Patel, D.J. (2007) Structure of two intramolecular G-quadruplexes formed by natural human telomere sequences in K+ solution. *Nucleic Acids Res.* **35**, 6517–6525

16. Ambrus, A., Chen, D., Dai, J., Bialis, T., Jones, R.A. & Yang, D. (2006) Human telomeric sequence forms a hybrid-type intramolecular G-quadruplex structure with mixed parallel/antiparallel strands in potassium solution. *Nucleic Acids Res.* **34**, 2723–2735

17. Dai, J., Carver, M., Punchihewa, C., Jones, R.A. & Yang, D. (2007) Structure of the hybrid-2 type intramolecular human telomeric G-quadruplex in K$^+$ solution: insights into structure polymorphism of the human telomeric sequence. *Nucleic Acids Res.* **35**, 4927–4740

18. Haider, S.M., Parkinson, G.N. & Neidle, S. (2003) Structure of a G-quadruplex-ligand complex. *J. Mol. Biol.* **326**, 117–125

19. Haider, S, Parkinson, G.N. & Neidle, S. (2008) Molecular dynamics and principal components analysis of human telomeric quadruplex multimers. *Biophys. J.* **95**, 296–311

20. Petraccone, L., Trent, J.O. & Chaires, J.B. (2008) The tail of the telomere. *J. Am. Chem. Soc.* **120**, 16530–16532

21. Campbell, N.H., Patel, M., Tofa, A., Ghosh, R., Parkinson, G.N. & Neidle, S. (2009) Selectivity in ligand recognition of G-quadruplex loops. *Biochemistry* **48**, 1675–1680

22. Parkinson, G.N., Ghosh, R. & Neidle, S. (2007) Structural basis for binding of porphyrin to human telomeres. *Biochemistry* **46**, 2390–2397

23. Parkinson, G.N., Cuenca, F. & Neidle, S. (2008) Topology conservation and loop flexibility in quadruplex-drug recognition: crystal structures of inter- and intramolecular telomeric DNA quadruplex–drug complexes. *J. Mol. Biol.* **381**, 1145–1156

24. Campbell, N.H., Parkinson, G.N., Reszka, A.P. & Neidle, S. (2008) Structural basis of DNA quadruplex recognition by an acridine drug. *J. Am. Chem. Soc.* **130**, 6722–6724

25. Read, M., Harrison, R.J., Romagnoli, B., Tanious, F.A., Gowan, S.H., Reszka, A.P., Wilson, W.D., Kelland, L.R. & Neidle, S. (2001) Structure-based design of selective and potent G quadruplex-mediated telomerase inhibitors. *Proc. Natl. Acad. Sci. U.S.A.* **98**, 4844–4849

26. Moore, M.J., Schultes, C.M., Cuesta, J., Cuenca, F., Gunaratnam, M., Tanious, F.A., Wilson, W.D. & Neidle, S. (2006) Trisubstituted acridines as G-quadruplex telomere targeting agents: effects of extensions of the 3,6- and 9-side chains on quadruplex binding, telomerase activity, and cell proliferation. *J. Med. Chem.* **49**, 582–599

27. Burger, A.M., Dai, F., Schultes, C.M., Reszka, A.P., Moore, M.J., Double, J.A. & Neidle, S. (2005) The G-quadruplex-interactive molecule BRACO-19 inhibits tumor growth, consistent with telomere targeting and interference with telomerase function. *Cancer Res.* **65**, 1489–1496

28. Soldatenkov, V.A., Vetcher, A.A., Duka, T. & Ladame, S. (2008) First evidence of a functional interaction between DNA quadruplexes and poly(ADP-ribose) polymerase-1. *ACS Chem. Biol.* **3**, 214–219

Biochem. Soc. Symp. 76
Citation reference: Biochem. Soc. Trans. (2009) **37**, 589–595.

10

The role of recombination in telomere length maintenance

Nicola J. Royle[1], Aarón Méndez-Bermúdez,
Athanasia Gravani, Clara Novo, Jenny Foxon,
Jonathan Williams, Victoria Cotton and
Alberto Hidalgo

*Department of Genetics, University of Leicester, University Road,
Leicester LE1 7RH, U.K.*

Abstract

Human telomeres shorten during each cell division, predominantly because of incomplete DNA replication. This eventually results in short uncapped telomeres that elicit a DNA-damage response, leading to cellular senescence. However, evasion of senescence results in continued cell division and telomere erosion ultimately results in genome instability. In the long term, this genome instability is not sustainable, and cancer cells activate a TMM (telomere maintenance mechanism), either expression of telomerase or activation of the ALT (alternative lengthening of telomeres) pathway. Activation of the ALT mechanism results in deregulation of recombination-based activities at telomeres. Thus ALT+ cells show elevated T-SCE (telomere sister-chromatid exchange), misprocessing of t-loops that cap chromosomes and recombination-based processes between telomeres or between telomeres and ECTRs (extrachromosomal telomeric repeats). Some or all of these processes underlie the chaotic telomere length maintenance that allows cells in ALT+ tumours un-limited replicative capacity. ALT activation is also associated with destabilization

[1] To whom correspondence should be addressed (email njr@le.ac.uk).

of a minisatellite, MS32. The connection between the minisatellite instability and the deregulation of recombination-based activity at telomeres is not understood, but analysis of the minisatellite can be used as a marker for ALT. It is known that telomere length maintenance in ALT+ cells is dependent on the MRN [MRE11 (meiotic recombination 11)–Rad50–NBS1 (Nijmegen breakage syndrome 1)] complex, but knowledge of the role of other genes, including the Werner's (*WRN*) and Bloom's (*BLM*) syndrome DNA helicase genes, is still limited.

Introduction to human telomeres

Human telomeric DNA comprises tandem arrays of the consensus sequence TTAGGG that is oriented 5′→3′ towards the terminus. The majority of the telomeric DNA is double-stranded, but at the terminus, the G-rich strand is longer than the C-rich strand, producing a 3′ single-stranded overhang of 100–300 nt. The double-stranded portion of the telomere varies in length (2–20 kb) between chromosome ends within a cell, between cells and between tissues (Figure 1a). A major contributor to the variation in telomere length is the inability of the cell to fully replicate a linear chromosome during lagging strand synthesis. In addition, other factors that damage telomeric DNA (such as oxidative damage) contribute to telomere length dynamics, but these events tend to be stochastic in nature. At the start of human telomere repeat arrays, there is often a region that contains DNA-sequence-variant repeats (such as TGAGGG, TCAGGG and TTGGGG) interspersed with consensus TTAGGG repeats [1–4]. The portion of the telomere that includes divergent repeats is variable, but, when present, these variant repeats are not usually found beyond 3 kb into the repeat array. The distribution of variant and TTAGGG repeats within these regions is highly variable between alleles (at a single telomere) within a population, which implies that there is a high underlying mutation rate. Consequently, these variable regions have been used as a tool to study mutation processes that operate on telomeric DNA [5,6].

The origin of the degenerate repeats is unknown, but it is likely that they arise from single base mutation events and, once present, the variant repeats can be propagated within the telomere primarily by intra-allelic processes such as slippage during replication or unequal sister-chromatid exchange. Population and pedigree analysis support the hypothesis that germline turnover of repeats within the proximal portion of the telomere is driven by intra-allelic processes, although rare recombination or conversion events cannot be excluded [2–4].

DNA damage and repair

The normal cellular response to damage that creates a DSB (double-strand break) in the DNA is cell-cycle arrest that can lead to repair of the DSB via NHEJ (non-homologous end-joining) or HRR (homologous recombination repair). The decision as to which repair pathway is selected is complex, but is partly

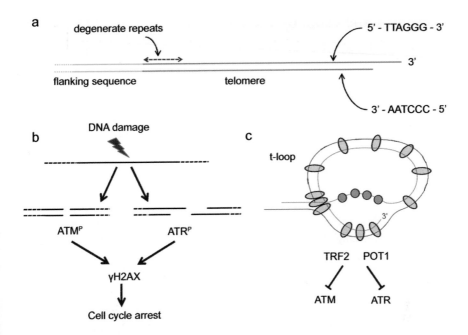

Figure 1. Telomere and avoidance of a DNA-damage response
(a) Representation of sequence organization in human telomeres. (b) Response to DNA damage located at an internal site on a chromosome. (c) Telomere capping is achieved via the shelterin complex of proteins bound to telomeric DNA. The presence of the TRF2 protein at telomeres inhibits the activation of ATM, whereas POT1 inhibits the activation of ATR.

dependent on the availability of a homologous sequence that can act as a template. Thus NHEJ is favoured in G_1- and early S-phase, whereas HRR is favoured during S- or G_2-phases of the cell cycle when sister chromatids are available [7,8]. When damage is detected at an internal location in the chromosome, a DNA-damage-response pathway is activated and orchestrated primarily through two serine/threonine protein kinases, ATM (ataxia telangiectasia mutated) and ATR (ATM- and Rad3-related). The current consensus is that ATM responds to damage that creates DNA DSBs (such as the damage caused by ionizing radiation), whereas ATR responds to the presence of single-stranded DNA (as might be generated if a replication fork stalls) [9]. Following recognition of these DNA lesions, ATM or ATR are activated by autophosphorylation and this results in the phosphorylation of histone H2AX on Ser^{139} in a large region of chromatin around the DNA damage site (Figure 1b). Subsequently, many other proteins are recruited to the damaged site and this facilitates the repair of the DNA damage. Coincident with the formation of DNA-damage foci, the cell cycle is arrested via ATM- or ATR-mediated activation of checkpoint kinases (Chk1 or Chk2), leading to activation of p53 (encoded by *TP53*) and expression of CDKN1A (cyclin-dependent kinase inhibitor 1A) (also known as p21) [8,9].

Telomeres and capping

The ends of human chromosomes must not be recognized as DNA DSBs, because inappropriate repair via NHEJ or HRR would cause chromosome and genome instability. Therefore a primary function of telomeres is to cap chromosomes, and the shelterin protein complex is essential for this capping function. Shelterin is composed of six proteins that only function at telomeres, but it can recruit a wide variety of other proteins to the telomere. Three of the shelterin components bind directly to telomeric DNA. The *TRF1* and *TRF2* genes (encoding telomeric-repeat-binding factor 1 and 2 respectively) are evolutionarily related and encode proteins that bind to double-stranded TTAGGG repeats as homodimers via their Myb DNA-binding domains [8]. The TRF2 protein preferentially binds at the end of the duplex telomeric repeats, adjacent to the single-stranded G-overhang. The single human *POT1* (protection of telomeres 1) gene [10] encodes a protein that binds to the TTAGGG single-stranded DNA via its two OB (oligonucleotide/oligosaccharide-binding)-fold domains. The three other protein components of shelterin [encoded by *RAP1* (repressor activator protein 1), *TPP1* (a POT1-binding partner) and *TIN2* (TRF1-interacting nuclear factor 2)] interact with one or several of the telomere DNA-binding proteins. Thus human Rap1 binds to TRF2, TPP1 interacts with POT1, and TIN2 is able to connect with all three DNA–binding proteins as it interacts directly with TRF1 and TRF2 and with POT1 via its interaction with TPP1 [8]. All of the shelterin components are essential for correct capping and telomere length regulation, as disruption of any of them results in altered telomere length dynamics.

Besides binding to duplex telomeric repeats, TRF1 and TRF2 can bend the DNA, thus forming loop structures [11]. The structures observed indicate that the G-rich single-stranded overhang inserts into the duplex DNA and pairs with the C-strand at the point of insertion, forming a D-loop. Moreover, TRF2 is required for D-loop formation. The factors that dictate the point of insertion are not known, but presumably this can be accomplished anywhere along the telomere length, including the stretches of TTAGGG repeats found among the degenerate repeats. These terminal t-loop structures or other structures, bound to the shelterin complex, therefore sequester the terminus of the chromosome and so suppress activation of ATM and ATR and activation of a DNA-damage response (Figure 1c).

Telomeres, replication and cellular senescence

Replication of telomeric DNA is problematic for several reasons. First, there is evidence in yeast that the initiation of replication occurs at an origin that lies internal to the telomere. As the replication fork hits the repetitive DNA, it may slow or even pause, possibly because it is necessary to remove the t-loop, or deal with secondary structures that form on the G-rich or C-rich strands. If the single replication fork stalls while travelling through the repetitive DNA it

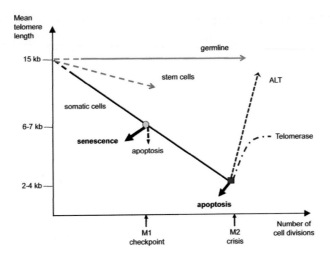

Figure 2. The telomere hypothesis of cellular senescence and immortalization

must be restarted to avoid loss of telomeric DNA [12,13]. Furthermore, it is not possible to replicate a linear DNA molecule fully via lagging strand synthesis, as removal of the most terminal RNA primer leaves a gap that cannot be filled (the 'end replication problem' [14]), so causing a gradual replication-dependent erosion of telomeric DNA. Following replication, it is necessary to process the terminus to generate G-strand overhangs required for capping and this resectioning also contributes to the erosion of telomeric DNA.

Expression of the enzyme telomerase, a reverse transcriptase that carries its own RNA template, enables a cell to overcome telomere attrition [12]. However, telomerase activity is tightly regulated, mainly via expression of the human *TERT* (telomerase reverse transcriptase) gene that encodes the reverse transcriptase component. In humans, telomerase activity is only sufficient to maintain telomere length fully in the germline (Figure 2); although telomerase activity can be detected in the progenitor cell compartment of tissues with a high cell turnover, the activity is insufficient to maintain telomere length over a human lifespan. In differentiated human cells, telomerase is inactive, and the gradual erosion of telomere length can be measured as a function of number of cell divisions and age [15].

In 1961, Hayflick and Moorehead [16] first described the limited replicative potential of normal somatic cells in culture, showing that they arrest after a defined number of PDs (population doublings), at the mortality 1 (M_1) check-point (also known as the Hayflick limit). At this checkpoint, most cells enter a senescent state. They stop dividing and show morphological and gene expression changes, including the expression of high levels of β-galactosidase in lysosomes [SA-β-galactosidase (senescence-associated β-galactosidase) is a marker of senescent cells]. It has been shown that there are several routes to the senescent phenotype [17,18], including telomere dysfunction, oxidative stress, DNA damage, oncogene activation and suboptimal growth conditions of cells in culture. These various stimuli seem to act through one of two signalling pathways: activation of tumour-suppressor protein p53 and/or the pRb (retinoblastoma protein) and their downstream cyclin-dependent kinase inhibitors p21 (CDKN1A) or p16 (CDKN2A). Thus various types of cellular stress can trigger senescence.

Recent advances have shown that telomere-dependent senescence arises when one or a few short telomeres that can no longer cap the chromosomes are present in the nucleus [19]. These uncapped or dysfunctional telomeres precipitate the formation of DNA-damage foci [20]. The content of these senescence-associated DNA-damage foci substantially overlaps with other DNA-damage foci, so includes phosphorylated ATM or ATR, γ-H2AX (phosphorylated histone H2AX) (bound to subtelomeric DNA) leading to phosphorylation of p53 and expression of p21 [18,20]. Following the onset of senescence, the telomere-induced DNA-damage foci persist, suggesting that senescent cells are in a state of continuous DNA damage response and therefore cell-cycle arrest.

Bypass of the M_1 checkpoint can be achieved by disruption of the signalling pathway (for example, loss or silencing of p53), this allows the cell to continue to replicate, but, in the absence of a TMM (telomere maintenance mechanism), telomeres continue to shorten, chromosomes fuse (via NHEJ) [21] and enter a cycle of breakage–fusion–anaphase bridge formation, and the genome becomes increasingly unstable. In the absence of a TMM, the majority of cells will undergo apoptosis at the stage known as M_2 or crisis (Figure 2).

Reactivation of telomerase in differentiated cells leads to the avoidance of senescence and therefore to immortality of cells in culture [22], but if accompanied by somatic mutations (oncogene activation and loss of tumour suppressor genes) in tissues, it leads to tumour formation. Furthermore, there is some evidence that genome instability, driven by dysfunctional telomeres as the cells approach crisis, can contribute to tumour formation, although eventually the genome must be stabilized by the activation of a TMM [23]. Telomerase is active in the majority of tumours ($\sim$85%), leading to the stabilization of mean telomere length. However, approx. 15% of tumours either have no known TMM or they activate the ALT (alternative lengthening of telomeres) mechanism [24].

Features of the ALT mechanism

ALT was first described in immortal cell lines that did not express telomerase [25]. The telomeres in these cell lines are very heterogeneous in length (<1 to >50 kb [24,26]) and contain single-stranded regions on the C-rich or G-rich strand [27]. The telomeres in ALT+ cell lines show gradual shortening due to incomplete replication, but they are also subjected to random events that suddenly shorten or elongate the repeat array. These features of telomeres in ALT+ cells resemble the telomere length dynamics in type II survivors of yeast that lack telomerase (see [28]). It is known that recombination-like processes underlie the telomere length maintenance in type II survivors as they are dependent on *RAD52* and other genes that are required for recombination. The first evidence that ALT in human cells is recombination-based came from telomere-tagging experiments in which a plasmid inserted into a telomere repeat array moved to other telomeres after a number of PDs, whereas a plasmid internal to the telomere did not [29]. Furthermore, analysis of the degenerate repeats in human telomeres revealed a class of complex telomere mutations only seen in ALT+ cells [5]. These complex mutations result in the truncation of the progenitor telomere (defined by the interspersion pattern of the degenerate repeats) and addition of a novel telomere repeat array (with a different interspersion pattern) distal to the breakpoint. Such complex mutations cannot be explained by intramolecular events such as slippage during replication, deletions or t-loop replication. Furthermore, they cannot be explained by equal or unequal sister-chromatid exchange and therefore arise by other intermolecular recombination-like processes (see below).

A subset of the nuclear bodies that contain the PML (promyelocytic leukaemia) protein are specific to ALT+ cells [APBs (ALT-associated PML bodies)], as they contain telomeric DNA and components of the shelterin complex in addition to PML and proteins involved in DNA repair, replication and recombination [24]. APBs are only present in a subset of ALT+ cells, and they are more abundant in the S/G_2-phases of the cell cycle, when it is thought that telomeres can be elongated. Moreover, some evidence shows that telomeres are closely associated with APBs at certain times [30], but, in contrast with this, there are cell lines and tumours that lack APBs, yet maintain telomeres by a recombination-based process [24]. Thus it is currently not clear what role APBs play in ALT+ cells, but there are three overlapping views: (i) they may be repositories for proteins that are required for telomere length maintenance; (ii) they may be the sites where telomere elongation occurs; and (iii) they may be the repository for by-products of telomere elongation that would otherwise cause cell-cycle arrest. Nonetheless, characterization of the content of APBs has given some indication as to the proteins that may be involved in telomere elongation in ALT+ cells.

Another feature of ALT+ cells is the presence of a ECTR (extrachromosomal telomeric repeat) that is present in multiple forms, including short linear molecules, a proportion of which are located in APBs [31], and relaxed circular molecules that can be single-stranded, double-stranded or indeed partially double-stranded [27,32]. It is thought that the ECTR is generated as a by-product of the recombination processes operating at telomeres in ALT+ cells, but it has also been proposed that the circular forms may sometimes act as substrates for telomere elongation.

A further marker of ALT+ cell lines and indeed some tumours that show telomere recombination is instability at a GC-rich minisatellite called MS32 (D1S8), which is located at an internal site 1q42 [26,33]. The mutation rate at this minisatellite varies between ALT+ cell lines, but is on average >50-fold higher than in telomerase+ or normal cell lines. It is unknown why this minisatellite is destabilized by activation of the ALT mechanism, but it appears to be a localized effect as none of the other minisatellites that have been investigated shows somatic instability in ALT+ cell lines ([33] and C. Novo and N.J. Royle, unpublished work). One hypothesis for the observed MS32 instability is that factors required for the correct replication of MS32 are recruited to telomeres in ALT+ cells and this causes incomplete replication or other errors at MS32 that are processed into DSBs. The subsequent repair by error-prone processes, that may involve the sister chromatid, then result in the loss, gain or other more complex rearrangement of repeats along the minisatellite.

Telomeres and recombination in ALT+ cells

With the exception of instability at MS32, there is no evidence of a general increase in recombination-like activity across the genome in ALT+ cells [34]. However, use of the CO-FISH (chromosome-orientation fluorescent *in situ* hybridization) technique with strand-specific probes [35] has shown that telomeres in ALT+ cells undergo an elevated level of post-replicative exchange, some of which appears to be unequal T-SCEs (telomere sister-chromatid exchanges) [36]). It has been proposed that unequal T-SCE could be the basis of telomere elongation in ALT+ cells, but a confounding problem is that unequal T-SCE does not result in a net gain of telomeric DNA as one sister chromatid is elongated at the expense of the other. Therefore T-SCE seem to contribute to the erratic telomere length dynamics in ALT+ cells, but other types of recombination-based event must also play roles (Figure 3).

Overexpression of a mutant form of TRF2 (TRF2ΔB) in telomerase+ cells led to the formation of extrachromosomal circles of telomeric DNA (t-circles). The mutant TRF2ΔB was able to suppress NHEJ between telomeres, but was not able to suppress misprocessing of t-loops [37]. This stochastic misprocessing resulted in t-loop excision, by a XRCC3 (X-ray repair complementing defective repair in Chinese-hamster cells 3)- and NBS1 (Nijmegen breakage syndrome 1)-dependent process, so releasing a t-circle and causing dramatic telomere shortening (Figure 3) [37,38]. Moreover, deletion of one of the two mouse POT1 genes (*Pot1a*) also led to increased T-SCE and to t-circle formation [39]. As T-SCE and t-circles are abundant in ALT+ cell lines, it seems probable that the capping function of TRF2, POT1 and possibly other shelterin components is dysfunctional in ALT+ cells.

As indicated above, the deregulation of recombination-like processes in ALT+ cells results in movement of telomeric sequence between chromosome ends [29]. The details of the mechanism that underlies these events are still unclear and several models have been proposed. One of the most attractive models is a type of BIR (break-induced replication), whereby the G-strand of a short 'recipient' telomere invades a longer 'donor' telomere and uses the C-strand as a template to extend the short telomere (Figure 3). The C-strand is then generated by lagging strand synthesis either concurrently or following G-strand synthesis [40]. The attraction of this model is the net gain of telomeric sequences, i.e. the

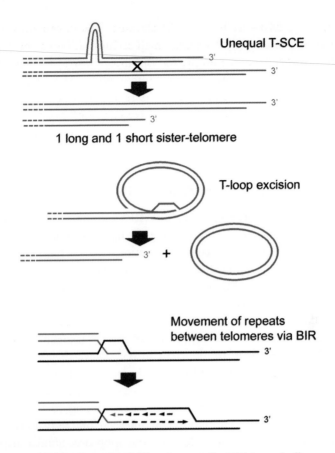

Figure 3. Recombination-based activities that are thought to underlie some of the known features of ALT+ cell lines

short recipient telomere is extended without loss of sequences from the donor telomere. Variants of this BIR model are also possible, such as strand invasion of extrachromosomal t-circles and copy from these via rolling circle replication [41] or roll and spread as seen in *Kluyveromyces lactis* [40,42], although it has also been shown that some human ALT+ cells can survive without t-circles [38]. Moreover, a type of unequal BIR between telomere sister chromatids can be envisaged, although it would not result in the movement of sequences between chromosomes ends. Finally, it has been proposed that t-loops themselves could be used for telomere extension. In this model, DNA synthesis would be initiated at the 3'-end of the G-strand within the D-loop. Replication would then proceed round the t-loop, extending the telomere by an intramolecular mechanism [24]. This process would not, however, move sequences between telomeres and so it cannot on its own explain all of the known features of telomeres in ALT+ cells.

In summary, ALT+ cells show: (i) elevated T-SCE, but no elevation of SCE across the genome; (ii) t-circles, which seem to arise via recombination-dependent misprocessing of t-loops; and (iii) movement of sequences between telomeres, either directly or via a t-circle intermediate. These features indicate that recombination-like mechanisms are deregulated at telomeres in ALT+ cells, but it is not yet clear whether telomere extension is dependent on one mechanism or whether several mechanisms can achieve telomere elongation within ALT+ cells.

DNA damage response in ALT+ cells

The wide range of telomere lengths within ALT+ cells plus the possible presence of stretches of single-stranded DNA along the repeat arrays indicate that some chromosomes in ALT+ cells have dysfunctional telomeres that will not be able to cap the chromosome. Indeed, TIFs (telomere-induced DNA-damage foci) can be detected in ALT+ cells throughout the cell cycle [41,43], and ATM appears to be permanently activated in ALT+ cell lines [44]. However, ALT+ cells survive and continue to divide, and so they must avoid a full-blown DNA-damage response, and corroboration of this comes from the observation that most ALT+ cell lines are deficient in p53. Nevertheless, there may be other routes to the management of the DNA-damage response in ALT+ cells. Disruption of TRF2 expression in telomerase+ p53-deficient cells leads to activation of ATM and downstream substrates, leading to loss of G-strand overhangs from telomeres and multiple telomere–telomere fusions via NHEJ. This precipitates an abrupt cell-cycle arrest and apoptosis. Similar disruption of TRF2 expression in an ALT+ cell line, which retains wild-type p53, showed a different response. Stable clones in which TRF2 expression was disrupted were generated, but at a reduced frequency; apoptosis was not induced, but, after a delay, there was an increase in p53/p21-mediated senescence. Finally, there was a significant loss of telomeric DNA from the TRF2-deficient ALT+ clones [44], although it is not known whether this loss was from the ECTR or from telomeres.

It is known that TRF1 and TRF2 can be post-transcriptionally modified by SUMO (small ubiquitin-related modifier) proteins. Moreover, disruption of the SUMOylation pathway in ALT+ cells leads to telomere shortening, the loss of APBs and an increase in cellular senescence [45]. Thus the muted response to TRF2 disruption in ALT+ cells compared with normal or telomerase+ cells may not be via alterations to the SUMOylation of telomere-binding proteins in ALT+ cells.

Genes involved in ALT

The MRN [MRE11 (meiotic recombination 11)–Rad50–NBS1] complex is required for HRR of DSBs at interstitial sites in the genome. Each component contributes different activities to the complex: MRE11 has exonuclease (3′-5′ *in vitro*) and endonuclease activities, and Rad50 has helicase activity. The third component NBS1 only associates with the MRE11 and Rad50 components at certain times of the cell cycle when it is thought to phosphorylate and thus activate the complex. Interestingly, the MRN complex associates with telomeres in normal cells at specific times during the cell cycle and it may play a role in the formation and disassociation of t-loops. Disruption of the MRN complex in ALT+ cells leads to telomere shortening and loss of APBs, so showing that it is required for telomere length maintenance in these cells [38,46,47].

The *RAD51D* gene, a member of a family of genes homologous with yeast RAD51, which is required for filament formation and strand invasion during HRR, has also been implicated in the ALT mechanism, although its role has not been fully determined [48]. More recently, the protein complex encoded by the *BLM* (Bloom's syndrome protein), *TOP3A* (topoisomerase IIIα) and *BLAP75* (BLM-associated polypeptide 75) genes [49,50] has been implicated in the ALT mechanism. Topisomerase IIIα localizes with TRF2 in ALT+ cells and siRNA (small interfering RNA) disruption of topoisomerase IIIα resulted in reduction of TRF2 levels, loss of G-strand overhangs and a reduction of ALT+ cell viability, but without induction of apoptosis.

Following the demonstration that the human ALT mechanism is recombination-based, a role for DNA helicase genes could be envisaged. Two members of the RecQ helicase gene family have been considered, the *BLM* and the *WRN* (Werner's syndrome protein) genes. Werner's syndrome patients (*WRN*$^{-/-}$) show genome instability, leading to increased cell loss resulting in a premature aging phenotype associated with predisposition to cancers, particularly sarcomas. Loss of WRN from mouse cells that lack telomerase led to genome instability, increased T-SCE and resulted in cells that were more readily immortalized in culture [51]. This indicates that WRN acts as a barrier to T-SCE in mouse cells, in addition to its role in telomere lagging strand replication. Bloom's syndrome patients (*BLM*$^{-/-}$) have a cancer-predisposition syndrome and show elevated levels of T-SCE, indicating that BLM is involved in regulating such exchanges. The fact that ALT+ cells show elevated T-SCE raises a question as to what, if anything, BLM does in the ALT mechanism. The evidence that disruption of topoisomerase IIIα has an impact on ALT+ cell survival also suggests that BLM plays a role in the ALT mechanism. Recently, we have been investigating the role of the *BLM* and *WRN* genes in ALT+ cells by examining the effect they have on minisatellite instability and on mutations in the telomere repeat array.

Note added in proof (received 6 April 2009)

Since submission of the present article, new data have been published which show that intratelomeric copying also contributes to telomere dynamics in ALT+ cells [52].

Funding

Research in N.J.R.'s group is supported by grants from the Medical Research Council and Cancer Research UK. J.W. is funded by a studentship from the Biotechnology and Biological Sciences Research Council, and A.K. is funded by Consejo Nacional de Cienca y Tecnologia (Mexico).

References

1. Allshire, R.C., Dempster, M. & Hastie, N.D. (1989) Human telomeres contain at least 3 types of G-rich repeat distributed non-randomly. *Nucleic Acids Res.* **17**, 4611–4627

2. Baird, D.M., Jeffreys, A.J. & Royle, N.J. (1995) Mechanisms underlying telomere repeat turnover, revealed by hypervariable variant repeat distribution patterns in the human Xp/Yp telomere. *EMBO J.* **14**, 5433–5443

3. Coleman, J., Baird, D.M. & Royle, N.J. (1999) The plasticity of human telomeres demonstrated by a hypervariable telomere repeat array that is located on some copies of 16p and 16q. *Hum. Mol. Genet.* **8**, 1637–1646

4. Baird, D.M., Coleman, J., Rosser, Z.H. & Royle, N.J. (2000) High levels of sequence polymorphism and linkage disequilibrium at the telomere of 12q: implications for telomere biology and human evolution. *Am. J. Hum. Genet.* **66**, 235–250

5. Varley, H., Pickett, H.A., Foxon, J.L., Reddel, R.R. & Royle, N.J. (2002) Molecular characterization of inter-telomere and intra-telomere mutations in human ALT cells. *Nat. Genet.* **30**, 301–305

6. Pickett, H.A., Baird, D.M., Hoff-Olsen, P., Meling, G.I., Rognum, T.O., Shaw, J., West, K.P. & Royle, N.J. (2004) Telomere instability detected in sporadic colon cancers, some showing mutations in a mismatch repair gene. *Oncogene* **23**, 3434–3443

7. Konishi, A. & de Lange, T. (2008) Cell cycle control of telomere protection and NHEJ revealed by a ts mutation in the DNA-binding domain of TRF2. *Genes Dev.* **22**, 1221–1230

8. Palm, W. & de Lange, T. (2008) How shelterin protects mammalian telomeres. *Annu. Rev. Genet.* **42**, 301–334

9. Shiloh, Y. (2003) ATM and related protein kinases: safeguarding genome integrity. *Nat. Rev. Cancer* **3**, 155–168

10. Baumann, P. & Cech, T.R. (2001) Pot1, the putative telomere end-binding protein in fission yeast and humans. *Science* **292**, 1171–1175

11. Griffith, J.D., Comeau, L., Rosenfield, S., Stansel, R.M., Bianchi, A., Moss, H. & de Lange, T. (1999) Mammalian telomeres end in a large duplex loop. *Cell* **97**, 503–514

12. Gilson, E. & Geli, V. (2007) How telomeres are replicated. *Nat. Rev. Mol. Cell. Biol.* **8**, 825–838

13. Verdun, R.E. & Karlseder, J. (2007) Replication and protection of telomeres. *Nature* **447**, 924–931

14. Olovnikov, A.M. (1973) A theory of marginotomy: the incomplete copying of template margin in enzymic synthesis of polynucleotides and biological significance of the phenomenon. *J. Theor. Biol.* **41**, 181–190

15. Harley, C.B., Kim, N.W., Prowse, K.R., Weinrich, S.L., Hirsch, K.S., West, M.D., Bacchetti, S., Hirte, H.W., Counter, C.M., Greider, C.W. et al. (1994) Telomerase, cell immortality, and cancer. *Cold Spring Harbor Symp. Quant. Biol.* **59**, 307–315

16. Hayflick, L. & Moorhead, P. (1961) The serial cultivation of human diploid cell strains. *Exp. Cell Res.* **25**, 585–621

17. Collado, M., Blasco, M.A. & Serrano, M. (2007) Cellular senescence in cancer and aging. *Cell* **130**, 223–233

18. von Zglinicki, T., Saretzki, G., Ladhoff, J., d'Adda di Fagagna, F. & Jackson, S.P. (2005) Human cell senescence as a DNA damage response. *Mech. Ageing Dev.* **126**, 111–117

19. Baird, D.M., Rowson, J., Wynford-Thomas, D. & Kipling, D. (2003) Extensive allelic variation and ultrashort telomeres in senescent human cells. *Nat. Genet.* **33**, 203–207

20. d'Adda di Fagagna, F., Reaper, P.M., Clay-Farrace, L., Fiegler, H., Carr, P., Von Zglinicki, T., Saretzki, G., Carter, N.P. & Jackson, S.P. (2003) A DNA damage checkpoint response in telomere-initiated senescence. *Nature* **426**, 194–198

21. Capper, R., Britt-Compton, B., Tankimanova, M., Rowson, J., Letsolo, B., Man, S., Haughton, M. & Baird, D.M. (2007) The nature of telomere fusion and a definition of the critical telomere length in human cells. *Genes Dev.* **21**, 2495–2508

22. Bodnar, A.G., Ouellette, M., Frolkis, M., Holt, S.E., Chiu, C.P., Morin, G.B., Harley, C.B., Shay, J.W., Lichtsteiner, S. & Wright, W.E. (1998) Extension of life-span by introduction of telomerase into normal human cells. *Science* **279**, 349–352

23. Chin, K., de Solorzano, C.O., Knowles, D., Jones, A., Chou, W., Rodriguez, E.G., Kuo, W.L., Ljung, B.M., Chew, K., Myambo, K. et al. (2004) *In situ* analyses of genome instability in breast cancer. *Nat. Genet.* **36**, 984–988

24. Henson, J.D., Neumann, A.A., Yeager, T.R. & Reddel, R.R. (2002) Alternative lengthening of telomeres in mammalian cells. *Oncogene* **21**, 598–610

25. Murnane, J.P., Sabatier, L., Marder, B.A. & Morgan, W.F. (1994) Telomere dynamics in an immortal human cell-line. *EMBO J.* **13**, 4953–4962

26. Jeyapalan, J.N., Mendez-Bermudez, A., Zaffaroni, N., Dubrova, Y.E. & Royle, N.J. (2008) Evidence for alternative lengthening of telomeres in liposarcomas in the absence of ALT-associated PML bodies. *Int. J. Cancer* **122**, 2414–2421

27. Nabetani, A. & Ishikawa, F. (2009) Unusual telomeric DNAs in human telomerase-negative immortalized cells. *Mol. Cell. Biol.* **29**, 703–713

28. Lundblad, V. (2002) Telomere maintenance without telomerase. *Oncogene* **21**, 522–531

29. Dunham, M.A., Neumann, A.A., Fasching, C.L. & Reddel, R.R. (2000) Telomere maintenance by recombination in human cells. *Nat. Genet.* **26**, 447–450

30. Molenaar, C., Wiesmeijer, K., Verwoerd, N.P., Khazen, S., Eils, R., Tanke, H.J. & Dirks, R.W. (2003) Visualizing telomere dynamics in living mammalian cells using PNA probes. *EMBO J.* **22**, 6631–6641

31. Fasching, C.L., Neumann, A.A., Muntoni, A., Yeager, T.R. & Reddel, R.R. (2007) DNA damage induces alternative lengthening of telomeres (ALT) associated promyelocytic leukemia bodies that preferentially associate with linear telomeric DN. *Cancer Res.* **67**, 7072–7077

32. Cesare, A.J. & Griffith, J.D. (2004) Telomeric DNA in ALT cells is characterized by free telomeric circles and heterogeneous t-loops. *Mol. Cell. Biol.* **24**, 9948–9957

33. Jeyapalan, J.N., Varley, H., Foxon, J.L., Pollock, R.E., Jeffreys, A.J., Henson, J.D., Reddel, R.R. & Royle, N.J. (2005) Activation of the ALT pathway for telomere maintenance can affect other sequences in the human genome. *Hum. Mol. Genet.* **14**, 1785–1794

34. Bechter, O.E., Shay, J.W. & Wright, W.E. (2004) The frequency of homologous recombination in human ALT cells. *Cell Cycle* **3**, 547–549

35. Bailey, S.M., Cornforth, M.N., Kurimasa, A., Chen, D.J. & Goodwin, E.H. (2001) Strand-specific postreplicative processing of mammalian telomeres. *Science* **293**, 2462–2465

36. Bailey, S.M., Brenneman, M.A. & Goodwin, E.H. (2004) Frequent recombination in telomeric DNA may extend the proliferative life of telomerase-negative cells. *Nucleic Acids Res.* **32**, 3743–3751

37. Wang, R.C., Smogorzewska, A. & de Lange, T. (2004) Homologous recombination generates T-loop-sized deletions at human telomeres. *Cell* **119**, 355–368

38. Compton, S.A., Choi, J.H., Cesare, A.J., Ozgur, S. & Griffith, J.D. (2007) Xrcc3 and Nbs1 are required for the production of extrachromosomal telomeric circles in human alternative lengthening of telomere cells. *Cancer Res.* **67**, 1513–1519

39. Wu, L., Multani, A.S., He, H., Cosme-Blanco, W., Deng, Y., Deng, J.M., Bachilo, O., Pathak, S., Tahara, H., Bailey, S.M. et al. (2006) Pot1 deficiency initiates DNA damage checkpoint activation and aberrant homologous recombination at telomeres. *Cell* **126**, 49–62

40. McEachern, M.J. & Haber, J.E. (2006) Break-induced replication and recombinational telomere elongation in yeast. *Annu. Rev. Biochem.* **75**, 111–135

41. Cesare, A.J. & Reddel, R.R. (2008) Telomere uncapping and alternative lengthening of telomeres. *Mech. Ageing Dev.* **129**, 99–108

42. Natarajan, S. & McEachern, M.J. (2002) Recombinational telomere elongation promoted by DNA circles. *Mol. Cell. Biol.* **22**, 4512–4521

43. Nabetani, A., Yokoyama, O. & Ishikawa, F. (2004) Localization of hRad9, hHus1, hRad1, and hRad17 and caffeine-sensitive DNA replication at the alternative lengthening of telomeres-associated promyelocytic leukemia body. *J. Biol. Chem.* **279**, 25849–25857

44. Stagno D'Alcontres, M., Mendez-Bermudez, A., Foxon, J.L., Royle, N.J. & Salomoni, P. (2007) Lack of TRF2 in ALT cells causes PML-dependent p53 activation and loss of telomeric DNA. *J. Cell Biol.* **179**, 855–867

45. Potts, P.R. & Yu, H. (2007) The SMC5/6 complex maintains telomere length in ALT cancer cells through SUMOylation of telomere-binding proteins. *Nat. Struct. Mol. Biol.* **14**, 581–590

46. Jiang, W.Q., Zhong, Z.H., Henson, J.D., Neumann, A.A., Chang, A.C. & Reddel, R.R. (2005) Suppression of alternative lengthening of telomeres by Sp100-mediated sequestration of the MRE11/RAD50/NBS1 complex. *Mol. Cell. Biol.* **25**, 2708–2721

47. Zhong, Z.H., Jiang, W.Q., Cesare, A.J., Neumann, A.A., Wadhwa, R. & Reddel, R.R. (2007) Disruption of telomere maintenance by depletion of the MRE11/RAD50/NBS1 complex in cells that use alternative lengthening of telomeres. *J. Biol. Chem.* **282**, 29314–29322

48. Tarsounas, M., Munoz, P., Claas, A., Smiraldo, P.G., Pittman, D.L., Blasco, M.A. & West, S.C. (2004) Telomere maintenance requires the RAD51D recombination/repair protein. *Cell* **117**, 337–347

49. Raynard, S., Zhao, W., Bussen, W., Lu, L., Ding, Y.Y., Busygina, V., Meetei, A.R. & Sung, P. (2008) Functional role of BLAP75 in BLM- topoisomerase IIIα-dependent holliday junction processing. *J. Biol. Chem.* **283**, 15701–15708

50. Mankouri, H.W. & Hickson, I.D. (2007) The RecQ helicase– topoisomerase III–Rmi1 complex: a DNA structure-specific 'dissolvasome'? *Trends Biochem. Sci.* **32**, 538–546

51. Laud, P.R., Multani, A.S., Bailey, S.M., Wu, L., Ma, J., Kingsley, C., Lebel, M., Pathak, S., DePinho, R.A. & Chang, S. (2005) Elevated telomere–telomere recombination in WRN-deficient, telomere dysfunctional cells promotes escape from senescence and engagement of the ALT pathway. *Genes Dev.* **19**, 2560–2570

52. Muntoni, A., Neumann, A.A., Hills, M. and Reddel, R.R. (2009) Telomere elongation involves intra-molecular DNA replication in cells utilizing alternative lengthening of telomeres. Hum. Mol. Genet. **18**, 1017–1027

Biochem. Soc. Symp. 76
Citation reference: Biochem. Soc. Trans. (2009) **37**, 597–604.
© The Authors. Journal compilation © 2009 The Biochemical Society

11

Understanding the functions of BRCA1 in the DNA-damage response

Maximina H. Yun[1] and Kevin Hiom

Division of Protein and Nucleic Acids Chemistry, MRC Laboratory of Molecular Biology, Hills Road, Cambridge CB2 0QH, U.K.

Abstract

Inheritance of a mutation in *BRCA1* (breast cancer 1 early-onset) results in predisposition to early-onset breast and ovarian cancer. Tumours in these individuals arise after somatic mutation or loss of the wild-type allele. Loss of BRCA1 function leads to a profound increase in genomic instability involving the accumulation of mutations, DNA breaks and gross chromosomal rearrangements. Accordingly, BRCA1 has been implicated as an important factor involved in both the repair of DNA lesions and in the regulation of cell-cycle checkpoints in response to DNA damage. However, the molecular mechanism through which BRCA1 functions to preserve genome stability remains unclear. In the present article, we examine the different ways in which BRCA1 might influence the repair of DNA damage and the preservation of genome integrity, taking into account what is currently known about its interactions with other proteins, its biochemical activity and its nuclear localization.

[1] *To whom correspondence should be addressed (email mhy26@cam.ac.uk).*

Introduction to *BRCA1* (breast cancer 1 early-onset)

BRCA1 is an important tumour-suppressor gene. Germline mutations in *BRCA1* are present in nearly 50% of inherited breast cancer cases, and the acquisition of a single defective allele leads to an elevated predisposition to both breast and ovarian cancer [1]. Evidence suggests that *BRCA1* may also be mutated in some sporadic breast cancer tumours [2].

A common feature of cancer cells is a profound increase in genome instability. Accordingly, cells defective for *BRCA1* exhibit elevated levels of chromosome aberrations, such as DNA breaks and chromatid exchanges, enhanced sensitivity to agents that damage DNA and defects in cell-cycle checkpoint function. Such changes are often associated with defects or loss of proteins involved in the detection and repair of DNA damage. It has therefore been proposed that *BRCA1* functions in the DNA-damage response as a caretaker of the genome [3].

Since its discovery, many studies have addressed the function of BRCA1 with a view to understanding how it contributes to the maintenance of genome stability and how defects in this process result in cancer progression. These studies have led to a series of discoveries that implicate BRCA1 in a multitude of different cellular processes. For example, there is now a large body of evidence supporting a direct role for BRCA1 in the repair of DNA damage by HR (homologous recombination). Not only is BRCA1 recruited to sites of DNA damage where it co-localizes with other proteins involved in the repair of DNA DSBs (double strand breaks) by HR, such as BRCA2 and Rad51 [4], but cells lacking functional BRCA1 are highly impaired for the homology-directed repair of defined DSBs, introduced into the genome by a restriction endonuclease [5]. BRCA1 has also been shown to be required for the activation of both S- and G_2/M-phase cell-cycle arrest after DNA damage, the latter being dependent on prior phosphorylation of BRCA1 by the master checkpoint kinase ATM (ataxia telangiectasia mutated) [6]. The observation that cells lacking full-length BRCA1 may also have multiple spindle poles has led to the proposal that BRCA1 contributes to the control of centrosome number [7]. Furthermore, BRCA1 is thought to be involved in transcriptional regulation. BRCA1 not only associates with RNA polymerase II [4], but also has been shown to activate the transcription of several genes, including *GADD45* (growth-arrest and DNA-damage-inducible protein 45) [4] and *SOX2* [SRY (sex determining region Y) box 2] [8]. Finally, BRCA1 has been implicated in two types of gene silencing: the inactivation of the X chromosome [9] and meiotic sex chromosome inactivation [10].

However, despite more than a decade of research, relatively little is known about how BRCA1 functions at the molecular level. Unravelling how BRCA1 contributes to some or all of the above functions has been very challenging, and many important issues remain unresolved. For instance, it is not yet clear whether BRCA1 functions through a specific enzymatic activity required for the

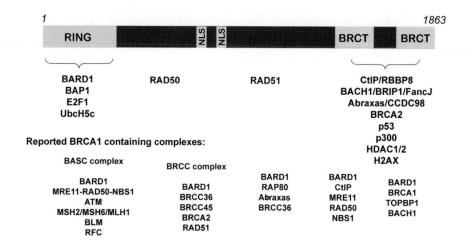

Figure 1. BRCA1-interacting proteins
Structure of full-length human BRCA1 protein. Coloured rectangles represent the previously characterized RING and BRCT domains, as well as two nuclear localization signals (NLS). BRCA1-binding partners are annotated below the domain in which the interaction is known to occur. Reported BRCA1-containing complexes are annotated at the bottom. BAP1, BRCA1-associated protein 1; BACH1/BRIP1, BRCA1-interacting protein-associated C-terminal helicase 1; BASC, BRCA1-associated genome surveillance complex; BLM, Bloom's syndrome protein; BRCC, BRCA1/BRCA2-containing complex; MLH, MutL homologue; MSH, MutS homologue; RBBP8, pRb-interacting protein 8; RFC, replication factor C; TOPBP1, topoisomerase II-binding protein 1.

repair of DNA lesions, as a global regulator controlling many different aspects of the DNA-damage response by modulating the activities of other proteins, or a combination of both.

What clues about the function of BRCA1 can we garner from its sequence? The *BRCA1* gene is organized in 24 exons encoding a protein of 1863 amino acids. Whereas conservation of the BRCA1 amino acid sequence varies among species, the N- and C-termini of the protein are highly conserved from nematode worms to humans [11]. These regions comprise two recognizable domains in BRCA1: a RING (really interesting new gene) finger domain at the N-terminus, and two C-terminal BRCT (BRCA1 C-terminal) domains (first identified in BRCA1, but subsequently found in a variety of DNA-repair proteins). Both domains mediate interactions with other proteins that may be important for BRCA1 function.

In fact, BRCA1 associates with a myriad of different proteins (Figure 1) whose interactions are not limited to the RING and BRCT domains. These proteins include transcription factors, such as E2F1 and pRb (retinoblastoma protein), chromatin-modifying proteins, such as HDAC (histone deacetylase) 1/2 and CBP [CREB (cAMP-response-element-binding protein)-binding protein]/p300, oncogenes such as *myc* and proteins involved in the DNA-damage response [4]. However, the contribution of many of these potentially interesting interactions to BRCA1 function remains unclear. On the other hand, studies on interactions mediated through the RING and BRCT domains of BRCA1 have been more informative. Therefore we will next focus on the proteins that interact with these domains.

Undoubtedly, the most important BRCA1-interacting protein is BARD1 (BRCA1-associated RING domain 1). Like BRCA1, BARD1 has a N-terminal RING domain and a pair of C-terminal BRCT domains. The association of BRCA1 with BARD1 is mediated through a pair of α-helices found adjacent to the RING domains of each protein [12]. In cells, the majority of BRCA1 is found associated with BARD1, suggesting that these proteins function together as a heterodimeric complex. Several other pieces of evidence support this view. First, the interaction of BRCA1 with BARD1 is required for its retention in the nucleus by blocking a nuclear export signal situated near the RING domain of BRCA1 [12a]. Secondly, in both the nematode worm *Caenorhabditis elegans* [11] and in the DT40 cell line, mutations in *bard1* phenocopy those in *brca1*, suggesting that these proteins act in the same functional pathways. Finally, the association of BRCA1 and BARD1 is required for the only biochemical activity ascribed to BRCA1, that of an ubiquitin ligase (E3) [13,14].

BRCA1–BARD1, an E3 ubiquitin ligase

The demonstration that BRCA1–BARD1 is able to ubiquitinate substrates including several histone proteins as well as itself (auto-ubiquitination) was an important breakthrough [14,15]. Although initial reports suggested that the RING domain of BRCA1 alone could confer E3 activity, subsequent studies revealed that this function is greatly enhanced by its association with the RING domain of BARD1. The potential importance of this activity in cells is supported by the fact that many mutations found in breast cancer patients, which map to the RING domain of BRCA1, cause defects in the ubiquitin ligase function [14]. Consequently, the discovery of this activity sparked a search for substrates for BRCA1-dependent ubiquitination that might explain its role as a caretaker of the genome.

Over the years, several potential substrates for BRCA1-dependent ubiqui-tination have been proposed. In 2001, considerable excitement was generated by the finding that mono-ubiquitination of FancD2 (Fanconi's anaemia comp-lementation group D2), a pivotal component of the Fanconi's anaemia pathway for the repair of replication-blocking lesions such as interstrand DNA cross-links, was greatly decreased in the BRCA1-defective cell line HCC1937 [16]. This observation provided an attractive link between BRCA1 E3 activity and the maintenance of genome stability *in vivo*. However, this was eventually ruled out by the demonstration that mono-ubiquitination of FancD2 was unperturbed in *brca1* mutant DT40 cells [17] and the identification of another component of the Fanconi's anaemia pathway, FancL (Fanconi's anaemia complementation group L), as the E3 ligase responsible for ubiquitination of FancD2 [18].

Other proteins reported as substrates for BRCA1 E3 function include nucleophosmin, γ-tubulin, topoisomerase II-α and RNA polymerase II. Perhaps the most interesting of these relates to the ubiquitination of γ-tubulin and nucleophosmin, as both proteins are known to be involved in the maintenance of centrosome number, a process that is disrupted in some BRCA1-defective cell lines [7]. Nevertheless, such a functional link has yet to be convincingly demonstrated.

CtIP [CtBP (C-terminal binding protein)-interacting protein], a protein involved in DNA repair by HR, is of particular interest because it has been shown to interact with the BRCT domains of BRCA1 in a cell-cycle-dependent manner and has been implicated in the control of G_2/M checkpoint function (see below) [19]. This protein too has been reported to be ubiquitinated by BRCA1–BARD1 [20]. Yu and Chen [19] proposed that ubiquitination of CtIP might be required for its retention on chromatin in IRIF (ionization-radiation-induced foci). In support, they found that expression of wild-type BRCA1, but not an ubiquitin ligase-defective mutant protein, restored G_2/M checkpoint function to a BRCA1-deficient cancer cell line. However, currently the ubiquitination of CtIP is the subject of a single report and genetic validation of its role in checkpoint function is lacking. Clearly further research is needed to establish this potentially important finding.

Since the discovery of the ubiquitin ligase activity of BRCA1, the identification of its targets and a demonstration of how it contributes to BRCA1 functions *in vivo* have been challenging and progress has been slow. One key reason has been the limitations of *in vitro* approaches. In common with other classes of enzymes, such as kinases, ubiquitin ligases are highly promiscuous *in vitro*, and the ubiquitination of a substrate under these conditions is a poor guide to its likely behaviour in cells. Consequently, screens for substrates, on the basis of ubiquitination *in vitro*, are of limited utility.

However, *in vivo* approaches are also fraught with difficulty. Many of the substrates identified by early *in vitro* work are ubiquitinated *in vivo* by more than one ubiquitin ligase. Perhaps the most likely means of identifying *bona fide* substrates for BRCA1–BARD1 is to undertake a systematic substrate screen in wild-type and BRCA1-defective cell lines. However, this is not straightforward as many mammalian cell lines defective for BRCA1 retain truncated forms of the protein including the RING domain. Moreover, even cells in which the RING domain has been deleted, such as in DT40 cells, reproducibly comparing patterns of ubiquitination across the whole proteome in different genetic backgrounds is likely to be technically challenging.

The picture has also been complicated by the atypical nature of the BRCA1-dependent ubiquitination. In classical ubiquitination, E3 ligases catalyse the transfer of ubiquitin from an ubiquitin-conjugating enzyme (E2) to a substrate to generate polyubiquitin chains. These chains are linked through Lys^{48} of neighbouring ubiquitin monomers and function by targeting the modified substrate for degradation by the proteasome. The major function of Lys[48] modifications is therefore to regulate protein turnover in the cell [21].

In contrast, BRCA1–BARD1 facilitates mono-ubiquitination of substrates *in vitro*, suggesting that modification of protein activity rather than regulation of protein turnover is its primary function [15]. This is complicated further by the fact that BRCA1–BARD1 also undergoes auto-polyubiquitination, which is thought to involve Lys[6]-linked chains [15,22]. Whereas non-Lys[48] chains have been detected in cells previously, e.g. the Lys[63] chains involved in regulation of PCNA (proliferating-cell nuclear antigen) during replication [23], the function of Lys[6]-linked chains remains unknown. However, one suggestion is that autoubiquitination of BRCA1 increases the efficiency at which it mono-ubiquitinates its substrate [15].

To complicate matters further, there is now conflicting evidence that BRCA1-dependent ubiquitination is important for the repair of DNA damage in cells. In support, Morris and Soloman [22] showed several years ago that conjugated ubiquitin is found in discreet nuclear foci at stalled replication forks and sites of DNA damage. These ubiquitin foci co-localize with BRCA1 and are depleted when BRCA1 levels are reduced using siRNA (small interfering RNA) [22]. Consistent with this, Boulton and colleagues have shown in *C. elegans* that the homologue of BRCA1 (named Brc) is required for the formation of conjugated ubiquitin foci at sites of DNA damage [24] and that this is dependent on the ubiquitin-conjugating enzyme UbcH5c, the E2 that supports BRCA1-dependent ubiquitination *in vitro* [15]. Nevertheless, a formal demonstration that BRCA1-dependent ubiquitination plays a role in the DNA-damage-repair response was lacking.

More recently, work by Ludwig and colleagues using BRCA1-deficient murine embryonic stem cells [24a] and our group using *brca1* mutant DT40 cells (K. Hiom, R. Franklin and M. Ferrer, unpublished work) have addressed this issue genetically. To do this, we took advantage of work by Brzovic et al. [25], who identified several key amino acids required for the interaction of BRCA1 with the E2 enzymes and are required for BRCA1-dependent ubiquitination. In particular, they showed that substitution of alanine for isoleucine at position 26 disrupted the interaction of canonical E2 enzymes with BRCA1, without perturbing the structure of the BRCA1–BARD1 complex [25]. By expressing this I26A mutant protein in a BRCA1-defective cell line, it was possible to ask whether BRCA1-dependent E3 function is required for survival of cells exposed to DNA damage and for repair of DNA breaks by HR. Surprisingly, the answer to both these questions appears to be no. An important caveat to these experiments is whether BRCA1 E3 function might interact with an E2 enzyme not disrupted by the I26A mutation. Despite this finding, it will also be important to determine whether mice expressing the I26A mutation in BRCA1 give rise to tumours and hence whether defects in DNA repair truly underlie the tumour-suppressor function of BRCA1.

BRCT domain-interacting proteins: insights into BRCA1 function

Although the contribution of the RING domains and the ubiquitin-ligase function of BRCA1 to the maintenance of genome stability remain uncertain, more can be learnt from the study of its BRCT domains. In patients, mutations in the BRCT domains of BRCA1 are represented among those that confer predisposition to cancer, suggesting that they play a role in the tumour-suppressor function of the protein [26]. Structurally, the two BRCT domains of BRCA1 sit adjacent to each other, forming a cleft that is required for the binding of specific phosphopeptides [27]. In human cells, this cleft has been shown to mediate interactions with several phosphoproteins involved in the repair of DNA damage, including FancJ (Fanconi's anaemia complementation group J; previously known as BACH1/BRIP1 for BRCA1-interacting protein-associated C-terminal helicase 1), CtIP and Abraxas, which all contain a pSer-Xaa-Xaa-Phe motif [28]. The potential importance of these interactions for the functions of BRCA1 is supported by the fact that mutations located at the interface between the two BRCT domains are represented among breast cancer cell lines derived from patients [29].

Although several groups have reported the interaction between BRCA1 and the phosphorylated form of FancJ, its functional importance is unclear. Genetic analysis, initially in DT40 cells and then in human cells, demonstrated that, although FancJ is an important component of the Fanconi's anaemia pathway for the repair of DNA cross-links, its function is completely independent of its interaction with BRCA [30]. More recently, FancJ has been shown to unwind G-quadruplex DNA *in vitro* and to be involved in the maintenance of genomic sequences with the G4 DNA signature in nematode worms and humans [31,32]. However, genetic evidence from *C. elegans* suggests that this role of FancJ functions outside the Fanconi's anaemia pathway. Further work will be needed to determine whether the association with BRCA1 contributes to this function.

CtIP (also known as RBBP8 for pRb-interacting protein 8) is a nuclear protein that is highly conserved among vertebrates. Mice that are heterozygous for CtIP develop multiple tumours, whereas homozygous disruption leads to early embryonic lethality [E (embryonic day) 4.0] [33]. Much like BRCA1, CtIP is thought to participate in multiple cellular processes, including regulation of the G_1/S transition, control of transcription and checkpoint activation [33]. More recently, CtIP and its homologues in yeast have been shown to be essential for repair of DNA damage by HR [34–36]. Knockdown of CtIP in human cells with siRNA leads to hypersensitivity to DSB-inducing agents and a decrease in the levels of HR. Moreover, as shown by their failure to recruit RPA (replication protein A), these cells appear to be impaired in the resection of broken DNA to generate the ssDNA (single-stranded DNA) tails required for both repair by HR and ATR (ATM and Rad3-related)-mediated checkpoint activation [35].

The role of CtIP in the resection of broken DNA ends is currently unclear. The amino acid sequence of CtIP provides no indication that it functions as a nuclease. Nevertheless, two groups have reported different nuclease functions for CtIP. In one study, CtIP was shown to possess a ssDNA exonuclease activity that could degrade a circular ssDNA phage. In a second study, Sae2, the yeast homologue of CtIP, was shown to have endonuclease activity by itself and to promote resolution of hairpin structures co-operatively with the MRX [MRE11 (meiotic recombination 11)–Rad50–Xrs2] complex [37].

Another possibility is that CtIP might modulate the activity of a different nuclease. The best candidate for this is the MRN [MRE11–Rad50–NBS1 (Nijmegen breakage syndrome 1)] complex. Several studies have demonstrated physical and functional interactions between CtIP and MRN in mammalian cells and also their yeast homologues Sae2 and MRX respectively [38,39]. Furthermore, MRE11 has been shown to posses both endo- and exo-nuclease activities, which are stimulated *in vitro* by CtIP [35]. Against this is the fact that resection by the MRE11 exonuclease occurs $3' \rightarrow 5'$, generating $5'$-ssDNA tails rather than the $3'$-ssDNA tails required for HR. However, more recent studies in yeast suggest that MRX might be involved in the generation of short ssDNA oligonucleotides that precede extensive resection [39a].

It is of note that BRCA1 has been shown to interact with both CtIP [19] and MRN [35,38] in a complex found in human cells shortly after irradiation and that mutation in any of these proteins causes defects in the repair of DSBs by HR. In support of a common function in HR, BRCA1 and BARD1 were shown by Nunez and co-workers to localize to regions of ssDNA after irradiation and that knockdown of BRCA1 reduces both the generation of ssDNA and the formation of Rad51 foci in response to ionizing radiation [40]. Together, this supports the notion that BRCA1 might act, alongside CtIP and the MRN complex, in the regulation of either the initial processing or resection of broken DNA ends.

As well as being a prerequisite for repair of DNA damage by HR, a role for BRCA1 in DNA end resection might also explain the defect in checkpoint activation observed in *brca1* mutant cells. Generation of ssDNA after DNA damage is not only required for nucleating the formation of Rad51 filaments for homology searching, but also, with RPA, acts as a signal for activation of cell-cycle checkpoints in both human and yeast cells [41]. Hence, two seemingly different phenotypes attributed to defects in BRCA1 can be explained by failures in just one function.

Recently, a third BRCA1 BRCT domain-interacting protein, Abraxas/ CCDC98 (coiled-coil domain-containing protein 98), was shown to play an important role in recruiting BRCA1 to sites of DNA damage [28,42]. Nevertheless, Abraxas interacts with BRCA1 independently of DNA damage, via an pSPTF (pSer-Pro-Thr-Phe) phosphopeptide motif, in the same way as CtIP. Cells in which Abraxas expression has been knocked down by siRNA display enhanced sensitivity to agents that induce DSBs and exhibit checkpoint defects, suggesting that this protein may function in a common pathway with BRCA1 for repair of DSBs [28]. Importantly, recruitment of BRCA1 to IRIF in these cells was also impaired, indicating that Abraxas functions upstream of BRCA1 and is needed for its recruitment to sites of DNA damage [42].

Abraxas itself is recruited to sites of DNA damage through its association with another protein, RAP80 (receptor-associated protein 80). Like Abraxas, knockdown of RAP80 in cells causes increased sensitivity to irradiation, reduced HR and defects in the G_2/M checkpoint. Significantly, the co-localization of BRCA1 and Abraxas in IRIF is abolished in RAP80-depleted cells, indicating that RAP80 is required for recruitment of the complex to DNA-damage sites [28].

What is then the signal for recruitment of the BRCA1–Abraxas–RAP80 complex to DNA-damage sites? A clue was provided by the presence of two UIMs (ubiquitin-binding motifs) at the N-terminus of RAP80. These UIMs exhibit strong binding to polyubiquitin chains of the Lys^6 and Lys^{63} type, suggesting that RAP80 might be recruited by polyubiquitination at the site of DNA damage [43,44]. The discovery of an E3 ubiquitin ligase, RNF8 (RING finger protein 8), that localizes to sites of DNA damage provided a mechanism for how this happens [45]. Soon after DNA damage, the variant histone H2AX is phosphorylated, and another mediator of the DNA-damage response, MDC1 (mediator of DNA-damage checkpoint 1), is recruited. RNF8 interacts with a phosphorylated form of MDC1, which, along with the E2 enzyme Ubc13, catalyses Lys^{63}-linked poly-ubiquitination of H2AX and H2A. It is these γH2AX (phosphorylated histone H2AX)-conjugated polyubiquitin chains that are thought to be recognized by the UIM domains of RAP80, which in turn recruits BRCA1–Abraxas. Consistent with these observations, depletion of RNF8 or Ubc13 depletion impairs DNA-damage-induced ubiquitin foci formation as well as BRCA1 and RAP80 recruitment [28,45]. Moreover, Ubc13 has been shown to be required for efficient repair by HR [46].

However, this model is not without its inconsistencies. First, cells depleted of RAP80 or Abraxas are phenotypically distinct from BRCA1-depleted cells. Although the former display increased sensitivity to ionizing radiation and failures in G_2/M checkpoint activation and in DSB repair by HR, these defects are far milder than for BRCA1-depleted cells. Perhaps Abraxas and RAP80 facilitate BRCA1 functions, but are not absolutely required [28]. Similarly, whereas *Brca1*-knockout mice exhibit early embryonic lethality, *Mdc1*- and *H2ax*-null mice are viable and their DNA-repair defects are less severe [47,48]. Finally, both BRCA1 and the MRN complex have been shown to localize at DNA damage sites in $H2AX^{-/-}$ mouse embryonic fibroblasts and cells lacking ATM [49], suggesting that recruitment of BRCA1 to sites of damage can occur even in the absence of the H2AX–RNF8–RAP80 system.

How could these observations be reconciled? Work by Lukas and colleagues [50] offers part of the answer. Through the use of laser micro-irradiation combined with confocal microscopy, they have shown that, after exposure to

DSB-inducing agents, the damaged nuclear area can be divided into at least two microdomains: a sub-chromatin area immediately flanking the break, usually containing ssDNA, and a second domain consisting of modified chromatin surrounding the break that spans up to 1 Mb from the lesion [50]. Consistent with the first domain representing the actual site of DSB repair, proteins recruited to it include BRCA2, Rad51 and Rad52. On the other hand, proteins that co-ordinate the repair of DSBs, such as ATM and MDC1, are recruited to the second domain where they co-localize with γH2AX. Interestingly, following irradiation, BRCA1 and MRN are found in both compartments [50].

Overall, these observations support the existence of two independent BRCA1-recruitment systems: one dependent on RAP80–Abraxas, which brings BRCA1 to the chromatin domain, and a second one involving the MRN complex and CtIP, which recruits BRCA1 to the area immediately flanking the DSB. Since each of these domains may have distinct structural and biochemical characteristics, it conceivable that BRCA1 might perform different functions in each one of them.

Towards an integrative model for BRCA1 function in DNA repair

Bringing together all these pieces of evidence, in combination with our current knowledge of the molecular events that occur soon after the induction of a DSB, we envisage the model depicted in Figure 2. Initial recognition of a DSB by the MRN complex leads to tethering of the broken ends and recruitment of ATM. This results in ATM autophosphorylation and dissociation from a dimer to monomer, leading to activation of its kinase function [51].

In the DSB nucleosome-free domain, MRN also recruits BRCA1 and CtIP (both ATM targets), leading to an increase in DSB end-processing, DNA resection and the generation of ssDNA. Binding of this ssDNA by RPA triggers both ATR/ATRIP (ATR-interacting protein)-mediated checkpoint activation and facilitates the subsequent formation of the Rad51 filament required for the repair of the break by HR. Although the molecular mechanism through which BRCA1 modulates end-processing and DNA resection is unclear, its association with CtIP exclusively during S- and G_2-phase is thought to play a pivotal role.

In the chromatin domain flanking the DNA break, ATM phosphorylation of the histone variant H2AX results in recruitment of MDC1 to the area, where it contributes to two signalling events. First, it binds to both MRN [through NBS1, via a series of phosphorylated SDT (Ser-Asp-Thr) repeats in MDC1] and ATM [via the MDC1 FHA (forkhead-associated) domain], which results in the phosphorylation of more H2AX, propagating the damage signal throughout the chromatin domain. The second event involves the recruitment of the E3 ligase RNF8, which, in conjunction with Ubc13, induces the conjugation of Lys^{63}-linked polyubiquitin to H2A and γH2AX. This prepares the ground for recruitment of BRCA1 via RAP80 and Abraxas.

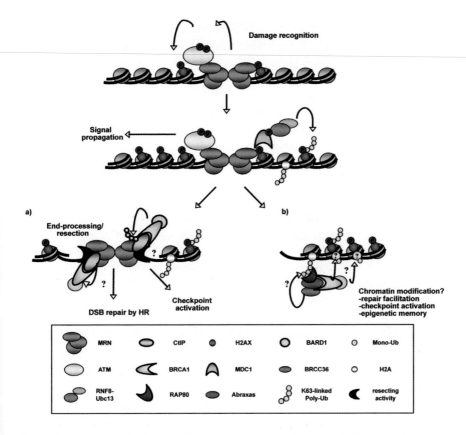

Figure 2. Model for BRCA1–BARD1 recruitment and functions in DSB repair

After induction of a DSB, the DNA ends are recognized by the MRN complex, leading to end-tethering and ATM dimer recruitment. The MRN–ATM interaction promotes ATM autophosphorylation at several sites (Ser[1981], Ser[367] and Ser[1893]), followed by monomerization. In this activated state, ATM phosphorylates several substrates, including histone H2AX. The latter recruits MDC1, which contributes to the propagation of the damage signal by recruiting more MRN (via NBS1) and ATM, expanding the phosphorylated H2AX region up to 1 Mb. This is also required for MDC1 phosphorylation by ATM. pMDC1 (phosphorylated MDC1) interacts with RNF8–Ubc13, which modifies histones H2A and H2AX by addition of Lys[63]-linked polyubiquitin chains. Recruitment of BRCA1 takes place by two independent mechanisms. (a) BRCA1–BARD1 is recruited to the DSB site via direct interaction with the MRN complex and CtIP, where it functions to regulate end-processing/strand resection, resulting in DSB repair by HR and checkpoint activation. BRCA1 could ubiquitinate CtIP, and this might be important for its retention at the site. Conversely, MRN or CtIP could modulate BRCA1 functions. (b) In the chromatin area surrounding the break, BRCA1–BARD1 is recruited through the formation if a complex with Abraxas and RAP80, which interacts with Lys[63]-linked polyubiquitin chains. The ubiquitin hydrolase BRCC36 (BRCA1/BRCA2-containing complex 36) is also present in the complex and may contribute to reverse histone modifications and confer temporality to the process. Once recruited, BRCA1–BARD1 could modify further as yet unknown targets in the chromatin, leading to repair facilitation, checkpoint activation and/or generation of an epigenetic memory. K63-linked Poly-Ub, Lys[63]-linked polyubiquitin; Mono-Ub, mono-ubiquitin.

The fact that cells defective in RAP80 and Abraxas show impaired DNA repair and checkpoint activation suggests that BRCA1 has an important function in the chromatin domain. Although the role of BRCA1 in this domain is not yet clear, one can envisage several possibilities.

One possibility is that BRCA1 might function as a part of a signal for the activation of other components of the DNA-checkpoint machinery within the chromatin domain. In support of this idea, loss of proteins involved in the recruitment of BRCA1 to the chromatin domain causes defects in checkpoint function. Although DNA repair defects are also observed, this may be an indirect result of impaired checkpoint function.

A second possibility is that BRCA1 may facilitate repair of DSBs by modifying chromatin structure surrounding the lesion. This might be achieved through the recruitment of chromatin-remodelling factors required for DNA repair such as the INO80 and the SWI/SNF remodelling complexes in yeast. Interestingly, BRCA1 has been shown to interact with a SWI/SNF-related chromatin-remodelling complex [52], as well as with HDAC1/2. Moreover, BRCA1 has been implicated in large-scale chromatin decondensation [53]. It is noteworthy that two other components of the chromatin domain complex, RNF8 and Ubc13, have been shown to ubiquitinate histones *in vivo*, which may also contribute to changes in chromatin structure in the damaged region.

Finally, a purely speculative suggestion is that chromatin modifications modulated by RNF8 and/or BRCA1 function to label regions of damaged (and subsequently repaired) DNA, where they might act as a cellular memory to preserve the original epigenetic status of the region. This might allow the recapitulation of the pre-damage epigenetic state of the chromatin following repair.

Conclusion

In all, despite many years of research, a key question still remains: how does BRCA1 participate in the DNA-damage response? Although BRCA1 has been shown to be involved in a large variety of processes and make many different physical interactions, there is very little mechanistic detail addressing its molecular function. It remains unclear whether the E3 ligase activity is the key effector of BRCA1 functions in the DNA-damage response or whether this has a different role, for example in regulation of transcription. However, the identification of several large complexes in which BRCA1 resides with many other DNA-repair-associated proteins provides many avenues for future discovery.

Funding

M.Y. is supported by the Milstein Studentship of the Darwin Trust, Edinburgh, Scotland.

References

1. King, M.C., Marks, J.H. & Mandell, J.B. (2003) Breast and ovarian cancer risks due to inherited mutations in *BRCA1* and *BRCA2*. *Science* **302**, 643–646

2. Staff, S., Isola, J. & Tanner, M. (2003) Haplo-insufficiency of *BRCA1* in sporadic breast cancer. *Cancer Res.* **63**, 4978–4983

3. Venkitaraman, A.R. (2002) Cancer susceptibility and the functions of BRCA1 and BRCA2. *Cell* **108**, 171–182

4. Scully, R. & Livingston, D.M. (2000) In search of the tumour-suppressor functions of BRCA1 and BRCA2. *Nature* **408**, 429–432

5. Moynahan, M.E., Chiu, J.W., Koller, B.H. & Jasin, M. (1999) *Brca1* controls homology-directed DNA repair. *Mol. Cell* **4**, 511–518

6. Xu, B., Kim, S. & Kastan, M.B. (2001) Involvement of *Brca1* in S-phase and G_2-phase checkpoints after ionizing irradiation. *Mol. Cell. Biol.* **21**, 3445–3450

7. Xu, X., Weaver, Z., Linke, S.P., Li, C., Gotay, J., Wang, X.W., Harris, C.C., Ried, T. & Deng, C.X. (1999) Centrosome amplification and a defective G_2–M cell cycle checkpoint induce genetic instability in *BRCA1* exon 11 isoform-deficient cells. *Mol. Cell* **3**, 389–395

8. Kondo, T. & Raff, M. (2004) Chromatin remodeling and histone modification in the conversion of oligodendrocyte precursors to neural stem cells. *Genes Dev.* **18**, 2963–2972

9. Ganesan, S., Silver, D.P., Greenberg, R.A., Avni, D., Drapkin, R., Miron, A., Mok, S.C., Randrianarison, V., Brodie, S., Salstrom, J. et al. (2002) *BRCA1* supports *XIST* RNA concentration on the inactive X chromosome. *Cell* **111**, 393–405

10. Turner, J.M., Aprelikova, O., Xu, X., Wang, R., Kim, S., Chandramouli, G.V., Barrett, J.C., Burgoyne, P.S. & Deng, C.X. (2004) BRCA1, histone H2AX phosphorylation, and male meiotic sex chromosome inactivation. *Curr. Biol.* **14**, 2135–2142

11. Boulton, S.J., Martin, J.S., Polanowska, J., Hill, D.E., Gartner, A. & Vidal, M. (2004) BRCA1/BARD1 orthologs required for DNA repair in *Caenorhabditis elegans*. *Curr. Biol.* **14**, 33–39

12. Brzovic, P.S., Rajagopal, P., Hoyt, D.W., King, M.C. & Klevit, R.E. (2001) Structure of a BRCA1–BARD1 heterodimeric RING–RING complex. *Nat. Struct. Biol.* **8**, 833–837

12a. Rodriguez, J.A., Schüchner, S., Au, W.W., Fabbro, M. and Henderson, B.R. (2004) Nuclear-cytoplasmic shuttling of BARD1 contributes to its proapoptotic activity and is regulated by dimerization with BRCA1. *Oncogene* **23**, 1809–1820

13. Lorick, K.L., Jensen, J.P., Fang, S., Ong, A.M., Hatakeyama, S. & Weissman, A.M. (1999) RING fingers mediate ubiquitin-conjugating enzyme (E2)-dependent ubiquitination. *Proc. Natl. Acad. Sci. U.S.A.* **96**, 11364–11369

14. Ruffner, H., Joazeiro, C.A., Hemmati, D., Hunter, T. & Verma, I.M. (2001) Cancer-predisposing mutations within the RING domain of BRCA1: loss of ubiquitin protein ligase activity and protection from radiation hypersensitivity. *Proc. Natl. Acad. Sci. U.S.A.* **98**, 5134–5139

15. Mallery, D.L., Vandenberg, C.J. & Hiom, K. (2002) Activation of the E3 ligase function of the BRCA1/BARD1 complex by polyubiquitin chains. *EMBO J.* **21**, 6755–6762

16. Garcia-Higuera, I., Taniguchi, T., Ganesan, S., Meyn, M.S., Timmers, C., Hejna, J., Grompe, M. & D'Andrea, A.D. (2001) Interaction of the Fanconi anemia proteins and BRCA1 in a common pathway. *Mol. Cell* **7**, 249–262

17. Vandenberg, C.J., Gergely, F., Ong, C.Y., Pace, P., Mallery, D.L., Hiom, K. & Patel, K.J. (2003) BRCA1-independent ubiquitination of FANCD2. *Mol. Cell* **12**, 247–254

18. Meetei, A.R., Yan, Z. & Wang, W. (2004) FANCL replaces BRCA1 as the likely ubiquitin ligase responsible for FANCD2 monoubiquitination. *Cell Cycle* **3**, 179–181

19. Yu, X. & Chen, J. (2004) DNA damage-induced cell cycle checkpoint control requires CtIP, a phosphorylation-dependent binding partner of BRCA1 C-terminal domains. *Mol. Cell. Biol.* **24**, 9478–9486

20. Yu, X., Fu, S., Lai, M., Baer, R. & Chen, J. (2006) BRCA1 ubiquitinates its phosphorylation-dependent binding partner CtIP. *Genes Dev.* **20**, 1721–1726

21. Hershko, A. & Ciechanover, A. (1998) The ubiquitin system. *Annu. Rev. Biochem.* **67**, 425–479

22. Morris, J.R. & Solomon, E. (2004) BRCA1: BARD1 induces the formation of conjugated ubiquitin structures, dependent on K6 of ubiquitin, in cells during DNA replication and repair. *Hum. Mol. Genet.* **13**, 807–817

23. Hoege, C., Pfander, B., Moldovan, G.L., Pyrowolakis, G. & Jentsch, S. (2002) RAD6-dependent DNA repair is linked to modification of PCNA by ubiquitin and SUMO. *Nature* **419**, 135–141

24. Polanowska, J., Martin, J.S., Garcia-Muse, T., Petalcorin, M.I. & Boulton, S.J. (2006) A conserved pathway to activate BRCA1-dependent ubiquitylation at DNA damage sites. *EMBO J.* **25**, 2178–2188

24a. Reid, L. J., Shakya, R., Modi, A.P., Lokshin, M., Cheng, J. T., Jasin, M., Baer, R. and Ludwig, T. (2008) E3 Ligase activity of BRCA1 is not essential for mammalian cell viability or humology-directed repair of double-strand DNA breaks. Proc. Natl. Acad. Sci. U.S.A. **105**, 20876–20881

25. Brzovic, P.S., Keeffe, J.R., Nishikawa, H., Miyamoto, K., Fox, 3rd, D., Fukuda, M., Ohta, T. & Klevit, R. (2003) Binding and recognition in the assembly of an active BRCA1/BARD1 ubiquitin-ligase complex. *Proc. Natl. Acad. Sci. U.S.A.* **100**, 5646–5651

26. Friedman, L.S., Ostermeyer, E.A., Szabo, C.I., Dowd, P., Lynch, E.D., Rowell, S.E. & King, M.C. (1994) Confirmation of BRCA1 by analysis of germline mutations linked to breast and ovarian cancer in ten families. *Nat. Genet.* **8**, 399–404

27. Yu, X., Chini, C.C., He, M., Mer, G. & Chen, J. (2003) The BRCT domain is a phospho-protein binding domain. *Science* **302**, 639–642

28. Wang, B., Matsuoka, S., Ballif, B.A., Zhang, D., Smogorzewska, A., Gygi, S.P. & Elledge, S.J. (2007) Abraxas and RAP80 form a BRCA1 protein complex required for the DNA damage response. *Science* **316**, 1194–1198

29. Williams, R.S., Green, R. & Glover, J.N. (2001) Crystal structure of the BRCT repeat region from the breast cancer-associated protein BRCA1. *Nat. Struct. Biol.* **8**, 838–842

30. Bridge, W.L., Vandenberg, C.J., Franklin, R.J. & Hiom, K. (2005) The BRIP1 helicase functions independently of BRCA1 in the Fanconi anemia pathway for DNA crosslink repair. *Nat. Genet.* **37**, 953–957

31. London, T.B., Barber, L.J., Mosedale, G., Kelly, G.P., Balasubramanian, S., Hickson, I.D., Boulton, S.J. & Hiom, K. (2008) FANCJ is a structure-specific DNA helicase associated with the maintenance of genomic G/C tracts. *J. Biol. Chem.* **283**, 36132–36139

32. Youds, J.L., Barber, L.J., Ward, J.D., Collis, S.J., O'Neil, N.J., Boulton, S.J. & Rose, A.M. (2008) DOG-1 is the *Caenorhabditis elegans* BRIP1/FANCJ homologue and functions in interstrand cross-link repair. *Mol. Cell. Biol.* **28**, 1470–1479

33. Chinnadurai, G. (2006) CtIP, a candidate tumor susceptibility gene is a team player with luminaries. *Biochim. Biophys. Acta* **1765**, 67–73

34. Limbo, O., Chahwan, C., Yamada, Y., de Bruin, R.A., Wittenberg, C. & Russell, P. (2007) Ctp1 is a cell-cycle-regulated protein that functions with Mre11 complex to control double-strand break repair by homologous recombination. *Mol. Cell* **28**, 134–146

35. Sartori, A.A., Lukas, C., Coates, J., Mistrik, M., Fu, S., Bartek, J., Baer, R., Lukas, J. & Jackson, S.P. (2007) Human CtIP promotes DNA end resection. *Nature* **450**, 509–514

36. Huertas, P., Cortes-Ledesma, F., Sartori, A.A., Aguilera, A. & Jackson, S.P. (2008) CDK targets Sae2 to control DNA-end resection and homologous recombination. *Nature* **455**, 689–692

37. Lengsfeld, B.M., Rattray, A.J., Bhaskara, V., Ghirlando, R. & Paull, T.T. (2007) Sae2 is an endonuclease that processes hairpin DNA cooperatively with the Mre11/Rad50/Xrs2 complex. *Mol. Cell* **28**, 638–651

38. Greenberg, R.A., Sobhian, B., Pathania, S., Cantor, S.B., Nakatani, Y. & Livingston, D.M. (2006) Multifactorial contributions to an acute DNA damage response by BRCA1/BARD1-containing complexes. *Genes Dev.* **20**, 34–46

39. Clerici, M., Mantiero, D., Lucchini, G. & Longhese, M.P. (2005) The *Saccharomyces cerevisiae* Sae2 protein promotes resection and bridging of double strand break ends. *J. Biol. Chem.* **280**, 38631–38638

39a. Zhu, Z., Chung, W. H., Shim, E.Y., Lee, S. H. and Ira, G. (2008) Sgs1 helicase and two nucleases Dna2 and Exo1 resect DNA double-strand break ends. Cell **134**, 981–994

40. Schlegel, B.P., Jodelka, F.M. & Nunez, R. (2006) BRCA1 promotes induction of ssDNA by ionizing radiation. *Cancer Res.* **66**, 5181–5189

41. Zou, L. & Elledge, S.J. (2003) Sensing DNA damage through ATRIP recognition of RPA–ssDNA complexes. *Science* **300**, 1542–1548

42. Liu, Z., Wu, J. & Yu, X. (2007) CCDC98 targets BRCA1 to DNA damage sites. *Nat. Struct. Mol. Biol.* **14**, 716–720

43. Yan, J., Kim, Y.S., Yang, X.P., Albers, M., Koegl, M. & Jetten, A.M. (2007) Ubiquitin-interaction motifs of RAP80 are critical in its regulation of estrogen receptor α. *Nucleic Acids Res.* **35**, 1673–1686

44. Sobhian, B., Shao, G., Lilli, D.R., Culhane, A.C., Moreau, L.A., Xia, B., Livingston, D.M. & Greenberg, R.A. (2007) RAP80 targets BRCA1 to specific ubiquitin structures at DNA damage sites. *Science* **316**, 1198–1202

45. Huen, M.S., Grant, R., Manke, I., Minn, K., Yu, X., Yaffe, M.B. & Chen, J. (2007) RNF8 transduces the DNA-damage signal via histone ubiquitylation and checkpoint protein assembly. *Cell* **131**, 901–914

46. Zhao, G.Y., Sonoda, E., Barber, L.J., Oka, H., Murakawa, Y., Yamada, K., Ikura, T., Wang, X., Kobayashi, M., Yamamoto, K. et al. (2007) A critical role for the ubiquitin-conjugating enzyme Ubc13 in initiating homologous recombination. *Mol. Cell* **25**, 663–675

47. Lou, Z., Minter-Dykhouse, K., Franco, S., Gostissa, M., Rivera, M.A., Celeste, A., Manis, J.P., van Deursen, J., Nussenzweig, A., Paull, T.T. et al. (2006) MDC1 maintains genomic stability by participating in the amplification of ATM-dependent DNA damage signals. *Mol. Cell* **21**, 187–200

48. Celeste, A., Petersen, S., Romanienko, P.J., Fernandez-Capetillo, O., Chen, H.T., Sedelnikova, O.A., Reina-San-Martin, B., Coppola, V., Meffre, E., Difilippantonio, M.J. et al. (2002) Genomic instability in mice lacking histone H2AX. *Science* **296**, 922–927

49. Celeste, A., Difilippantonio, S., Difilippantonio, M.J., Fernandez-Capetillo, O., Pilch, D.R., Sedelnikova, O.A., Eckhaus, M., Ried, T., Bonner, W.M. & Nussenzweig, A. (2003) H2AX haploinsufficiency modifies genomic stability and tumor susceptibility. *Cell* **114**, 371–383

50. Bekker-Jensen, S., Lukas, C., Kitagawa, R., Melander, F., Kastan, M.B., Bartek, J. & Lukas, J. (2006) Spatial organization of the mammalian genome surveillance machinery in response to DNA strand breaks. *J. Cell Biol.* **173**, 195–206

51. Uziel, T., Lerenthal, Y., Moyal, L., Andegeko, Y., Mittelman, L. & Shiloh, Y. (2003) Requirement of the MRN complex for ATM activation by DNA damage. *EMBO J.* **22**, 5612–5621

52. Bochar, D.A., Wang, L., Beniya, H., Kinev, A., Xue, Y., Lane, W.S., Wang, W., Kashanchi, F. & Shiekhattar, R. (2000) BRCA1 is associated with a human SWI/SNF-related complex: linking chromatin remodeling to breast cancer. *Cell* **102**, 257–265

53. Ye, Q., Hu, Y.F., Zhong, H., Nye, A.C., Belmont, A.S. & Li, R. (2001) BRCA1-induced large-scale chromatin unfolding and allele-specific effects of cancer-predisposing mutations. *J. Cell Biol.* **155**, 911–921

Biochem. Soc. Symp. 76
Citation reference: Biochem. Soc. Trans. (2009) **37**, 605–613.
© The Authors. Journal compilation © 2009 The Biochemical Society

12

PCNA on the crossroad of cancer

Ivaylo Stoimenov* and Thomas Helleday*†[1]

Department of Genetics, Microbiology and Toxicology, Stockholm University, S-106 91 Stockholm, Sweden, and †Gray Institute for Radiation Oncology and Biology, Old Road Campus Research Building, Roosevelt Drive, University of Oxford, Oxford OX3 7DQ, U.K.

Abstract

Cancer is caused by genetic changes that often arise following failure to accurately replicate the DNA. PCNA (proliferating-cell nuclear antigen) forms a ring around the DNA to facilitate and control DNA replication. Emerging evidence suggests that PCNA is at the very heart of many essential cellular processes, such as DNA replication, repair of DNA damage, chromatin structure maintenance, chromosome segregation and cell-cycle progression. Progression of the DNA replication forks can be blocked by DNA lesions, formed either by endogenous damage or by exogenous agents, for instance anticancer drugs. Cellular response often results in change of PCNA function triggered either by specific post-translational modification of PCNA (i.e. ubiquitylation) or by exchange of its interaction partners. This puts PCNA in a central position in determining the fate of the replication fork. In the present article, we review PCNA modifications and interaction partners, and how those influence the course of events at replication forks, which ultimately determines both tumour progression as well as the outcome of anticancer treatment.

---

[1] *To whom correspondence should be addressed (email thomas.helleday@rob.ox.ac.uk).*

Introduction

The accurate transmission of genetic material to daughter cells is critical for the control of cell proliferation and survival. Loss of accurate replication results in mutations that, in certain unfavourable circumstances, allow cells to bypass normal growth control and genome stability checkpoints. Such changes are sufficient to transform a normal cell into a cancer cell.

Understanding the regulation of DNA replication is not only essential for gaining insights into tumour development, but it is also critical in cancer treatments. The majority of drugs used for cancer treatments result in DNA damage, which in turn causes more toxic lesions during DNA replication. Replicating cells will obtain more toxic lesions that trigger cell death which results in tumour shrinkage, while non-dividing healthy cells are spared.

It is clear that there are several choices for the damaged replication forks: the replication fork may either pause in front of the damage to allow repair [1] or it may bypass the damage using specific polymerases [2], or it may convert the damage into a second lesion that in turn will either trigger a different DNA-repair pathway or will activate programmed cell death [3]. Emerging evidence suggests that modifications of a key replication protein, PCNA (proliferating-cell nuclear antigen) play an important role in deciding which pathway is to be used.

PCNA is an evolutionarily well conserved protein found in all eukaryotic species from yeast to humans, as well as in archaea. PCNA functions are associated not only with DNA replication, but also with other vital cellular processes such as chromatin remodelling, DNA repair, sister-chromatid cohesion and cell-cycle control. PCNA was originally described as an antigen for autoimmune disease in systemic lupus erythematosus patients, detected only in the proliferating-cell populations [4]. Later it was shown that expression levels of PCNA during cell cycle are differential and associated with proliferation or transformation [5,6]. In the following years, much has been done to uncover the role of PCNA in DNA replication, and one of the first functions assigned was a sliding clamp for DNA polymerase δ [7,8]. However, the progress in the field not only strengthened the importance of PCNA, but also even placed PCNA at the crossroad of many essential pathways. The crucial involvement of PCNA in cellular proliferation and its tight association with cancer transformation resulted in the frequent use of PCNA as a diagnostic and prognostic cell-cycle marker [9]. As a protein with significant clinical importance, extensive research has been dedicated to determine PCNA structure, function and therapeutic applications.

Structural considerations for PCNA functions

Alignment of amino acid sequences of PCNA from different species shows considerable homology and evolutionary conservation (Figure 1A). Even more striking is the similarity in molecular structure: yeast and human PCNA share

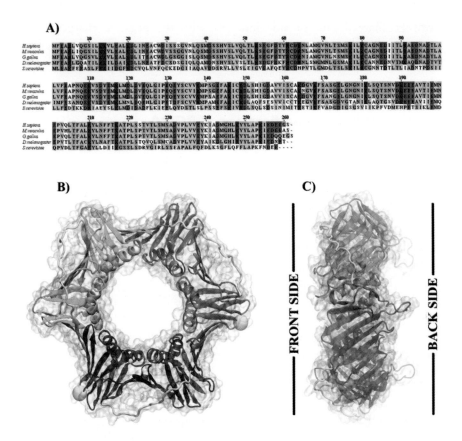

Figure 1. Sequence and structural features of PCNA

(**A**) Amino acid sequence alignment of PCNA from human (*Homo sapiens*), mouse (*Mus musculus*), chicken (*Gallus gallus*), *Drosophila melanogaster* and *Saccharomyces cerevisiae*. (**B**) Front view of the three-dimensional structure of human PCNA, different subunits are coloured red, green and blue, interdomain connecting loop is coloured yellow, and important amino acid residues are designated with yellow balls (small balls indicate Tyr[211], and big balls indicate Lys[164]). (**C**) Side view of human PCNA showing a smooth front side and visible protrusions in the back side.

35% amino acid sequence identity, but their three-dimensional structure is highly superimposable [10].

The eukaryotic PCNA consists of three identical monomers, interacting head-to tail and forming a homotrimer with an overall toroidal shape (Figures 1B and 1C). Each monomer has two very similar domains linked by an interdomain connecting loop (Figure 1B). Interaction between those domains clearly resembles the interaction between individual monomers, which gives the molecule a pseudo-hexagonal symmetry. The homotrimer has a distinguishable front and back side (Figure 1C). The front side is believed to be the interface for protein interactions, whereas the back side might have a different function (see below).

The overall surface of the PCNA molecule has a negative charge; however, many amino acid residues facing the hole form a positive potential field. The positively charged interior side interacts with the negative charges of the sugar-phosphate backbone of DNA and that interaction is believed to facilitate sliding of PCNA along DNA [11].

Post-translational modifications of PCNA

PCNA is the subject of several post-translational modifications that affect its function. Although the vast majority of PCNA molecules in the cell are not post-translationally modified, it is believed that PCNA is ubiquitylated, phosphorylated, acetylated, methylated and even SUMOylated.

One of the well-documented post-translational modifications of PCNA is ubiquitylation. First described in yeast and later found in mammalian cells [12–14], ubiquitylation is targeted on a highly conserved lysine residue at position 164. There are two distinct ubiquitylation events: attachment of a single ubiquitin moiety (mono-ubiquitylation) and building of a polyubiquitin chain via an 'unusual' Lys[63] interubiquitin linkage (Lys[63] polyubiquitylation) [12]. Each of these requires a separate set of modification enzymes and each is believed to result in different protein interactions. Mono-ubiquitylation is achieved by consequent action of an ubiquitin-activating enzyme E1, specific ubiquitin-conjugation enzyme E2 (which in humans might be either hRad6A or hRad6B) and RING (really interesting new gene)-finger-containing E3 ubiquitin ligase (Rad18). Building a polyubiquitin chain requires the heterodimeric ubiquitin-conjugation enzyme Ubc13–Mms2 and a specific RING-finger-containing E3 ubiquitin ligase. In yeast, this ligase is believed to be Rad5, whereas, in humans, three different enzymes are shown to polyubiquitylate PCNA on position 164 by Lys[63] linkages, SHPRH (SNF2 histone linker PHD RING helicase), HLTF (helicase-like transcription factor) and RNF8 (RING finger protein 8), at least *in vitro* [15–18]. However, it is currently unknown whether mono-ubiquitylation always precedes PCNA polyubiquitylation. Attachment of a single ubiquitin molecule results in a new surface property of PCNA and induces a change in the interaction partners. This is a key concept in the proposed polymerase-switch during one of the DNA-damage-avoidance pathways: TLS (translesion synthesis).

In yeast, another PCNA modification, targeted on the same conservative lysine residue at position 164, has been described [12]. This modification involves attachment of a protein, designated as SUMO (small ubiquitin-related modifier). SUMOylation of PCNA in yeast might also occur at another position, Lys[127], which is not present in higher eukaryotes (Figure 1A). Attachment of a SUMO on yeast PCNA is a signal for recruitment of a specific helicase (ySrs2), which blocks recombinational events during replication [19]. However, SUMOylation of PCNA has not yet been characterized in mammals, and the precise function of this modification remains to be uncovered. In yeast, even a poly-SUMOylation on PCNA has been described recently [20]. Poly-SUMOylation is controlled by DNA and is proposed to be a consequence of PCNA loading on DNA [21].

The data on modification of PCNA by phosphorylation are contradictory. The first report on PCNA phosphorylation [22] was investigated further by Naryzhny and Lee [23]. The conclusion in the latter paper was that a highly phosphorylated protein was co-purified with PCNA, and Naryzhny and Lee [23] argued that phosphorylation on PCNA does not happen *in vivo*. It should be noted that both research groups used cells derived from different mammals. However, more recent data clearly show phosphorylation on Tyr[211] [24]. Using electrospray ionization MS/MS (tandem MS), phosphorylation on Tyr[211] in both human and mouse cells was demonstrated, strengthened by the use of phospho-specific antibodies. It is estimated that approx. 6% of chromatin-bound PCNA is subjected to phosphorylation on Tyr[211]. This modification has been suggested to stabilize chromatin-bound PCNA as opposed to polyubiquitylation [24].

Acetylation is another modification detected on PCNA [23]. Analysis of high-resolution two-dimensional protein electrophoresis shows the presence of three forms of PCNA, two of which correspond to acetylation and hyperacetylation. The presence of the acetylated and hyperacetylated PCNA on the chromatin and localization of the non-acetylated form in the nucleosol clearly suggests a dynamic PCNA translocation dependent on acetylation status [23]. The only detailed report speculates about the involvement of PCNA acetylation in the initiation of DNA replication [23].

A new modification on PCNA has also been described: methyl esterification on many glutamic acid and aspartic acid residues [25]. Interestingly, PCNA methylation is associated with breast cancer and is believed to be cancer-specific [26]. This fact points to a possible new cancer marker; however, it is currently not known what aspect of PCNA metabolism could be altered. Methylated PCNA is commonly referred as csPCNA (cancer-specific PCNA).

PCNA-interacting partners and corresponding PCNA-interaction motifs

PCNA interacts with a plethora of proteins that are involved in many vital cellular processes (summarized in Figure 2). These include DNA replication proteins, proteins of DNA-repair machineries, cell-cycle regulators, chromatin remodelling and assembly factors, sister-chromatid cohesion proteins, transcription and translation factors, metabolic enzymes and even membrane and cytoskeletal proteins. Many of these interactions are well characterized, but it should be pointed out that some of them are only detected *in vitro* and their functional significance in cells remains to be discovered.

From the two PCNA-specific binding motifs described, the better studied and widely represented in proteins is the PIP-box (PCNA-interaction protein box). The consensus sequence of the PIP-box is QXX(M/L/I)XX(F/Y)(F/Y), although it sometimes might be N-terminally flanked by a KAX sequence [27]. The PIP-box has an unusual secondary structure: a 3_{10}-helix that fits quite well in the hydrophobic pocket of PCNA, which is situated in the interdomain

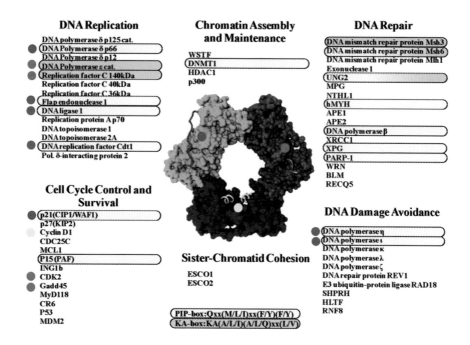

DNA Replication
- DNA polymerase δ p125 cat.
- DNA Polymerase δ p66
- DNA Polymerase δ p12
- DNA Polymerase ε cat.
- Replication factor C 140kDa
- Replication factor C 40kDa
- Replication factor C 36kDa
- Flap endonuclease 1
- DNA ligase 1
- Replication protein A p70
- DNA topoisomerase 1
- DNA topoisomerase 2A
- DNA replication factor Cdt1
- Pol. δ-interacting protein 2

Chromatin Assembly and Maintenance
- WSTF
- DNMT1
- HDAC1
- p300

DNA Repair
- DNA mismatch repair protein Msh3
- DNA mismatch repair protein Msh6
- DNA mismatch repair protein Mlh1
- Exonuclease 1
- UNG2
- MPG
- NTHL1
- hMYH
- APE1
- APE2
- DNA polymerase β
- XRCC1
- XPG
- PARP-1
- WRN
- BLM
- RECQ5

Cell Cycle Control and Survival
- p21(CIP1/WAF1)
- p27(KIP2)
- Cyclin D1
- CDC25C
- MCL1
- P15 (PAF)
- ING1b
- CDK2
- Gadd45
- MyD118
- CR6
- P53
- MDM2

Sister-Chromatid Cohesion
- ESCO1
- ESCO2

PIP-box: Qxx(M/L/I)xx(F/Y)(F/Y)
KA-box: KA(A/L/I)(A/L/Q)xx(L/V)

DNA Damage Avoidance
- DNA polymerase η
- DNA polymerase ι
- DNA polymerase κ
- DNA polymerase λ
- DNA polymerase ζ
- DNA repair protein REV1
- E3 ubiquitin-protein ligase RAD18
- SHPRH
- HLTF
- RNF8

Figure 2. PCNA-interacting proteins
Surface model of PCNA is shown with individual monomers coloured red, green and blue. Characteristic interfaces on PCNA are emphasized: interdomain connecting loop (purple), C-terminal tail (orange) and inner α-helices (yellow). For clarity, only one interface per subunit is shown. Different interacting proteins are grouped by function, their respective PCNA-interactive domains are denoted by coloured boxes, and the respective PCNA interface (if known) is presented as a coloured circle. BLM, Bloom's syndrome protein; CDC25C, cell-division cycle 25C; HLTF, helicase-like transcription factor; hMYH, human MutY homologue; ING1b, inhibitor of growth 1b; MCL1, myeloid cell leukaemia sequence 1; MDM2, murine double minute 2; MPG, methylpurine-DNA glycosylase; NTHL1, nth endonuclease III-like 1; PAF, PCNA-associated factor; PARP-1, poly(ADP-ribose) polymerase 1; Pol., polymerase; RNF8, RING finger protein 8; SHPRH, SNF2 histone linker PHD RING helicase; UNG2, uracil-DNA glycosylase 2; WRN, Werner's syndrome protein; WSTF, Williams–Beuren syndrome transcription factor.

connecting loop [28]. Interactions involving the PIP-box are hydrophobic and as such they are highly favourable in water solvents. Another PCNA-binding motif which is related to the canonical PIP-box is termed the KA-box [KA(A/L/I)(A/L/Q)XX(L/V)]. Although theoretically each PCNA trimer could interact with three different proteins at the same time and even through different PCNA-binding motifs, sometimes the size of the interacting proteins or complexes makes this scenario impossible. However, in archaea, PCNA is a heterotrimer, and each subunit shows binding preferences for either DNA polymerase, FEN1 (flap endonuclease-1) or DNA ligase I [29], suggesting a model of co-operative action. Eukaryotic PCNA, on the other hand, is a homotrimer and binding preferences are not observed, although similar co-operation between DNA polymerase, FEN1 and DNA ligase I cannot be excluded.

PCNA interactions play a key role in DNA replication

Interestingly, existing evidence suggests interaction with PCNA occurs only at the front side of the homotrimer. This makes interactions mutually exclusive when the PCNA partner is a huge protein complex. A binary mode of those interactions places PCNA at the cross-point of the several switching events that are associated with the progression of the replication forks. The very first of these events concerns exchange of the priming replicative enzyme, DNA polymerase α-primase, with a processive DNA polymerase. The general model of DNA replication involves DNA polymerase α-primase as a complex, which initiates DNA synthesis. This is achieved by synthesis of a short RNA primer (~ 10 nucleotides), later extended with a short DNA sequence of an additional ~ 20 nucleotides. The polymerase α-primase complex, however, has a high error rate owing to a lack of proofreading and possesses limited processivity. In contrast with many other DNA polymerases, DNA polymerase α-primase does not need PCNA to function, and furthermore, PCNA might even repulse it from the replication fork. When priming of DNA is complete, processive DNA synthesis is needed in order to finish replication, which includes the activity of two additional polymerases: polymerase δ and ε. Growing evidence suggests that each of these polymerases has a distinct role at the fork. Both of them are highly processive owing to PCNA assistance and both have high fidelity, but polymerase δ is believed to be involved in discontinuous replication of the lagging strand and polymerase ε is thought to continue the replication of the leading strand [30]. The exchange of polymerases at the replication forks involves PCNA, but there is a topological problem: normally, PCNA is a homotrimer in solution with a ring-shaped structure and cannot encircle DNA by itself. This problem is solved by the use of a helper protein commonly designated as clamp loader. In eukaryotes, the PCNA clamp is loaded around DNA by an RFC (replication factor C) protein complex. This is achieved by temporarily breaking interactions between subunits of PCNA and reassembling the homotrimer structure around DNA. The subunits hRFC140, hRFC36 and hRFC40 interact with the front side of PCNA in an ATP-dependent manner. The whole complex is recruited to DNA, where the RFC–PCNA complex is able to bind the template–primer junction generated by polymerase α-primase [31]. The binding of RFC and the loading of PCNA on to the DNA displaces polymerase α-primase. However, the front side of PCNA, which is the side for interaction with polymerase δ or ε, is blocked by the bulky RFC complex. A conformational change in RFC facilitated by ATP hydrolysis disrupts the RFC–PCNA complex and clears the way for PCNA and polymerase δ/ε interaction. In this manner, PCNA, with the help of RFC, conveys the DNA synthesis from one polymerase (α) to another one (δ or ε).

Another event orchestrated by PCNA during DNA replication is the maturation of Okazaki fragments. These fragments are remnants of discontinuous synthesis of the lagging strand. When the polymerization of a newly primed fragment reaches the primer of the previous fragment, several enzymatic activities are needed to complete the replication, all stimulated by PCNA. Polymerization continues with a strand displacement of the ribonucleotides of the old primer by a process called nick translation. This is carried out by the replicative polymerase in conjunction with a helicase/nuclease yDNA2. Displaced nucleotides form a flap structure, which hinders the polymerase processivity and eventually triggers dissociation of the DNA polymerase from PCNA. Another PCNA-interacting protein is recruited, FEN1, which cleaves the flap overhang. The enzymatic activity of FEN1 is stimulated by PCNA interaction, and the result of the reaction is a nick in the double-stranded DNA. That nick is sealed by yet another PCNA-interacting enzyme: DNA ligase I. The analysis of three-dimensional structures suggests the binding of DNA ligase I to PCNA via a PIP-box. This interaction is believed to trigger a conformational change that allows DNA ligase I to adopt a more organized structure around DNA and will eventually lead to the nick being sealed. It appears that co-ordination of Okazaki fragment maturation occurs in a stepwise fashion and each step might involve a different PCNA interaction.

PCNA at the crossroad of the DNA-damage-avoidance switch

Conveying replication initiation to elongation and later to the final ligation step (once in the leading strand synthesis and multiple times in the lagging strand) is not the only process for PCNA to co-ordinate. However, this is believed to happen under normal circumstances of undisturbed DNA replication. If DNA contains damage once replication has begun, the replication fork may encounter that damage, and it may stall and eventually might collapse. Stalled replication forks are the signal for activation of special pathways involved in DNA-damage avoidance. Again, the control is believed to be carried out through interactions with PCNA; however, the key step is a post-translational modification of the PCNA molecule. The current model suggests that, at the stalled replication forks, PCNA becomes mono-ubiquitylated in a Rad6A (or Rad6B)–Rad18 dependent manner on an evolutionarily conserved position: a lysine residue at position 164. This is a signal for recruitment of a special polymerase, which is able to continue DNA replication even on a damaged template. Humans, together with other eukaryotes, have several such polymerases commonly referred as TLS polymerases [32]. Mono-ubiquitylation of PCNA is a key event in the exchange of the conventional replicative polymerase (δ or ε) with a TLS polymerase, since this modification increases the affinity of the TLS polymerase for PCNA [33]. Indeed, UBMs (ubiquitin-binding motifs) are found in many TLS polymerases involved in DNA damage bypass mechanisms, for example in Y-family TLS polymerases (η, ι and κ and Rev1), together with PIP-boxes in some polymerases (η and ι) or another domain in other polymerases [BRCT (*BRCA1* C-terminal) domain in Rev1]. However, the initial hypothesis that the PCNA-interaction motif and UBM co-operate in the recruitment of TLS polymerases at sites of damage has recently been challenged. The latest results suggest the more important role of the PCNA-interaction motif and assign a secondary function to UBM [34]. However, mono-ubiquitylation of PCNA might be the mechanism of repulsion of the replicative polymerase and a platform for recruitment of accessory proteins in order to bypass a DNA lesion. Although TLS polymerases can bypass damaged bases, their processivity and fidelity are very low, which imposes the idea that these polymerases act on a short sequence around the damage. Little is known of whether there is a back switch to a replicative polymerase (δ or ε) or whether TLS polymerases are simply filling gaps simultaneously and/or behind the replication forks; however, it has been proved that mono-ubiquitylation of PCNA is directly reversible at least after UVC damage [35]. The presence of a deubiquitylating enzyme in humans, which can act on PCNA (ubiquitin-specific protease 1) implies a mechanism for recycling of intact PCNA [35].

TLS is one of the two main pathways of DNA-damage avoidance during replication. The second pathway is poorly characterized, but is believed to involve a recombination event around the forks, which is independent of Rad52 [36]. However, from genetic studies and models in yeast, it is proposed that this pathway requires a modification of PCNA, but this time that is polyubiquitylation on the same residue: Lys^{164}. Building a polyubiquitin chain on PCNA is achieved by the consecutive action of specific enzymes and results in a chain where the ubiquitins are linked via the 'unusual' Lys^{63} position. This is not a signal for proteasome degradation, but rather for recruitment of recombinational factors. However, the levels of PCNA polyubiquitylation in mammals are extremely low, and usually only mono-ubiquitylation is easily detectable, which might be a direct result of different utilization of the DNA-damage-avoidance pathways or the existence of another model in higher eukaryotes.

The model built from yeast studies suggests an elegant mechanism for PCNA in conveying the replication to one or another DNA-damage-avoidance pathway [37]. If the fork encounters damage, which obstructs the replication progression, the cellular machinery utilizes the quicker but error-prone pathway (TLS) by mono-ubiquitylation of PCNA. If that is enough, the damage is bypassed and replication continues. If none of the TLS polymerases is able to cope with the problem, a second more massive protein modification event takes place: polyubiquitylation of PCNA. This is believed to recruit factors for recombinational avoidance of the damage and is generally considered to be error-free. PCNA SUMOylation is suggested to be a mechanism for suppression of unwanted recombination during replication, since it is normally detected in S-phase or it might be an event which places the PCNA ubiquitylation in another phase of the cell cycle.

More recently, new insights were added to the model, suggesting coupling between DNA-damage-avoidance pathways and DNA replication [38]. Accumulation of ssDNA (single-stranded DNA) regions after replication fork stalling might be the primary signal for recruitment of the PCNA ubiquitylation machinery. Those ssDNA regions are quickly covered by RPA (replication protein A). RPA may function as a mediator for recruitment of the PCNA ubiquitin ligase Rad18 at the replication forks [38].

PCNA is an indispensable factor for DNA repair

The role of PCNA in replication seems to be important in many aspects; however, that is not the only function of the protein. PCNA is an indispensable part of several repair pathways such as MMR (mismatch repair), NER (nucleotide excision repair) and BER (base excision repair).

MMR is a mechanism to correct misincorporated bases (mismatches) or insertion/deletion loops generated after imprecise replication. In MMR, PCNA is required not only for the actual repair synthesis, but also in the initial step of damage recognition [39]. MMR needs to discriminate between the original and newly synthesized strand in order to function properly. PCNA provides this opportunity simply because of the interactions being directional, occurring on the face of the molecule. Since PCNA is loaded on the DNA in the only possible orientation, facing the 3'-end of the daughter strand, discrimination is possible and indeed exonuclease excisions of incorrectly incorporated nucleotides in the growing strand are carried out in the 5'-3' direction. PCNA interacts with MSH3 (MutS homologue 3), MSH6 (MutS homologue 6), MLH1 (MutL homologue 1) and EXO1 (exonuclease 1), components of MMR, from which at least MSH3, MSH6 and MLH1 have a PIP-box. Later in the pathway, repair synthesis takes place, which also depends on PCNA. However, all of these interactions are believed to be mutually exclusive, suggesting that PCNA is conveying the function from the sensor proteins (MSH3, MSH6 and MLH1) to the actual excision effectors (EXO1) and later to the polymerases [40].

NER is a pathway which deals with bulky DNA lesions, generated after interaction of DNA with certain chemicals and UV-irradiation. PCNA is proven to interact with a PIP-box of at least one of the NER proteins, the endonuclease XPG (xeroderma pigmentosum complementation group G) [41]. The main role of PCNA in NER is associated with the repair synthesis, which occurs after the reaction catalysed by XPG. However, the interaction between PCNA and XPG suggests a cross-talk between the proteins involved in different stages of NER. Mutations in XPG may cause a disorder referred to as xeroderma pigmentosum, which is tightly associated with cancer. Indeed, some of those mutations in XPG are in close proximity to the PCNA-binding site or cause a truncated protein unable to bind PCNA. There exists a patent application claiming a method for purifying csPCNA, on the basis of its specific interaction with XPG [42].

The pathway for the repair of small chemical alternation of nucleotides after exposure to oxidating, reducing or alkylating agents as well as of detected misincorporated uracils is denoted as BER. There are two modes of BER: short-patch and long-patch. The role of PCNA is associated with the repair of DNA synthesis in the long-patch, carried by DNA polymerase δ or ε. However, PCNA is recruited to the BER machinery in the steps of damage recognition before the actual repair synthesis takes place. As can be seen in Figure 2, PCNA interacts with proteins involved in all steps of BER: glycosylases [UNG2 (uracil-DNA glycosylase 2), MPG (methylpurine-DNA glycosylase), NTHL1 (nth endonuclease III-like 1) and hMYH (human MutY homologue)], AP-endonucleases (APE1 and APE2), polymerases (DNA polymerase β, δ and ε) and even a repair cofactor XRCC1 (X-ray repair complementing defective repair in Chinese-hamster cells 1). It is possible that PCNA functions as a bridge between different BER proteins, stimulates their activities and co-ordinates the whole process.

PCNA in chromatin assembly and maintenance

More enigmatic is the role of PCNA in chromatin assembly and maintenance. The organization of genetic material in eukaryotes is a real barrier for many aspects of DNA metabolism, which imposes dynamic changes in the chromatin structure, especially while the cell is dividing. During DNA replication, chromatin is completely disrupted in front of the replication fork, but is quickly restored when the fork passes. At present, it is not clear how big a region around the fork is remodelled; however, it is known that at least the nucleosomal organization is restored once the replication machinery leaves behind a couple of hundred nucleotides [43]. This suggests a very tight regulation between chromatin remodelling and DNA replication. Indeed, among the many chromatin-remodelling factors, several are believed to function around the forks. One of them is the histone chaperone complex known as CAF1 (chromatin assembly factor 1). Interestingly enough, a protein of the complex (CAF1 subunit A) possesses a PIP-box and is found to interact with the front side of PCNA. There have been studies exploring that interaction and also suggesting a mechanism for coupling of chromatin remodelling with DNA replication. The working model is based on the observation that PCNA might function as a double trimer *in vivo* [44,45]. The double-trimer formation is possible if two PCNA molecules are interacting with their back sides. Site-directed mutagenesis experiments mapped this interaction between the conserved Arg[5] and Lys[110] [44]. All known PCNA interactions are believed to happen on the front side of the homotrimer, which is rather surprising considering the number of possible choices and the fact that many are mutually exclusive. Double-trimer formation proposes an elegant model for explanation of the current data. There is some evidence for a simultaneous binding of both DNA polymerase δ and CAF1 subunit A to PCNA; however, no crystallographic data of the common complex are available [44]. Speculation of double-trimer formation places PCNA in the crossroad of genetic and epigenetic inheritance, with DNA replication proceeding in a chosen direction and nucleosomal assembly happening behind the fork. These two processes involve front-side PCNA interactions, but at possibly different molecules of the double trimer. Although double-trimer formation is highly speculative, it might describe some specific situation. One of the challenges of the model is to explain simultaneous loading of two PCNA molecules around DNA in opposite direction.

There are several other PCNA-interacting proteins, whose function is dedicated to chromatin remodelling and maintenance (Figure 2), although the role of the corresponding interactions has not been clearly defined. For example, DNMT1 (DNA methyltransferase 1) is an enzyme which has a PIP-box and which function is related to replication. DNMT1 methylates semi-methylated CpG sequences, resulting from semi-conservative DNA replication, which is a function dedicated to preserve the epigenetic methylation pattern. This pattern is directly connected to the chromatin structure. Another example is HDAC1 (histone deacetylase 1). HDAC1 interacts directly with PCNA *in vitro*, and this interaction is a proposed mechanism for recruitment of HDAC1 into distinct foci *in vivo* [46]. HDAC1 is involved in gene silencing by deacetylation of the core histone components and, as such, altering epigenetic information and chromatin structure.

PCNA is involved in establishment of sister-chromatid cohesion

Successful replication of the genome is one of the important steps required in cell division, while the next step is a segregation of the genetic material into progeny cells. A special structure is involved in keeping the homologous chromosomes together, termed the sister-chromatid cohesion complex (or simply cohesin). Cohesin is already established in S-phase of the cell cycle, coupling the DNA replication to sister-chromatid cohesion. An essential protein for cohesin assembly in yeast is yEco1 [in humans, the family contains ESCO (establishment of cohesion) 1 and 2] and that protein was shown to bind PCNA via a defined PIP-box [47]. Since the human protein ESCO2 was also shown to interact with PCNA, there is a clear intersection at PCNA between the two processes, building the sister-chromatid cohesion and progression of the replication forks.

Cell-cycle regulators interact with PCNA

In higher eukaryotes, PCNA functions are regulated by an interaction with one of the cell-cycle inhibitors, p21[CIF1/WAF1]. Binding of p21 to PCNA is mediated by a PIP-box (Figure 2), and it is one of the strongest PCNA interactions. The experimental results show that, *in vitro*, p21 abrogates DNA replication and MMR, but does not interfere with PCNA-dependent NER. A proposed explanation is a competitive binding on the same PCNA interface:interdomain connection loop and stronger affinity for p21 in comparison with the competitors such as DNA polymerase δ p66 subunit, FEN1, DNA ligase I and the replication factor Cdt1. Stable quaternary complexes between p21, PCNA, CDK (cyclin-dependent kinase) and cyclins were reported, which suggests a more complex model of regulation. In fact, PCNA can bind CDK–cyclin couples separately from p21. For example, CDK2–cyclin A, stimulated by PCNA, is able to phosphorylate RFC, DNA ligase I and FEN1. Interestingly enough, PCNA forms complexes with cyclins alone, and, for D-type cyclins, the interactions have been mapped in a very distinct PCNA region: interior α-helices (Figure 2, yellow dot).

Cell-cycle regulators such as CDK–cyclins as well as the inhibitors of the cell cycle such as p21 and p27 are crucial components of the checkpoint system, a barrier very often overcome in the progression of cancer. It seems that extensive cross-talk, mediated by PCNA, exists between cell-cycle regulation, DNA replication and repair.

Another process related to cell-cycle-checkpoint control is apoptosis. It has been shown that PCNA participates actively in the regulation of damage-induced apoptosis, by inducing programmed cell death, either by stimulating proteins such as ING1b (inhibitor of growth 1b) or suppressing anti-apoptotic proteins such as Gadd45 (growth-arrest and DNA-damage-inducible protein 45), MyD118 (myeloid differentiation factor 118) and CR6. An interesting fact is that the interaction between Gadd45 and PCNA involves a different interface, a C-terminal tail of PCNA (Figure 2, orange dot), which is in close proximity to the interdomain connecting loop, but is a separate region. Thus integration of all processes in cell-cycle progression might involve distinct parts of the PCNA molecule: interdomain connecting loop, C-terminal tail or interior α-helices (Figure 2). There is a correlation between the PCNA interface and the motifs present in PCNA-interacting proteins; however, the current knowledge is insufficient for drawing a strong conclusion.

Conclusion and future perspectives

PCNA is at the very heart of many essential cellular processes such as DNA replication, repair of DNA damage, chromatin structure maintenance, chromosome segregation and cell-cycle progression and can be regarded as one of their common integrators. In order to achieve this goal, PCNA must interact with many proteins, either simultaneously or separately in a mutually exclusive manner. In the process of the replication of DNA, many lesions, formed accidentally by environmental factors or intentionally by anticancer drugs, might block the progression of the replication forks. The cellular response to this often results in a change of PCNA function triggered either by a specific post-translational modification of PCNA (i.e. ubiquitylation) or by a change of its interaction partners, making PCNA determine the fate of the replication fork. Successful repair of the lesion and restart of the replication, or alternatively failure of the DNA repair machinery or even cell death, might ultimately be translated into a simple question of whether a patient will die from cancer or respond to anticancer therapy.

The role of PCNA is established through its interaction partners; however, little is known about the compartmentalization of the respective interactions. It is very likely that we have many subpopulations of PCNA, dedicated to a particular process. The logic implies that there are at least three main fractions of PCNA: a cytosolic fraction produced after translation, a nucleosolic pool and, most importantly, a chromatin-bound PCNA pool. From published work, it is known that even chromatin-bound PCNA is not a homogeneous fraction, as, depending on the methods of fixation or extraction procedures, at least two populations could be described [48]. The mechanical model of a replication fork suggests that PCNA on the leading and lagging strands might be different: one should stay with the polymerase until termination occurs, the other should be loaded and unloaded constantly at each Okazaki fragment. Despite this, PCNA is engaged in processes other than mere DNA replication.

All of these predicates allow us to speculate that every set of PCNA molecules is unique with respect to its properties. One possible explanation for such a variety is the change of the post-translational status of PCNA by different modifications (phosphorylation, ubiquitylation, SUMOylation, acetylation and methylation), which might result in different interaction affinities and different intracellular localizations. An example for importance of post-translational modifications of PCNA is the existence of csPCNA, which is methylated [25]. However, the post-translational modifications occur as a consequence of protein interactions with the respective modifying enzymes. It is tempting to believe that we have a chain of events (localization, interaction, modification, change of interacting partners or localization) and a new sequence of events. Since the chain is highly branched, the result will be a different subset of PCNA molecules dedicated to a particular cellular process.

A critical issue that needs to be addressed in future experiments is revealing how different anticancer drugs influence PCNA modifications or interactions. Since the choice of error-prone or error-free DNA-damage avoidance is believed to be dependent on the simple switch between mono- and poly-ubiquitylation of PCNA, guidance of anticancer therapy in one or another direction might be achieved in the near future. However, it is currently unknown how different cancers will respond to chemicals knocking down a particular PCNA-related function. The wide variety of anticancer drugs exhibit highly different activities in different tumours, despite many of them being alkylating agents producing DNA adducts. Thus it is likely that specific DNA lesions will signal for different PCNA modifications which may be of importance for the outcome of the treatment. Furthermore, it is possible that genetic and epigenetic difference among tumours influences the modifications of PCNA, which is an area that needs further attention.

Acknowledgements

We apologize to those scientists whose work we were unable to cite in the present article. We thank Dr Anne Lagerqvist for critically reading the manuscript before submission.

Funding

We thank the Swedish Cancer Society, the Swedish Children's Cancer Foundation, the Swedish Research Council, the Swedish Pain Relief Foundation and the Medical Research Council for financial support.

References

1. Mirkin, E.V. & Mirkin, S.M. (2007) Replication fork stalling at natural impediments. *Microbiol. Mol. Biol. Rev.* **71**, 13–35
2. Prakash, S., Johnson, R.E. & Prakash, L. (2005) Eukaryotic translesion synthesis DNA polymerases: specificity of structure and function. *Annu. Rev. Biochem.* **74**, 317–353
3. Helleday, T., Lo, J., van Gent, D.C. & Engelward, B.P. (2007) DNA double-strand break repair: from mechanistic understanding to cancer treatment. *DNA Repair* **6**, 923–935
4. Miyachi, K., Fritzler, M.J. & Tan, E.M. (1978) Autoantibody to a nuclear antigen in proliferating cells. *J. Immunol.* **121**, 2228–2234
5. Bravo, R., Fey, S.J., Bellatin, J., Larsen, P.M. & Celis, J.E. (1982) Identification of a nuclear polypeptide ("cyclin") whose relative proportion is sensitive to changes in the rate of cell proliferation and to transformation. *Prog. Clin. Biol. Res.* **85**, (Part A), 235–248
6. Celis, J.E., Bravo, R., Larsen, P.M. & Fey, S.J. (1984) Cyclin: a nuclear protein whose level correlates directly with the proliferative state of normal as well as transformed cells. *Leuk. Res.* **8**, 143–157
7. Prelich, G., Tan, C.K., Kostura, M., Mathews, M.B., So, A.G., Downey, K.M. & Stillman, B. (1987) Functional identity of proliferating cell nuclear antigen and a DNA polymerase-δ auxiliary protein. *Nature* **326**, 517–520
8. Tan, C.K., Castillo, C., So, A.G. & Downey, K.M. (1986) An auxiliary protein for DNA polymerase-δ from fetal calf thymus. *J. Biol. Chem.* **261**, 12310–12316
9. Elias, J.M. (1997) Cell proliferation indexes: a biomarker in solid tumors. *Biotech. Histochem.* **72**, 78–85
10. Gulbis, J.M., Kelman, Z., Hurwitz, J., O'Donnell, M. & Kuriyan, J. (1996) Structure of the C-terminal region of p21$^{\mathrm{WAF1/CIP1}}$ complexed with human PCNA. *Cell* **87**, 297–306
11. Podust, L.M., Podust, V.N., Floth, C. & Hubscher, U. (1994) Assembly of DNA polymerase δ and ε holoenzymes depends on the geometry of the DNA template. *Nucleic Acids Res.* **22**, 2970–2975
12. Hoege, C., Pfander, B., Moldovan, G.L., Pyrowolakis, G. & Jentsch, S. (2002) RAD6-dependent DNA repair is linked to modification of PCNA by ubiquitin and SUMO. *Nature* **419**, 135–141
13. Watanabe, K., Tateishi, S., Kawasuji, M., Tsurimoto, T., Inoue, H. & Yamaizumi, M. (2004) Rad18 guides polη to replication stalling sites through physical interaction and PCNA monoubiquitination. *EMBO J.* **23**, 3886–3896
14. Kannouche, P.L., Wing, J. & Lehmann, A.R. (2004) Interaction of human DNA polymerase η with monoubiquitinated PCNA: a possible mechanism for the polymerase switch in response to DNA damage. *Mol. Cell* **14**, 491–500
15. Motegi, A., Sood, R., Moinova, H., Markowitz, S.D., Liu, P.P. & Myung, K. (2006) Human SHPRH suppresses genomic instability through proliferating cell nuclear antigen polyubiquitination. *J. Cell Biol.* **175**, 703–708
16. Unk, I., Hajdu, I., Fatyol, K., Szakal, B., Blastyak, A., Bermudez, V., Hurwitz, J., Prakash, L., Prakash, S. & Haracska, L. (2006) Human SHPRH is a ubiquitin ligase for Mms2–Ubc13-dependent polyubiquitylation of proliferating cell nuclear antigen. *Proc. Natl. Acad. Sci. U.S.A.* **103**, 18107–18112
17. Unk, I., Hajdu, I., Fatyol, K., Hurwitz, J., Yoon, J.H., Prakash, L., Prakash, S. & Haracska, L. (2008) Human HLTF functions as a ubiquitin ligase for proliferating cell nuclear antigen polyubiquitination. *Proc. Natl. Acad. Sci. U.S.A.* **105**, 3768–3773

18. Zhang, S., Chea, J., Meng, X., Zhou, Y., Lee, E.Y. & Lee, M.Y. (2008) PCNA is ubiquitinated by RNF8. *Cell Cycle* **7**, 3399–3404

19. Pfander, B., Moldovan, G.L., Sacher, M., Hoege, C. & Jentsch, S. (2005) SUMO-modified PCNA recruits Srs2 to prevent recombination during S phase. *Nature* **436**, 428–433

20. Windecker, H. & Ulrich, H.D. (2008) Architecture and assembly of poly-SUMO chains on PCNA in *Saccharomyces cerevisiae*. *J. Mol. Biol.* **376**, 221–231

21. Parker, J.L., Bucceri, A., Davies, A.A., Heidrich, K., Windecker, H. & Ulrich, H.D. (2008) SUMO modification of PCNA is controlled by DNA. *EMBO J.* **27**, 2422–2431

22. Prosperi, E., Scovassi, A.I., Stivala, L.A. & Bianchi, L. (1994) Proliferating cell nuclear antigen bound to DNA synthesis sites: phosphorylation and association with cyclin D1 and cyclin A. *Exp. Cell Res.* **215**, 257–262

23. Naryzhny, S.N. & Lee, H. (2004) The post-translational modifications of proliferating cell nuclear antigen: acetylation, not phosphorylation, plays an important role in the regulation of its function. *J. Biol. Chem.* **279**, 20194–20199

24. Wang, S.C., Nakajima, Y., Yu, Y.L., Xia, W., Chen, C.T., Yang, C.C., McIntush, E.W., Li, L.Y., Hawke, D.H., Kobayashi, R. & Hung, M.C. (2006) Tyrosine phosphorylation controls PCNA function through protein stability. *Nat. Cell Biol.* **8**, 1359–1368

25. Hoelz, D.J., Arnold, R.J., Dobrolecki, L.E., Abdel-Aziz, W., Loehrer, A.P., Novotny, M.V., Schnaper, L., Hickey, R.J. & Malkas, L.H. (2006) The discovery of labile methyl esters on proliferating cell nuclear antigen by MS/MS. *Proteomics* **6**, 4808–4816

26. Malkas, L.H., Herbert, B.S., Abdel-Aziz, W., Dobrolecki, L.E., Liu, Y., Agarwal, B., Hoelz, D., Badve, S., Schnaper, L., Arnold, R.J. et al. (2006) A cancer-associated PCNA expressed in breast cancer has implications as a potential biomarker. *Proc. Natl. Acad. Sci. U.S.A.* **103**, 19472–19477

27. Xu, H., Zhang, P., Liu, L. & Lee, M.Y. (2001) A novel PCNA-binding motif identified by the panning of a random peptide display library. *Biochemistry* **40**, 4512–4520

28. Bruning, J.B. & Shamoo, Y. (2004) Structural and thermodynamic analysis of human PCNA with peptides derived from DNA polymerase-δ p66 subunit and flap endonuclease-1. *Structure* **12**, 2209–2219

29. Dionne, I., Nookala, R.K., Jackson, S.P., Doherty, A.J. & Bell, S.D. (2003) A heterotrimeric PCNA in the hyperthermophilic archaeon *Sulfolobus solfataricus*. *Mol. Cell* **11**, 275–282

30. Pursell, Z.F., Isoz, I., Lundstrom, E.B., Johansson, E. & Kunkel, T.A. (2007) Yeast DNA polymerase epsilon participates in leading-strand DNA replication. *Science* **317**, 127–130

31. Bowman, G.D., O'Donnell, M. & Kuriyan, J. (2004) Structural analysis of a eukaryotic sliding DNA clamp–clamp loader complex. *Nature* **429**, 724–730

32. Loeb, L.A. & Monnat, Jr, R.J. (2008) DNA polymerases and human disease. *Nat. Rev. Genet.* **9**, 594–604

33. Bienko, M., Green, C.M., Crosetto, N., Rudolf, F., Zapart, G., Coull, B., Kannouche, P., Wider, G., Peter, M., Lehmann, A.R. et al. (2005) Ubiquitin-binding domains in Y-family polymerases regulate translesion synthesis. *Science* **310**, 1821–1824

34. Acharya, N., Yoon, J.H., Gali, H., Unk, I., Haracska, L., Johnson, R.E., Hurwitz, J., Prakash, L. & Prakash, S. (2008) Roles of PCNA-binding and ubiquitin-binding domains in human DNA polymerase η in translesion DNA synthesis. *Proc. Natl. Acad. Sci. U.S.A.* **105**, 17724–17729

35. Huang, T.T., Nijman, S.M., Mirchandani, K.D., Galardy, P.J., Cohn, M.A., Haas, W., Gygi, S.P., Ploegh, H.L., Bernards, R. & D'Andrea, A.D. (2006) Regulation of monoubiquitinated PCNA by DUB autocleavage. *Nat. Cell Biol.* **8**, 339–347

36. Zhang, H. & Lawrence, C.W. (2005) The error-free component of the RAD6/RAD18 DNA damage tolerance pathway of budding yeast employs sister-strand recombination. *Proc. Natl. Acad. Sci. U.S.A.* **102**, 15954–15959

37. Ulrich, H.D. (2005) The RAD6 pathway: control of DNA damage bypass and mutagenesis by ubiquitin and SUMO. *Chembiochem* **6**, 1735–1743

38. Davies, A.A., Huttner, D., Daigaku, Y., Chen, S. & Ulrich, H.D. (2008) Activation of ubiquitin-dependent DNA damage bypass is mediated by replication protein A. *Mol. Cell* **29**, 625–636

39. Umar, A., Buermeyer, A.B., Simon, J.A., Thomas, D.C., Clark, A.B., Liskay, R.M. & Kunkel, T.A. (1996) Requirement for PCNA in DNA mismatch repair at a step preceding DNA resynthesis. *Cell* **87**, 65–73

40. Lee, S.D. & Alani, E. (2006) Analysis of interactions between mismatch repair initiation factors and the replication processivity factor PCNA. *J. Mol. Biol.* **355**, 175–184

41. Gary, R., Ludwig, D.L., Cornelius, H.L., MacInnes, M.A. & Park, M.S. (1997) The DNA repair endonuclease XPG binds to proliferating cell nuclear antigen (PCNA) and shares sequence elements with the PCNA-binding regions of FEN-1 and cyclin-dependent kinase inhibitor p21. *J. Biol. Chem.* **272**, 24522–24529

42. Hickey, R.J., Malkas, L.H., Schnaper, L., Bechtel, P.E., Park, M., Hoelz, D.J. & Tomic, D. (2007) *Method for purifying cancer-specific proliferating cell nuclear antigen*, U.S. Pat. 7,294,471

43. Lucchini, R., Wellinger, R.E. & Sogo, J.M. (2001) Nucleosome positioning at the replication fork. *EMBO J.* **20**, 7294–7302

44. Naryzhny, S.N., Zhao, H. & Lee, H. (2005) Proliferating cell nuclear antigen (PCNA) may function as a double homotrimer complex in the mammalian cell. *J. Biol. Chem.* **280**, 13888–13894

45. Naryzhny, S.N., Desouza, L.V., Siu, K.W. & Lee, H. (2006) Characterization of the human proliferating cell nuclear antigen physico-chemical properties: aspects of double trimer stability. *Biochem. Cell Biol.* **84**, 669–676

46. Milutinovic, S., Zhuang, Q. & Szyf, M. (2002) Proliferating cell nuclear antigen associates with histone deacetylase activity, integrating DNA replication and chromatin modification. *J. Biol. Chem.* **277**, 20974–20978

47. Moldovan, G.L., Pfander, B. & Jentsch, S. (2006) PCNA controls establishment of sister chromatid cohesion during S phase. *Mol. Cell* **23**, 723–732

48. Toschi, L. & Bravo, R. (1988) Changes in cyclin/proliferating cell nuclear antigen distribution during DNA repair synthesis. *J. Cell Biol.* **107**, 1623–1628

Keyword index

activation-induced cytidine deaminase (AID), 61
Aicardi–Goutières syndrome, 15
alternative lengthening of telomeres (ALT), 113
anaphase bridge, 47, 113
aprataxin, 91
archaeon, 37
ataxia oculomotor apraxia, 91
ataxia telangiectasia, 1, 15, 77, 91, 113, 137

bacteria, 23
B-cell, 61
Bloom's syndrome protein (BLM), 47, 113, 127, 143
Bloom's syndrome, 47, 113, 127
breast cancer 1 early-onset (BRCA1), 37, 47, 127

cancer, 1, 37, 47, 101, 113, 127, 143
cancer risk, 1
cell-cycle control, 1, 143
checkpoint kinase, 2
checkpoint homologue, 1
Chl1, 37
chromatin modification, 127, 143
chromatin structure, 77, 127, 143
chronic checkpoint activation, 15
class switch recombination, 61

damage-response signalling, 77
DinG (damage-inducible G) helicase, 37
DNA-damage response, 101, 113, 127
DNA 3' exonuclease, 15
DNA ligase, 23, 91, 143
DNA polymerase III, 15
DNA repair, 1,15, 23, 37, 47, 123, 143
DNA replication, 15, 23, 37, 143
DNase III, 15
double-strand break, 1, 23, 37, 77, 91, 113, 127
double-strand break repair, 37, 77, 91
drug binding, 101

evolution, 23, 37, 47, 61, 143
extrachromosomal telomeric repeats, 113

Fanconi's anaemia, 37, 127
Fanconi's anaemia complementation group D, 127
Fanconi's anaemia complementation group J, 37, 127
Fanconi's anaemia complementation group L, 127
fragile site, 47

G-quadruplex, 1, 47, 101, 127

helicase, 37, 47, 113, 127, 143
heterochromatin, 77
heterochromatin protein, 1 (HP1), 77
histone deacetylase 1/2, 77
Holliday junction dissolution, 47
homologous recombination, 1, 13, 37, 47, 113, 127

iron–sulfur-cluster-binding domain, 37

KAP-1 [KRAB domain-associated protein 1], 77
Ku, 23

lung cancer, 1

minisatellite, 113
molecular epidemiology, 1
molecular evolution, 37
molecular model, 101
MRN–Rad50–NBS1 complex, 113
mycobacteria, 23

NHEJ polymerase, 23
non-homologous end-joining (NHEJ), 1, 23, 61, 77, 113

phosphorylation, 1, 23, 47, 61, 77, 113, 127, 143
poly(ADP-ribose) polymerase-1, 101